Doubling for
McQueen and Redford

Doubling for McQueen and Redford

The Stunt Careers of Loren Janes and Mickey Gilbert

JAMES C. UDEL

McFarland & Company, Inc., Publishers
Jefferson, North Carolina

LIBRARY OF CONGRESS CATALOGUING-IN-PUBLICATION DATA

Names: Udel, James C., 1959– author.
Title: Doubling for McQueen and Redford : the stunt careers
of Loren Janes and Mickey Gilbert / James C. Udel.
Description: Jefferson, North Carolina : McFarland & Company, Inc.,
Publishers, 2022 | Includes index.
Identifiers: LCCN 2021030276 | ISBN 9780786497775 (paperback : acid free paper) ∞
ISBN 9781476642727 (ebook)
Subjects: LCSH: Stunt performers—Interviews. | James, Loren, 1931-—
Inverviews. | Gilbert, Mickey, 1936-—Interviews. | Stunt performers—United
States. | BISAC: PERFORMING ARTS / Film / History & Criticism
Classification: LCC PN1995.9.S7 U34 2021 | DDC 791.4302/80922—dc23
LC record available at https://lccn.loc.gov/2021030276

BRITISH LIBRARY CATALOGUING DATA ARE AVAILABLE

ISBN (print) 978-0-7864-9777-5
ISBN (ebook) 978-1-4766-4272-7

© 2022 James C. Udel. All rights reserved

*No part of this book may be reproduced or transmitted in any form
or by any means, electronic or mechanical, including photocopying
or recording, or by any information storage and retrieval system,
without permission in writing from the publisher.*

Front cover: Pulling off one of stuntdom's greatest moments, Loren Janes leaps
from a moving train onto a thirty-foot tall saguaro cactus
in *How the West Was Won*, 1962 (author's collection)

Printed in the United States of America

*McFarland & Company, Inc., Publishers
Box 611, Jefferson, North Carolina 28640
www.mcfarlandpub.com*

Table of Contents

Acknowledgments   vii
Preface   1
Introduction   3

Part I: Loren Janes

1. Childhood and the Early Days   5
2. Going Professional   12
3. Age of the Flying Cowboys   19
4. Wrestling Anacondas, Stunt Associations and McQueen   23
5. When the World Wasn't Padded   27
6. *The Misfits, Taras Bulba* and *The Greatest Story Ever Told*   35
7. Western Classics: *McLintock!* and *The Sons of Katie Elder*   40
8. G-Men, *Camelot* and More   46
9. From Apes to Frank Bullitt and Beyond   63
10. Tentpoles and Bogdanovich's Masterpiece Plus Custer's Last Stand   72
11. Life as a Pro   80
12. A Hard Day's Night   88
13. McQueen's Best and Last   98
14. New Beginnings of a Journeyman Player   107
15. Cold, Cold, Cold Around the Heart   114
16. Master of the Tinseltown Universe   119

Part II: Mickey Gilbert

17. Birth of a Champion   127
18. A Career Begins: *Alvarez Kelly* and Peckinpah   132
19. *Cleopatra* to *Return of a Man Called Horse*   139
20. All in a Day's Work   153

21.	Sydney Pollack, Redford and Belushi	162
22.	Stunt Heaven and Helicopters	168
23.	Old Gringo Rides	172
24.	Return of the Westerns	179
25.	The Fat Lady Sings	191

Glossary   197

Index   205

Acknowledgments

After writing this book, a laundry list of thanks is required.

First, I would like to note that without my publishers at McFarland (specifically Susan Kilby), this book would most likely not exist. Their unwavering support of the work has not only been a boost to my writing, but was an act of true compassion, allowing me to keep going while I was seriously ill.

I would like to congratulate my wife of more than 33 years, Maryann, for not banishing me to life in my car while writing this thing. She is truly aces.

I also acknowledge the input of my dear son Douglas. From massages to quell cramping hands to late-night coffee-sharing as I bounced ideas off him, the man was truly a muse and always motivated me to do my best. It is for Douglas that I write my books.

I would be totally remiss if I did not mention the other world-class stunt players I interviewed in cross-checking research and compiling this book. From Terry Leonard and Roydon Clark to Bob Herron and good friend Gene LeBell, these folks were invaluable in fact-checking my stories. LeBell was my guiding barometer of all things true in my research, vs. the half-true accounts one can get if not careful. I used his name in my cold introductions, and not one person he referred me to told me to get lost.

Once again, I find myself saluting the Internet Movie Database's wonderful research engine. I adore the IMDb's backbone of content which keeps my interviews flowing.

Thanks must go my three cats, Malcolm, Morty and Miles. Malcolm made hourly visits to my writing desk with gentle clawing paws reminding me to take a break; and the other boys made sure I was okay enough to feed them during those breaks. The hairy fellows have had my back in the writing process.

I must thank Loren Janes and his bright and supportive wife Jan for the dozen-plus interviews they sat through for the book. Loren suffered from Alzheimer's; she believed in letting *him* tell me the stories and she did her best to help our weekly conversations with gentle reminders and love for the man.

I never underestimated Loren during the interview process, and I was glad to hear that he was still full of life's spice after we parted: Handled a bit too abruptly by an orderly at a local hospital, the 80-plus-year-old Janes instinctively Judo-flipped the fellow—over his shoulder into a wall. Thank goodness, no one was harmed. All parties on Loren's floor were apprised *not* to grab him from behind without permission. Loren Janes passed away on June 24, 2017. He left life as he lived it, full bore and ready for any challenge. May God grant him serenity.

Another huge Stetson tip is offered to Mickey Gilbert. He was generous with stories until he had no more to share. His memories and career history are the stuff of legend.

Finally, I must acknowledge the sweat equity of the industry that has given me much of what I care about today. Working in the Hollywood trenches for the better part of 30 years as a studio grip, my ability to have a family, love a wife, care for our child, and strive past my educational level to produce good works, are all underlined through my living made in Los Angeles. I've had the good fortune to collaborate in the making of movies and television shows, and that's made me a better person from the effort of creation that the craft requires.

Preface

This book is a five-decade walk through the pre–CGI landscape of motion picture action, as experienced by two extraordinary stuntmen who lived it. Loren Janes tells stories of everything from Richard Brooks' *Blackboard Jungle* to Kubrick's *Spartacus*, Disney's *Swiss Family Robinson* and Hollywood's first multi-directorial mega-picture, *How the West Was Won*. In his early career, Mickey Gilbert's stunt path went from Edward Dmytryk's *Alvarez Kelly* and Ivan Tors' *Africa: Texas Style* (roping lions and Cape buffalos), to Sam Peckinpah's *The Wild Bunch*.

Working the Who's Who of A-list stunt assignments, Loren Janes doubled the likes of Kirk Douglas, Glenn Ford, Jack Lemmon, Paul Newman, Tony Curtis, Jack Nicholson, Frank Sinatra and Yul Brenner—not to mention Steve McQueen during the actor's entire 23-year career, from *Bullitt* and *Papillon* to *The Hunter*.

First mentored by silent era stunt legend Richard Talmadge (think swordfights and rope swings from ships' masts for Errol Flynn), Janes spent four years on Cal Poly's water polo teams, including championships in both diving and gymnastics in 1950. In 1956, Janes was the first civilian to enter the United States Olympic trials in Modern Pentathlon, a grueling summer event that combines riding, fencing, shooting, swimming and running. He repeated the accomplishment in 1964. Janes co-founded the Stuntmen's Association in 1961 along with Carey Loftin, George Robotham, Dale Van Sickel, Gil Perkins, Red Morgan, Regis Parton and Fred Krone. He worked such '60s classics as *Taras Bulba*, *Our Man Flint*, *The Dirty Dozen*, *It's a Mad, Mad, Mad, Mad World*, *The Sons of Katie Elder*, *Nevada Smith* and *Bullitt*, to list a tiny fraction of his early history, and worked as an acclaimed master of his craft into the early 21st century.

Mickey Gilbert flourished under the watchful eye of his mentor (and father-in-law) Joe Yrigoyen. He earned his keep on pictures like *Rio Lobo*, *The Undefeated*, *Beneath the Planet of the Apes* and *Butch Cassidy and the Sundance Kid* (doubling Robert Redford in the famous cliff jump). The Redford relationship continued through the later pictures *Brubaker* and *The Electric Horseman*. He spent five years on TV's *The Fall Guy*; his other movies include *Return of a Man Called Horse* and director Michael Mann's *The Last of the Mohicans*. Mickey Gilbert became a "name" in Hollywood's stunt world.

Janes and Gilbert had the amazing fortune of making their own breaks. Like climbers scaling Mount Everest, they made it to the top of their profession. From the great age of Westerns (both big- screen and small-screen), to the swashbucklers and war pictures audiences consumed from the mid–1950s onward, these fellows performed during a time of dynamic storytelling, often delivered with violence. And that required stuntmen who could gallop a horse, fall off a roof, give or take a punch, and dive off a 90-foot cliff—sometimes all in one day. Janes got his first break on *Jupiter's Darling*: In a spectacular feat

Early in the history of the Stuntmen's Association (ca. 1961), this photo of its founder was taken. Front row, left to right, Red Morgan, Regis Parton, Fred Krone and Loren Janes. Back row, left to right, Carey Loftin, George Robotham, Dale Van Sickel and Gil Perkins.

of courage, he doubled Esther Williams in a high dive from one of Catalina Island's soaring cliffs, saving two others who attempted the high fall with him but were injured on impact with the water.

This book, covering roughly 1950 to 2000, is the project-by-project history of these two exceptional stunt players from that time. They not only excelled at the craft, but ultimately did so with the kind of creativity that redefined the trade. This book celebrates their spirit and it hopes to illuminate the extraordinary techniques of their daily doings while working on some of the most iconic motion pictures Movieland ever presented.

Introduction

Interviewing Loren Janes and Mickey Gilbert in their respective homes, days turned to weeks and months became four years before all the work was done, getting these stories right. From researching hundreds of films chronologically by production date and title (then organizing facts such as hiring stories, filming locations, shooting dates and intended stunts onto numerous legal pads), I reviewed countless pictures for stunt content, then compiled *all* into a series of notebooks. Conducting the interviews with this timeline allowed me to dig deeply into the background of nearly every major motion picture these men had ever done.

Loren Janes in particular was assisted by the method, as he was suffering the early and then the later stages of Alzheimer's disease. Portals of his memory would glide open as I showed him the photographic evidence of his amazing career. From the cactus leap in *How the West Was Won* to his 23 years with McQueen that culminated with *The Hunter*, he would "play back" the substance of his fondest memories in response to a movie title, actor name or storyline; this resulted in clarity that could last from several moments to a half-hour, during which he could recall everything from the heights of stunt jumps to how much he was paid during his Warner Bros. days. The stuff was challenging to extract, but golden in content when analyzed! He would withdraw once the moment's vision had passed, but then we would review another photograph and the process would begin anew.

Mickey Gilbert's sessions were Sunday morning smooth. Over countless cups of coffee at his Santa Barbara ranch, the kid had a storytelling style that was all cowboy charm. Having labored for years as a Hollywood grip myself, I knew some of the hows and whys of the stunt craft. What I didn't know was the back stories to his iconic moments on screen. And Mickey was nice enough to fill me in! Gilbert was every bit as mathematically brilliant as Janes (who held a teaching degree in advanced calculus), but Mickey's intelligence lay with his knowledge of horses, motivation of people, falling objects and the occasional flying car. And while Janes was the everlasting professor to his final interview, it was Gilbert's easy "aw shucks" persona that compelled me to keep asking questions about his extraordinary career. Mickey's method of communication was more like a good poker player. Little was said until it mattered, and then it was good stuff indeed. For example, explaining to this writer about the imagined and probable path of a Ford Mustang launched into a wagon-load of watermelons for TV's *The Fall Guy*, Gilbert drew an imaginary arc through the air with a quick slash of his hand. "The ramp *had* to be positioned here," he gently lectured on the calculations he took to figure the jump. "And the car needs to be doing 60 miles an hour as it hits the pitched ramp. It was like a golfer's chip shot, up like a mortar then down to the green."

"The Mustang stuck like glue," Gilbert said, his voice finishing like a preacher on the pulpit, all quiet humility. "And that little gag landed me *Fall Guy* for five years."

This book begins where my first book left off. I published *The Film Crew of Hollywood* in 2013 with one chapter on the charming king of stunts, Gene LeBell. My relationship with him grew to a real brotherhood. Hearing from him of the great masters still deserving of literary celebration in Hollywood, I began a second tome hoping to interview a dozen. That was not to be, for practical reasons, so I chose the two most iconic fellows still around. Famous players of the stunt craft (Buddy Joe Hooker, Roydon Clark, Bob Yerkes, Conrad Palisano, Chuck Hicks, Vic Armstrong, Gary Davis, May Boss, Debbie Evans, Ronnie Rondell, the Gill Brothers, Charlie Picerni, Terry Leonard, Hal Needham) seemed obvious "legends" for focus; but further examination found Janes and Gilbert to be the most prolific subjects of their generation.

And speaking of the next generation, Mickey's sons Troy, Tim and Lance have followed in Dad's footsteps: All are successful Hollywood stunt players and coordinators. Mickey Gilbert remains in love and married to Yvonne Yrigoyen since 1962, some 59 years ago. Retired and living the good life of the gentleman rancher, grandfather and former stunt master of the equine realm, he calls his relationship with God, clean living and the love of family his treasures, and the secret to a good life.

PART I: LOREN JANES

1

Childhood and the Early Days

Few are truly born to a motion picture profession, or earn the rank of "legend" in a career. One practitioner of stunt-craft who forged his own way to action stardom was athlete extraordinaire Loren Janes. He was born on October 1, 1931, in Sierra Madre, California, to parents Loren Sr. and Marjorie Smailes, who lived the rugged life of ranchers tending a 20,000-acre spread in the middle of present-day Lake Piru. Growing up the sole male child on a large homestead enabled the boy to experience bronc and bull riding, days in the saddle locating lost calves, sun that blistered uncovered scalps, and cold that could freeze a sick steer solid. By eight, he was an able hand.

The bank foreclosed on their home during the Depression, and money remained tight. His mother found work as administrative assistant to the president of Cal-Tech while Dad got seasonal assignments as a yearbook photographer for Los Angeles prep schools. Despite being a loner from age ten, young Loren was an avid Boy Scout, YMCA attendee and a member of Pasadena's hiking club. Academically bright while attending Sierra Madre Elementary, his adolescence was filled with tumbling and gymnastics involvement via YMCA classes that made him an athletic standout.

The December 7, 1941, Pearl Harbor attack and the onset of World War II changed the family dynamic forever. Janes Sr. enlisted with the 1st Marine Division in August 1942 and soon found in himself in the thick of Guadalcanal's fierce fighting, which claimed his life by February 1943. His world shattered after the loss of his father, Loren strove to succeed in all he did, both physically and mentally. Testing himself with solo treks along the Sierra Madre's treacherous passes, he hiked or rode the entire John Muir Trail (aboard his horse Hah-Ka-Nah) four times from age 12 to 17. He found an abandoned cabin stocked with Tarzan novels. Absorbing the rich Fred Arting illustrations and Edgar Rice Burroughs' prose, Loren was soon emulating all that he read. Launching self-guided excursions into the wilderness at 12, he walked barefoot into the mountains clothed only in shorts and hunting knife in a homemade sheaf, with a .22 caliber rifle slung over his shoulder. He set up camp complete with pup tent, rabbit spit fireplace and fresh water nearby. Comfortable and secure for days, Loren would bivouac and harvest the bounty of the region. He bagged and dressed deer in secluded sections of the Muir trail; the meat helped feed his mother and extended family in summers.

While attending Sierra Madre Elementary in the fall of '45, the teenager was placing cash in parental palms by milking cows at a dairy. Aching for a creative outlet, he volunteered for drama club plays, first designing sets, then acting. His initial tastes of audience-to-performer contact thrilled the youngster. By 13, he had a substantial paper route serviced by horseback aboard Hah-Ka-Nah. The horse would pause at each intended address, triggering the half-asleep boy's automatic throwing reflex of a rolled paper. Advancing at the dairy via lack of manpower due to war shortages, he reported for school exhausted and milk-stained after his shifts.

After the war, things started looking up. Loren attended the prestigious Pasadena High School (City College) between 1945 and 1947, flourishing as a student. He majored in biological sciences (plant and animal origins) and had a brilliant mind for math. Receiving varsity letters in a variety of athletics, gymnastics, diving, swimming and tumbling, Janes also led hiking and surfing clubs. Captain of the swim and diving teams, winner of state trampoline competitions, lettering in everything, he was the school's MVP. He was known for daredevil stunts, like taking a 60-foot swan dive from a bridge into less than ten feet of water. His fame led to summer lifeguard gigs in Santa Cruz between '49 and '53, and he made the newspaper when he saved a young girl from drowning.

Diver Helen Crlenkovich of 1936 Olympics fame mentored Janes by hiring him for "water shows" throughout 1950 and '51. His act included high-diving stunts, swimming

Doubling Esther Williams as "Amytis" in Director George Sydney's *Jupiter's Darling* (ca. 1955), Loren Janes (in white circle) leaps from a 90-foot cliff into the sea below Catalina Island's southern expanse. Performing a swan dive just meters ahead of Hannibal's heavies (including famous carnival diver Al Lewin and his cousin George), Janes' palm-down entry into the sea was perfect while the others broke back and skull. Janes saved them, keeping them both afloat until help could arrive, and his diving and deeds of salvation became the talk of town.

1. Childhood and the Early Days

demonstrations and audience challenges of speed and duration. Loren was also a Mount Baldy ski instructor.

Joining the Marine Corps First Division in February 1951, Loren broke Camp Pendleton's obstacle course record during basic training. He was assigned to famed grunt Chesty Puller's offices until an underwater demolitions accident left him with a severe concussion leading to medical discharge in January 1952. Attending Cal State Poly San Luis Obispo on the G.I. Bill later that year, he majored in biological sciences while tearing up the athletic departments: He lettered in water polo, gymnastics, trampoline, tumbling and floor exercises.

Working more water shows with Helen Crlenkovich through 1953, Loren graduated from Cal Poly with a degree in Biological Studies. Hired by Sherman Oaks' prestigious Saunders School for Boys and Girls, an exclusive enclave for kids of Hollywood parentage, Janes taught advanced mathematics including trigonometry and calculus, occasionally performing high-diving exhibitions and acrobatic gags for school fund raisers.

The mathematician's foray into Tinseltown's stunt world was about to begin. He nailed a triple somersault off the high-dive in the school's massive Olympic pool during a swim team drive, amazing students and faculty alike. Movie producers learned of the daring math teacher's exploits, and within a few weeks, a stuntman was born. In the summer of '54, MGM producer George Wells was searching for a skilled high-diver for the Esther Williams vehicle *Jupiter's Darling* and having no luck peddling the 90-foot cliff plunge to stunt regulars around town. (In the scene, Williams is fleeing from Hannibal's troops, who are approaching from the rear.) Wells finally gave in to his son George Jr.'s insistence that he knew the only person in America who could do it: his math teacher!

Stuntman Richard Talmadge is in his prime in this early publicity shot. Years after his acting and stunting heyday, he mentored Loren Janes.

Following a meeting at MGM and an agreement of $250 per dive, Loren Janes shook hands with Wells and assured him that such a stunt was possible. Janes doubled Esther Williams plummeting over the cliff on horseback, with two of Hannibal's henchmen following suit. The heavies were played by well-known platform specialist Al Lewin (signing on for a flat rate of $500 a day) and his third cousin Walter, a naval reservist. The 90-foot descent from Catalina's tallest rise into the churning sea was sobering to observe. It was the equivalent of dropping from a ten story building. The gag would kill most divers unless they were trained in specific techniques to reduce impact. In the case of Lewin and Cousin Walt, the results were less than stellar. Al landed awkwardly after a successful separation from his dropping horse; the plunge left him unconscious with a broken back, sinking slowly beneath the sea's surface. Also knocked cold, his cousin was severely concussed, and also fractured his collarbone and three cervical vertebrae.

Despite blinding wig and restrictive breast enhancements, Janes tucked his chin against his chest and employed cleaving hands to pass through the water with a professional's precision and poise (an ability honed in dozens of high-dive exhibitions). He jetted down 26 feet before reaching zero buoyancy and rising. He reflexively worked his neck and shoulders while ascending toward the surface. Clutching Lewin's seemingly lifeless body, he broke the surface with Lewin in one arm and supporting Cousin Walt with the other; he kept both injured men afloat for several minutes until help arrived. Janes was experienced with high diving from grade school pranks off bridges and platform exhibitions while at Pasadena City College. He was also a student of the famous Acapulco cliff divers, reading voraciously of their exploits and method.

Legendary stuntman–second unit director Richard Talmadge witnessed Loren's heroics and mentored him for years to come. Talmadge became famous in the swashbuckling pictures of the 1920s and '30s, doubling icons Barrymore, Fairbanks

Glenn Ford throws Janes through an open classroom window in *Blackboard Jungle*.

1. Childhood and the Early Days

and Flynn. On the heels of *Jupiter's Darling*'s successful shoot, Loren returned to teaching flush with cash and wanting more. Working at the school offered a predictable, comfortable income but he was excited with the idea of pulling off cliff leaps that others refused. The movies promised adventure and fame. He enjoyed his reputation at MGM as the "new stuntman" who did the big dive and saved two guys in the process. Janes was lured from his advanced calculus class (he took "sick days") to double Glenn Ford in director Richard Brooks' tough, fight-laced drama *Blackboard Jungle* (1955).

Ford starred as a war vet newly hired as an English instructor at a rough inner-city school. Hearing about Loren from fellow producer Wells, *Blackboard Jungle* producer Pandro Berman kept him at MGM as personal trainer to actor Louis Calhern. Promoted to fight coordinator, then stunt double for Ford, Loren displayed a lean realness to his movement that directors like Brooks loved. The fights were as close to real as safety would allow. The film also featured Sidney Poitier, Anne Francis, Richard Kiley and Vic Morrow (the latter beat Steve McQueen for the part of Artie West).

Loren's phone was soon ringing off the hook with offers. As westerns comprised the bulk

Top and above: **Blackboard Jungle star Glenn Ford (in jacket and tie) and Janes mixed it up for over an hour before 16 takes provided director Richard Brooks the coverage he desired.**

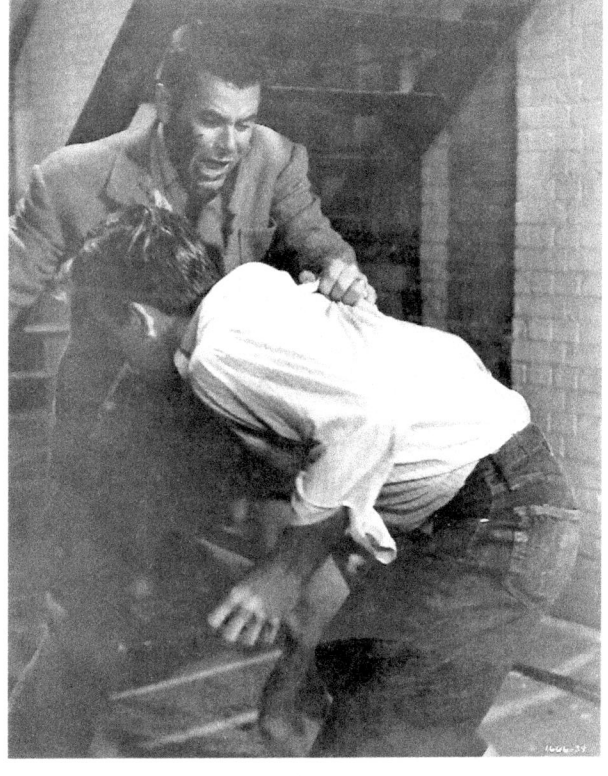

of Hollywood production from the postwar era to the 1960s, Janes was soon in the saddle on television series like Ziv's *The Cisco Kid*.

Fate would nearly have it be his *only* ride. Though Loren was awarded several pages of dialogue and title listing in the opening credits as character Tim Siebert (owing to the producer's necessity to fill the screen after the show's star, Duncan Renaldo, was injured in a boulder-jump stunt gone bad), even mogul Jack Warner's insistence failed to land Loren to a contract. Attempting to sign Loren by way of advancing his character to "side-kick," (removing the focus on Renaldo whose recovery had waned), Warner's office offered brighter stardom if he would play ball.

Informed the deal's only strings were managerial, he was told two things must be taken seriously for his new life to proceed. First was a manager: Henry Willson. Second was political affiliation: Communist. Attending his first meeting for prospective party members, after hearing an hour of Stalinist rhetoric he turned and goose-stepped out of the hall. Willson was not so lucky. When the notorious predator cornered Janes with his much used "I'll scratch your back you scratch mine" pitch, Janes yanked the agent's suit jacket over his arms then shoved him in the coat closet, locking it before tossing the key in the waste basket—as muffled pleas inside begged for release.

The Cisco Kid (1950–1956). Searching for a new co-star to help the show's falling ratings out of a rut (following Duncan Renaldo's injury from a boulder-fall), Loren Janes (playing Tim Siebert) was later picked by studio boss Jack Warner as his new "It guy."

Security chaperoned Janes to Warner's offices before he could leave the lot. He was confronted by the studio head after being ushered inside by a nervous secretary, owing to the bigshot's dislike of those refusing his entreaties. Informed Loren was failing to "play ball" (with Willson or the Party), the studio boss switched to threats to get his man. Lectured to play along and get rich or resist and get banned from Hollywood for life, Janes balked at Warner's idea of talent contracts. Disgusted by the movie czar's deception and political ideology equally, Loren hastily walked out the door and off the lot. Strolling past the guards at gate three without glancing back, he rescued his automobile from the Forest Lawn parking as the choice he had just made hit home. He said *no* to the deal.

Blackballed by Jack Warner as promised throughout 1955, Janes soon found himself living in his '49 Chevrolet coupe—parked near a stream in Mulholland Canyon, surviving during summer hiatus from Saunders School on a busboy job at a nearby Golden Bull restaurant (eating "canyon-stew" with bagged squirrel and rabbit when all else failed). Jack Warner's influence was wide and few dared to buck him. Technically, Janes would not work for Warner Bros. again until hired for *Laramie* in 1959. Banished and finding few stunt jobs in town once coordinators heard the news, he was part of the laundry list of crew including actors, writers, and action-players who continued on Warner's blacklist until Jack sold creative control to Seven Arts ten years later. With Warner rapidly losing his juice to enforce superficial grudges by '56, however, stuntmen like Loren dared pursue their careers without fear of reprisal.

And Janes dared with vengeance. Vindication came five years hence as a founding member of the Stuntmen's Association, signaling the end of studio-controlled action players forever.

2

Going Professional

Janes returned to teaching calculus in January '56. As his reputation grew, so did the number of "sick days" he had to take. The Hollywood newbie's talents increased with every stunt he did.

He was brought in for risky wagon turn-overs and horse gags by director Byron Haskin for *The First Texan* in January 1956 (fellow stuntman Bob Morgan, the movie's stunt coordinator, tipped Janes off about the job). Huge battle scenes were staged in Agoura Hills' North Ranch in the movie's recreation of the Alamo. Blasted off galloping horses as both Mexican soldier and Texan volunteer, he was blown from trampolines simulating cannon explosions, and bayonetted off siege ladders, two stories up from the ground. Used throughout filming in multiple guises and makeups, Loren became indispensable to Morgan, who placed him in every big stunt. In the battle sequences when Sam Houston's (Joel McCrea) forces overwhelm General Santa Ana's Mexican regulars, Loren gaffed a wagon blown into the air with him flying out as it exploded. Using a hidden trampoline and exceptional acrobatic ability, Janes launched himself 15 feet above the buckboard with a somersault flourish on the descent, landing on pads that were beneath the dirt. He performed many horse drags: one of the stuntman's feet is stirrup-bound and he is dragged along the ground attached to a running horse. One day, he was shot as a fleeing Mexican cavalryman, then re-costumed and fought hand to hand doubling James Griffith as Davy Crockett and bayoneting three Mexican soldiers. Sword-stabbed, trampled, lanced, sniped and otherwise dispatched, Loren made a good impression, leaving his bits of blood, sweat and leather in the soil of the Janss Conejo ranch in Thousand Oaks. And that good impression got him more work.

Loren was flown to Tucson aboard a drafty war surplus DC-3 to work *Walk the Proud Land* in April '56. He had been hired by coordinators Joe Yrigoyen and Clem Fuller, drafted into the Universal Western for his unparalleled horse work. Helmed by "saddle-picture" vet Jesse Hibbs, it featured war hero Audie Murphy and Anne Bancroft, plus Jay Silverheels as Geronimo and Sailor Vincent as a barfly. It was cowboys-and-Indians fare with lots of hand-to-hand fighting, stirrup-drags, arrow shots, wagon turn-overs and gunplay; Janes did everything from being shot off galloping horses backward to taking falls from 30-foot-high boulders. He was cast as an Apache and his wardrobe including loincloths, head bands and sleeveless vests provided little protection when performing the stunts. Loren doubled Audie Murphy in the film's climactic knife fight vs. Tommy Rall. The action entailed flips, gut punches and kicks to the chin before the hero ended the argument with a blade in the ribs.

"Indian" gags were usually painful, and thus reserved for newcomers. Rewarded with "good guy" assignments too, Loren was shot off a running horse following multiple arrow hits to his back. After he was fitted with a wooden backboard hidden beneath his uniform, real arrows were fired into him by an archery expert from the effects department. Next, he was required to do a face-first fall from the horse, to avoid dislodging the shafts.

One particularly brutal day, Loren had been beaten up multiple times, rolled over by a horse, then nearly drowned when pinned under a wagon in a stream. He recalled supporting player Jay Silverheels telling him in his Tonto voice, "Me think Loren need better agent … who you with now, Kemosabe?"

"I represent myself," Loren piped up, laughing.

"Better to fire self than work for fool," Silverheels joked. "Even the Lone Ranger's horse, Silver, have an agent these days! Trade ego for accountant. Bottom line better…. Parts, too!"

In the spring of '56, Loren was referred by his mentor Richard Talmadge to ABC-TV's *The Adventures of Jim Bowie*, where he could help filling the historical episodic's weekly need for trappers, traders and Indians good and bad. Janes was tasked with supporting Scott Forbes, who starred as the venerable Bowie. His roles included a trapper robbed and killed by renegades (with Janes back-stabbed while holding off a trio of braves with a Kentucky long rifle). His favorite role was that of a fake preacher smuggling stolen gold, attacked by a grizzly for his trouble. Loren worked with a Rudd Weatherwax–trained bear in the sequence: The back of his neck was smeared with peanut butter to get the animal to "fake bite" him. With cameras rolling at the Iverson Ranch, the grizzly paw-grabbed Loren by the head and licked his neck with reckless abandon, instead of mauling him as rehearsed. Instantly consumed with giggling, director Lewis Foster cut the scene as cast and crew broke up laughing.

Consistently working westerns due to his varied stunt abilities, Janes was soon faced with a Saunders School ultimatum: teach full time or take a leave of absence. Leveraging the guarantee of a $9000-a-year teaching job against Hollywood's earnings and fame, Loren traded academia for Tinseltown without looking back. Allowing three years to decide whether to make his stunt work permanent or return to teaching, Janes set an initial goal of $20,000 annually. He then took any call offered, no matter the learning curve required to pull it off.

Janes got jobs on better pictures and added new skills to his repertoire. He doubled Jack Palance in director Robert Altman's World War II action-drama *Attack* (co-starring Lee Marvin, Eddie Albert, Buddy Ebsen, Richard Jaeckel and Strother Martin); it was shot in 32 days, and Janes earned $4500 in the process. He and 40 other action players worked on producer-director Cecil B. DeMille's *The Ten Commandments*; he suffered everything from spear impalement as an Egyptian soldier (via a plywood torso worn beneath his tunic), to being run over by a horse-drawn chariot before engulfment by a wall of water (in the parting of the Red Sea gag). For the latter sequence, 60,000 gallons of water were pumped into the massive set in the studio tank. Horses and stunt players found themselves beneath the surface in the process. Lifeguards pulled them from the "sea" after each take.

In mid–1956, another stunt legend, Tap Canutt, hired Janes to work on director William Wyler's Civil War movie *Friendly Persuasion*, starring Gary Cooper and Anthony Perkins. Shot by Ellsworth Fredricks around Canoga Park's Rowland (and M and T ranches in Chino), its epic battle scenes had Loren saber-fighting on horseback, shot, stirrup-dragged and trampled as both Union and Confederate soldiers—doubling anyone under six feet tall who gets dispatched. He became friendly with star Cooper (both liked chess, history and horses), and by picture's end they were pals who sang Christmas carols together each holiday for years to come. Janes was also befriended by *Friendly Persuasion* producer Walter Mirisch, who became a lifelong supporter of his career. Working multiple horse falls and a major stampede, Janes stayed on the Allied Artists project until completion. "Wading through a stampede on horseback is like stepping across a fast-moving brook," said Janes. "No fast moves, you just go with the flow."

On Warner Brothers' Burbank lot, Janes appeared in the pilot episode of the Western series *Sugarfoot* with Will Hutchins. The cast also included Jack Elam, Slim Pickens, Dennis Hopper and a young Kurt Russell. Loren mastered stair falls (shot or shoved), banister flips and roof rolls and worked with real bronco riders Robert Terhune, Roydon Clark and Bob Herron. On a later *Sugarfoot* episode, "The Wizard," Janes was befriended by Efrem Zimbalist, Jr.; years later, they worked together on Zimbalist's hit show *The F.B.I.* In the summer of '56, he was hired by stunt coordinator Leonard Geer for producer Walter Mirisch's *The Tall Stranger*. Janes was back in his saddle in this post–Civil War action story. Loren did running horse mounts, got shot off roofs and performed galloping action sequences as a multitude of characters. As he perfected wagon flip-overs,

In an episode of TV's *Broken Arrow*, Janes grabs the shirtless Michael Ansara by the arm during a knife-fight challenge. This was obviously shot on a stage with a painted backdrop and trucked-in hay grass.

stirrup drags and saddle-jerks under Geer's watchful eye, his stunt portfolio was expanding with marketable gags.

Chosen by *Blackboard Jungle* producer Pandro Berman to handle the fight staging for MGM's *Jailhouse Rock,* Loren was a good physical match for the 22-year-old star of the musical, Elvis Presley. It was shooting in May and June 1956. Berman used Janes' realistic approach to film violence in the picture's penitentiary sequences (all sets at MGM), to sell the angel-faced singer as a believable scrapper.

Janes was thrilled when coordinator Fred Carson called upon his horse skills and he joined the crew of the Western television series *Broken Arrow,* filming at the Walker ranches and Fox backlot, as well as Vasquez Rocks. He played cavalrymen and Apache Indians. Guesting on the series: various TV stars in the making, including Robert Blake and Leonard Nimoy. (Nimoy played an Apache brave so scrawny, Blake offered him *his* boxed fried chicken lunch in jest.) Janes was blasted off horses riding bareback; this required strength in the core and legs to grip the animal, then propel oneself clear of churning hoofs. He took falls one steps further by back-flipping as he was shot. He would land after a complete revolution at 25 MPH (palms and knees to the dirt—facing the horse's rear); a miscalculation could cause loss of teeth, cuts, fractures or worse if kicked hard enough.

Loren was hired by producer John Robinson to double a relative unknown, Steve McQueen, who played the leading role of bounty hunter Josh Logan on CBS-TV's *Wanted: Dead or Alive.* He got the job (starting on the pilot) only because stuntman Richard Farnsworth was too tall. "Steve and I hit it off," Janes said. "We both shared a love of automobiles. And suffered tough childhoods. Physically, we were a perfect body match. Five foot ten, 175 pounds, blond-haired and blue-eyed lean."

Location shoots took place at Simi Valley's Corriganville Ranch, as well as the popular Vasquez Rocks; interiors and western street scenes were photographed at CBS (the former Republic lot). It was the beginning of a 25-year friendship and professional bond between Janes and McQueen. Loren tutored the actor in riding and on-set fighting. McQueen loyally used Janes for decades to come, never arguing about his double's price.

Containing new stunt concepts, from realistic hand-to-hand fighting to men blasted off running horses and multi-camera bar brawls, *Wanted: Dead or Alive* had that unmistakable whiff of cool (generated by McQueen) that audiences loved. The series helped him hone his less-is-more style.

Applying past expertise when faced with new challenges, Janes' next learning curve was underwater in Robert Wise's submarine classic *Run Silent Run Deep.* Shot in October late '56, the Cold War classic used practical locations aboard the U.S.S. *Redfish* on the Salton Sea's frigid October waters. A San Diego submarine base and personnel (including Rear Admiral Roy McGregor) were utilized to train actors on technical details of Navy protocol. Featuring Clark Gable, Burt Lancaster, Jack Warden, Brad Dexter and Don Rickles as quartermaster Ruby in his cinema debut, the Russell Harlan-lensed action-drama pushed Loren, J.D. Skidmore and Billy Babcock to unparalleled risks. Doubling Lancaster in an underwater plunge beneath the *Redfish,* Janes recalled the Navy's refusal to allow their divers to work the picture, requiring him to swim the murky depths of Imperial County's waters for days on end to get the sequences.

Returning to stunt mentor Richard Talmadge to work on 20th Century–Fox's *From Hell to Texas* during November '56, Loren was now a far more seasoned player than when he made his first picture, *Jupiter's Darling.* Janes labored through frigid mornings in Lone

Pine's Alabama Hills as well as teeth-chipping horse work at Chatsworth's Iverson Ranch. He recalled box lunches consumed while overlooking Lone Pine's picturesque vistas. Actors Chill Wills and Dennis Hopper were lounging in the shade of massive Ponderosa pines, away from the rest of the company. Janes sat within earshot while polishing off the last of his fried chicken. Overhearing Hopper tell Wills that he wanted an apple for dessert but was too comfortable to fetch one, Loren reached in his pocket and silently removed a glistening McIntosh. Hiding behind the trunk of a huge tree, he tossed the fruit up, unobserved. It landed in Hopper's lap with a thud, and the wide-eyed actor held it aloft for his friend to see. "That's the first time I ever saw a pine tree drop an apple," Wills laughed. Realizing they were not alone, Hopper continued the joke, calling out, "Thanks for the apple, o genie. How about some cash?" Responding in a falsetto voice, Janes said, "I'm a bit short 'til payday. Would a check be okay?"

Comfortable with talent *and* stunt-folk, Janes was a natural when it came to placing others at ease. His playful and gentle sense of humor was found refreshing; people enjoyed working with him, and it was poised to pay off.

Director Jack Arnold's *High School Confidential!* (1958) starred Russ Tamblyn, Mamie Van Doren, Jerry Lee Lewis, Michael Landon and Jackie Coogan. Loren recalled the young, pug-nosed Tamblyn as athletically gifted and taught him stage combat, melding both in the picture's fight scenes. Tamblyn's balance-bar gags in the schoolyard were a testament to Loren's training, and served the actor well four years later in Robert Wise's *West Side Story*. According to Janes, Landon was a "nice boy," Jerry Lee Lewis riveting but wild, and Mamie Van Doren was attended by hubby Mickey Hargitay day and night. Janes' real focus was high-speed driving runs done for the picture's action sequences. Behind the wheel of the era's hottest cars via motor-heads George Barris and pals, Loren put the pedal to the metal in '55 Chevys and Dodges, producing 300 horsepower and speeds in excess of 120 MPH. Loren and Regis Parton brought a realistic tone to the picture's violence. Given a speaking part as "Bert," Loren was a quick study with lines, knowing his and everyone else's dialogue in the script.

Janes was included in a gymnastic Who's Who when drafted for *The Buccaneer*, filmed in 1957, produced by Cecil B. DeMille and directed by his son-in-law Anthony Quinn; the latter had second unit boss Arthur Rosson find acrobats for the swashbuckling gags needed in the film. A wide audition net was cast for tumblers, divers, high-wire walkers and circus performers; Loren was called by stunt coordinator Preston Peterson, who had seen his chariot hijinks in *The Ten Commandments*. He did somersaults 60 feet in the air from the picture's tall-ship rigging staged at Paramount, and a backflip from yardarm to mast, swooping over the decks on a rope, kicking four bad guys overboard. Janes palled with actor Woody Strode, and the two formed a bond that would continue through *Spartacus* and 16 other films. He attributed the friendship to their shared athletic past. "Once you've competed on an Olympic level, you respect others who have traveled the same path. Woody was a state decathlon champ, pro-wrestler, and one of the first black players in national football, by 1946. We respected each other's past, and commitment to being the best we knew how regardless of job titles."

Janes was surviving his first year of separation from Saunders School by way of personal leave with increasing stunt work. The initial struggle was replaced by momentum's arc of the committed. Required to re-apply for temporary separation classification as a full-time teacher on continuing leave in order to keep his position open, Loren renewed for a second year's absence with few reservations. Then he did not work for the first two months of 1958, after putting money down for a better car and moving to an apartment closer to the studios.

He felt desperate and thought about more part-time work to stem the flow of his meager savings. A 7 a.m. phone call from a second unit director with a thick Prussian accent caused him to throw down the morning classifieds and listen intently to his proposal. Empowered by Seven Arts to hire acrobatic stunt actors for *Thunder in the Sun,* Erich von Stroheim retained Janes and two others for specialized trampoline shots in the film.

A powerful director during Hollywood's silent era, the Austrian's fall from grace occurred during a spate of box office disappointments between *Queen Kelly* in 1929 and *Walking Down Broadway* a decade later. He was often over-budget, unbendable with talent, and unwilling to change. His movie *Greed* (1924) ran ten hours before MGM cut it to three. The once famous director was on a downward spiral that lasted until Billy Wilder cast him in *Sunset Blvd.* (1950). Von Stroheim acted disagreeably towards Janes; the stuntman received constant put-downs and ridicule from cinematographer Stanley Cortez as well.

A member of a cutting-edge acrobatic group of stunt players utilizing circus trampolines to produce flying action for motion pictures, Loren was encouraged by Richard Talmadge to learn the new skill. It involved jumping from elevated platforms onto angled trampolines; the resulting bounce would catapult stuntmen vertically through the air at twice the distance and speed of a fall. No wires, no upside-down camera tricks, no obvious platform dives used in the past to simulate flight. It was employed for years in explosions for war movies, hurling stuntmen skyward. Later mortar and air ram variants were capable of 20-foot flying launches.

Thunder in the Sun was filmed amid the boulders of Lone Pine's Alabama Hills (except for matching stage sets with stucco rocks, real trees and specially lit backings used for vertical leaps deemed too dangerous to shoot on location). The cast yodeled a weird Basque settlers' yell with each gag.

Pulling off 30-foot "ramp launches," sailing laterally through space, Janes would seemingly fly off boulders (Superman position) parallel to the horizon in full frame. He landed below the frame line on hidden pads with a front-roll flourish into a standing position. Playing an Indian bad guy, he plummeted from a 30-foot cliff into cardboard boxes buried beneath packed dirt and covered with carpet. The impact would purge a strong man's wind like a heavyweight's punch, every take.

Playing a renegade brave making a knife attack, Janes performed a vertical leap from a cave roof 15 feet off the ground. Flying over a granite knoll, he would have been severely injured had he failed to land on his mark. Doubling Jeff Chandler in all of his fights, he did an airborne horizontal tackle of a bad guy catapulting 20 feet; both dropped into a net rigged below the frame line. He intercepted two buckboard-stealing Indians with a 30-foot horizontal trampoline swoop, knocking the stunt players clean off the wagon seat. In this movie, he was part of a trio of stunt legends to be: Loren worked the film with Hal Needham and Roydon Clark.

In early '58, Loren was handpicked by director George Marshall to do stunts on the Debbie Reynolds "war of the sexes" romp *The Mating Game.* He opened the film doubling Paul Douglas, jumping a horse over a convertible driven by Tony Randall. The saddle gag was more dangerous than it looked. Setting Randall's speed at a constant 14 MPH, Loren's leap required six inches of clearance and precise timing. "Aiming the horse ahead of the car is vital," said Janes. "That and explosiveness of command, so the animal doesn't hesitate when his reflexes tell him he should."

Loren was also given a small supporting role as Sherm. It was his first time working with Debbie Reynolds, whom he later doubled in *How the West Was Won*. She was impressed by the difficult stunts he did. Required to dive head-first from a second story barn loft into bales of hay, the belly landings put the tough guy in cowboy traction by day's end. Queried as to how one avoids serious damage from these impacts, Janes revealed tucking his chin against his chest prevented the cervical vertebra from hyperflexion (a broken neck). In another scene, he gets a hammer-shot on the toe from little Ricky Murray followed by a shovel to the face at the hands of Una Merkel; Loren does a knocked-cold face-fall too realistic for comfort. During a free-for-all ruckus between Randall, Reynolds and William Smith, the stuntman donned specially padded costumes and took the rough falls for Reynolds. Janes was taunted by cast and crew alike when he sat down for supper in costume (blond wig, foam-breasted blouse, tie-on hat and apron). Posing for pictures and accepting the ribbing good-naturedly, he had the final laugh in 1963 when he doubled Debbie during *How the West Was Won*'s stampede sequences, at twice the rate, wearing much the same wardrobe.

3

Age of the Flying Cowboys

Again banking on his acrobatic skills, Loren was called by coordinator Whitey Hughes for Walt Disney's live-action *Darby O'Gill and the Little People* (1959). The inland valley sequences were shot at the Rowland Ranch in Canoga Park and the Albertson spread in Triunfo, California. Loren was doing his usual circus-level back-flips, somersaults, headstands and trampoline leaps among little people opposite the "giant," Sean Connery. Mixing midgets in the foreground with full-sized actors like Janes along the same focal plane but at a different depth, d.p. Winton Hoch's live-action photographic efforts using forced perspective plates were a near seamless success, believably bringing writer Herminie T. Kavanagh's vision of leprechauns to the screen. Loren recalled Walt Disney supplying voluminous storyboards with rich illustrations detailing the precise action in every shot. Adhering to the highly detailed game plan, director Robert Stevenson availed himself of Loren's springboard and trampoline mastery (as well as Loren's great suggestions) to keep the stunt schedule moving along well. This was noticed by Disney, who clicked with the soft-spoken Janes, and kept hiring him for years to come.

In late '58, Janes was drafted by stunt coordinator Henry Wills for more cowboy action (the gold standard of television throughout the decade): TV's *Laramie* was photographed by Ray Rennahan on Universal's back lot as well as Red Rock State Park and the Corriganville Ranch. The Revue production was a cattle car of Tinseltown talent, from Ernest Borgnine and Charles Bronson to Lee Van Cleef, Harry Dean Stanton, Ben Johnson and Brian Keith. The series was little more than a vehicle for stunt brawls and stagecoach attacks including horse action with shot-off, trampled or dragged cowboys. Stunt coordinators Paul Baxley and Hal Needham would hire him often in the future.

Among the plethora of cowboy content occupying Loren's "test year," independent features and episodics like *Bat Masterson, The Rebel Breed* and *Pony Express* filled his stunt dance card. Lensed by cinematographer Monroe Askins (of later *Gunsmoke* fame), *Bat Masterson* starred Gene Barry as the dandy-crimefighter, with Janes laboring on the NBC series via horse gags, fights, stair falls and wagon work.

The Ziv series filmed on locations including the Paramount, Corrigan, Iverson and Castle ranches. Working on the series led directly to a stint on Desilu's *Pony Express*. Janes was charged with stunt coordination on a few episodes, from wagon wrecks to four-legged flourishes like mounting a running horse, catapulting side to side between saddles or standing while galloping (straddling two at once, Roman-style). *Pony Express'* reliance on bar fights, cowboy punches and equestrian style stretched Janes' understanding of stunts as never before, despite the program's dismal ratings. Loren sporadically taught while also stunting, to keep all options open.

When *Pony Express* was cancelled suddenly, without a call, Janes took whatever he could find. Tasked with pulling off believable gang fight choreography for director Richard Bare's *This Rebel Breed,* Loren was uncomfortable seeing blackface makeup applied to white actors. Challenged with depictions of gang fighting including knives, he taught the kids Marine Corps hand to hand, enlarging and slowing the movements and enabling d.p. Monroe Askins' camera to catch the action. Even the talents of Rita Moreno and Dyan Cannon could not make that turkey fly.

Janes worked for half the going rate on the low-budget show in desperation. He was running out of money. He thought he had hit the jackpot with *Pony Express*, and its sudden cancellation made him quite unsure of his future.

Then fate's fickle finger dialed his number: He was called by Paul Baxley, who was putting together 200 stunt players at Universal for an open call under the direction of Yakima Canutt (of *Ben-Hur* chariot race fame).

The studio was seeking body builders, gymnasts, swordfighters, wrestlers and all-around tough guys for a historical epic helmed by Stanley Kubrick, *Spartacus*. First in line for the obstacle course the morning of try-outs, Loren showed the stuff of his Marine Corps days: outrunning, climbing, ducking, slashing and hustling any who tried. At day's end, candidates were lined up for review by the producer-star Kirk Douglas. Sauntering down the line of exhausted stunt players arranged by height like a general reviewing troops, he paused before Loren, motioning him to step forward. Standing five feet ten inches stretched over 170 well-muscled pounds, with a boxer's shoulders and cleft chin,

During the making of Stanley Kubrick's *Spartacus*, Janes (center, back to camera) went through a ducking and jumping drill at the Universal back lot's Gladiator Camp. To the left is star Kirk Douglas in midair. On the extreme left, athlete-actor Woody Strode observes the action while awaiting his turn.

steel blue eyes framed by a shock of tawny blond hair swept back over his forehead, Janes was nearly a mirror vision of the actor. Circling him with a quizzical look, Douglas asked him if he was up to working as his stunt double on the show. Turning to Canutt and Baxley standing to the producer's side, Loren graciously answered, "So long as it's okay with these gents."

Janes went from broke-ish to booked. His starting pay for the picture in 1959 was $200 a day ($1,885 in 2021 dollars). He was responsible for the lion's share of combat instruction including gladius swords, tridents, thrown nets and hand-to-hand. Experience gained in Pentathlon competition during the 1956 Olympics in events such as fencing, pistol shot, javelin and skiing qualified him as an expert when translated to gladiatorial skills. Answering to Baxley and Canutt while demonstrating extraordinary athletic prowess, Janes was a taskmaster to guide the stunt troops, numbering 187 by filming's end. Leading morning calisthenics via his old Marine Corps protocol including push-ups, deep-knee bends, jumping jacks and sword exercises, he was 20 yards ahead of the group during its two-mile run before breakfast. Then he was first through the chow line with two large glasses of milk, a plate full of eggs, bacon, biscuits and fruit.

Bringing horse craft to the picture's forefront driving chariots, Loren performed bumps (collisions on cue) and piloted wagon turn-overs and rode multiple mounts bareback and Roman style in battle sequences. He performed a "running horse" sequence up a flight of stairs during the climax. Loren spoke of the methods used to train an animal to bound up 30 feet of inclined marble (shot at Hearst Castle); when instinct would normally prevent trying. Ever the teacher, he revealed, "The trick is to walk the horse up the landings a dozen times, nice'n'easy. Slowly speed up the process until it can trot. Then, begin again, riding. The final stroke is to approach the stairs like they don't exist; then giddy-up the sucker and let nature take its course."

Cast as Thracian slave general, Roman soldier and gladiator, Loren was featured throughout the film. It cost $40,000 (about $375,000 in 2021 dollars) to build the ten-acre gladiatorial camp on Universal's back lot. It employed all types of replicated training devices. Real and accurately rendered of heavy wood and iron, they could maim or kill a person if the wielder was not cautious. From spinning wooden roundels wielding chained balls to obstacle courses with swinging weights, Russell Metty—the temperamental lenser of such classic fare as *Bringing Up Baby* and *Touch of Evil*—included all in his rendition of the massive outdoor sets (and was awarded a Best Cinematography Oscar for his efforts). Kubrick, an accomplished d.p. in his own right, designed, storyboarded and/or photographically controlled a great deal of the picture himself. Often arguing over set-ups, Metty was known to storm off on early lunch breaks, important phone calls or mysterious meetings to make his displeasure known.

There were six weeks of massive Roman battles on Spain's central plains (representing the 3rd Seville War of revolting Thracian slaves vs. Rome in 71 A.D.). Kubrick enlisted 8500 Spanish infantrymen costumed as Roman Legionnaires. The scenes were as realistic as Canutt and Baxley could safely coordinate. Loren recalled that Kubrick could move 8000 people for a shot (a two-hour effort was required to make it work). World War II veteran turned stuntman Bill Raisch (a Ziegfeld dancer before losing an arm) was featured in a visceral battle sequence where he was rolled over by a flaming log in closeup. Many late mornings saw stunt players rush to remove their raggedy slave trappings and spray-on body dirt, then report in the afternoon wardrobed as clean-shaven Romans with armor and brass helmets.

Janes saved more than $1000 a week on *Spartacus* with continued "bumps" (bonus cash for specialized or dangerous stuff like chariot flip-overs, horse-falls and fire). The extra monies earned Janes the equivalent of a judge's pay. He was working what would prove to be the breakthrough of his early career (both rate and reputation). *Spartacus*' 167 shooting days and contacts gave him the push to stay in the game. He was able to make far more than a teacher and enjoy the adrenal rush of Hollywood and all its trimmings. For the first time since taking personal leave from Saunders, Loren realized he might never return.

Finally out of the woods after *Spartacus* and rooming with fellow stunter Jack Williams at the City View Apartments on San Carlos Street in a modern two-bedroom walk-up, Loren ultimately bought property in Santa Clarita's Sand Canyon area, building a fine home with friends' help. When he installed a phone in the cabin where he lived during construction, the first call to his number was from Steve McQueen, who wanted Loren on his next feature, *The Magnificent Seven*, a western re-working of Kurosawa's masterpiece *The Seven Samurai*. Cinematographer Charles Lang and director John Sturges agreed that Loren's likeness to McQueen was startling and signed him to double the star at nearly $1500 a week. It was scheduled to start on March 1, 1960, in Morales, Mexico, for desert work. McQueen's castmates included Yul Brynner, Eli Wallach, Charles Bronson, James Coburn, Brad Dexter and Robert Vaughn. Stunt coordinator Henry Wills failed to fill the production needs of Sturges' violent vision by only suppling a half-dozen proven Hollywood stuntmen. Battle sequences were filmed with Mexican villagers blasted from thatched roofs, trampled, horse-dragged and blown from wagons. When more willing locals from Churubusco Studios could not be found, Loren and fellow stunt players Larry Duran, Jerry Gatlin, Jack Williams, Bob Terhune and Wills himself donned sombreros, Mexican ponchos, droopy mustaches, dark makeup and hair pieces, playing the parts of bad guys *and* victims.

Receiving his first paycheck while on location in Mexico, Loren sent a letter of resignation via telegram to the Saunders Day School headmaster, on the same day that *Spartacus* came to theaters, October 7, 1960. Grossing $1611 a week on *The Magnificent Seven*, Loren no longer thought of himself as a calculus teacher. He was a full-time stuntman, earning four times as much, with no regrets. Janes doubled McQueen whenever danger was present.

Loren worked as a bad guy, performing patented horse gags (pulling the animal down by virtue of reins and saddle control to simulate being shot). He also did reverse saddle tumbles (blasted backwards, head over heels, from a running horse, and landing face down on the ground). There were also multiple high-falls off two-story adobe buildings, incorporating flourishes like half-gainer flips, diving-board hesitations and roof-rolls. Pads beneath the dirt softened the landings.

Loren laughed that he was killed in the picture numerous times by each star, dying by Coburn's thrown knife, Vaughn's twin Colt revolvers, and bullets from the guns of Dexter, Brynner and Bronson. Henry Wills joked that Janes should *really* be shot, to allow others a crack at the stunt pay. Janes continued bonding with McQueen during the six weeks of filming; in the evenings, the two had time to swap stories of difficult childhoods.

4

Wrestling Anacondas, Stunt Associations and McQueen

In May 1959, Loren was engaged by second unit helmer Yakima Canutt to travel to the British West Indies for Walt Disney's action-thriller *Swiss Family Robinson*. Doubling James MacArthur, he was nearly drowned on the Tobago Islands performing the "rafting the breakers" sequence, as the family first approaches land upon losing their ship.

Janes was sailing in a hand-built skiff he had constructed (idle during three days of continuous downpour). The rain-swelled sea made passing through riptides during the morning's shooting quite dangerous. His craft struck coral reefs and jutting shoals hidden below the churning white water, launching him headfirst into the surf. Fighting

Pictured here doubling *Swiss Family Robinson*'s James MacArthur sailing through fierce breakers, Janes takes his raft over dangerous coral reefs despite consequence.

to break surface despite the undertow, Loren kept his composure clinging to the reef's rocky edge. Diving beneath the current, Janes surfaced in a calmer spot a few yards away, dazed and cut along the forehead. Canutt requested another take. Cleaned up and ready for camera (bleeding stanched with Vaseline), he was boated back to the first position, his raft tethered behind. Janes was required to man the rig for another three days of shooting in the treacherous sea before director Ken Annakin was satisfied he had his coverage (and Canutt his action). Loren was so exhausted from filming that he collapsed on his base camp cot after wrapping and slept 11 hours straight, missing breakfast the following morning. A production assistant was sent to fetch him, Janes was greeted upon at arrival on set by a rousing cast and crew ovation led by MacArthur, saluting his labors.

Drafted for water-wrangler duties during the picture's comedic ocean-ferry of the Robinsons' animal menagerie. Loren was responsible for a gaggle of geese, 40 monkeys, a Texas longhorn, eight Great Danes, two baby elephants, a half-dozen ostriches, a burro, goats and hogs (with attached floatation barrels, as pigs swim poorly). Two days of soggy shooting tested the stuntman's endurance. Devising harness and leads for all, Janes was required to swim underwater and guide the elephants, as well as the pigs and burro, in the proper direction. While the geese were at home in the sea, the monkeys clung to floating boxes (prepared by Loren, and laced with favorite foods by

In the British West Indies for Walt Disney's *Swiss Family Robinson*, Janes (right) and stunt partner Chuck Courtney (left) prepare to wrestle a 27-foot-long anaconda in its native habitat.

their trainers). The stuntman recalled being skull-pecked by nervous ostriches as he tread water in their midst to lead them. "Each shot smarted," he remarked, and added with a boyish smile, "After ten takes, it wasn't fun any more."

Given the job of wrestling a 27-foot anaconda the following day, Loren longed for the ostriches from the morning before. The snake had been captured by a platoon of natives for the movie company (they corralled it into a massive burlap sack during a four-hour struggle); it required 16 strong men to carry the temporarily subdued serpent to the lagoon where the scene was to be filmed. They were shooting amid a tropical storm's aftermath, and the inland's freshwater channels and lagoons were swollen and turned an angry brackish brown. The storm destroyed all crew quarters (palm-thatched huts with hammocks and plank floors); the intended treehouse set for the boa fight was also lost. In its place, a partially enclosed bog with lush jungle vegetation was chosen. The location was primordial in both setting and danger; the "snake porters" were required to keep the constrictor from dragging stuntmen to an underwater grave. Loren and Chuck Courtney (doubling John Mills) actually wrestled the slithering giant in the water; the filming lasted nearly two days owing to the brute's strength and its refusal to cooperate. It was capable of crushing human bones in seconds, and of inflicting severe bites with tortoise-like jaws.

Enticed with $200 cash "bumps" each day, the stuntmen did the best they could. Guarding each other's backs with lengths of hardwood cut from acacia trees, they directed blows at the snake's body, which was their only means of control. Skin on Loren's neck and arms chafed raw and bruised purple from the constriction of the massive specimen. The footage was spectacular. *Swiss Family Robinson* was in theaters by Christmas 1960; audiences sat frozen in fear during the watery battle until cheering the snake's retreat at the fight's end.

Not all of the picture's gags were so extreme. Ramrodding the "family animal race sequence"—jockeying everything from zebras and ostriches to adolescent elephants—Janes somehow always knew what to do during the three weeks of filming. Referring to ostriches as "nasty birds," Janes said that one must get on quickly from the side when mounting; a trainer secures the ostrich's neck to avoid head-butting. And be wary of strong legs (which can knock a large man down with a single kick), as well as sharp pecking beak and clawed feet capable of cleaving flesh like a can opener.

Special trainer Fez Reynolds showed Janes the finer points of controlling zebras. He described a method of grabbing a zebra's mane, to deter it from biting (which they can manage with greater flexibility than horses). "You couldn't really ride far," Loren remembered of the animal race. "The gag was to stay on long enough for [cinematographer] Harry Waxman to grab some footage. They cut the race out of 15-second snippets. Only the elephants were predictable. The ostriches and zebras were not really tame."

During *Swiss Family Robinson*'s pirate fight sequences, Janes was featured in stunts like "shoot-downs" from palm trees, falling 30 feet into buried pads, blasted backwards off 60-foot cliffs, and dodged rolling boulders tumbling down a hill. He also performed a spectacular "log roll-over gag" with Paul Stader, Chuck Courtney and Ken Buckle as pirates. The foursome was "taken out" at the bottom of a steep ravine by a cloth and rubber tree prop built for the scene. Its weight (only 300 pounds, vs. the real McCoy's two tons) meant no broken bones or loss of life getting the shot.

Once again Richard Talmidge's first pick, Loren doubled Elvis Presley in 20th Century–Fox's cowboys-and-Indians story, *Flaming Star*. Shot in Utah and the Janss Conejo

Ranch, it was Presley's second film with Janes (after *Jailhouse Rock* in '57). With Don Siegel helming, it was straight drama. Executing galloping horse falls at 20 MPH, Janes was ordered by the realist director to do six takes before he was satisfied. "The ground was hard and we had no time to prepare it [loosen the soil, rake, then re-pack]. By day's end, my butt hurt," he laughed.

Loren was next attached to a motion picture that would forever change the form and function of stuntmen and the organization of their craft. While little-known, Don Taylor's *Everything's Ducky* was the pivotal moment. Released in December '61, it starred Mickey Rooney, Buddy Hackett and Jackie Cooper and told a farcical tale of ducks in the Navy. Working the film as a stuntman held few laughs. Engaged in a barroom brawl with a dozen Marines fighting as many sailors, Rooney received an errant head punch and the star shut down production by refusing to continue. He was struck by an amateur "extra-action-player" cheaply employed by producers Allen Barron and Red Doff at a fraction of the cost to pay a real stuntman. The resulting fracas led to Columbia's recognition of Dale Van Sickel's newly formed Stuntmen's Association, with Chuck Hayward, Glen Wilder and Janes in major roles.

Next for Loren: Steve McQueen's riveting war drama *Hell Is for Heroes,* lensed in the fall of 1961; coordinator Guy Way assigned him to do all the rising star's action work. Featuring Fess Parker, Bobby Darin, James Coburn, Bob Newhart, L.Q. Jones, Harry Guardino and Nick Adams as the Polish hanger-on Homer Janeczek, the picture, set toward the end of World War II, was a darkly gritty look at a frontline American infantry squad. Fighting the enemy and themselves, heavily outmanned by Germans, they must take a fortified emplacement.

Covering two weeks of exteriors doubling McQueen's climactic attack on the Pill Box, Loren utilized his remarkable likeness to the actor running uphill through hundreds of squibs replicating machine-gun fire, inches from buried exploding charges. With director Don Siegel insisting on survivable reality, the effects department's liberal use of charges singed Loren's face and neck while blinding debris had to be wiped from his eyes after each take. The temperature was in excess of 115 degrees during the day and remained near 100 into the night. The Cottonwood, California, location offered other challenges: baked ground and shrapnel-like stones piercing costumes and flesh alike. Janes and Vince Deadrick Sr., Fritz Ford, Richard Elmore, Chuck Hicks, David Pena and Jesse Wayne went above and beyond; by picture's end, all had dropped 15 pounds and truly looked the part of beleaguered soldiers. Loren recalled a camaraderie growing between McQueen and James Coburn that started on *The Magnificent Seven*. "Steve was very competitive," Loren said. "With Coburn, however, it was more like one-upsmanship on who could be cooler. He either liked you or not. If he thought you were okay, he could be playful. Otherwise, he'd look right through you."

5

When the World Wasn't Padded

Janes returned to the familiar hills of Lone Pine after being hired by Richard Talmadge to work 20th Century–Fox's *North to Alaska* (1960), producer-director Henry Hathaway's spoof of the California Gold Rush and two pals trying to strike it rich. It was lensed by old-school ace Leon Shamroy (*Cleopatra*, *Planet of the Apes*). John Wayne and Stewart Granger are comedic as one man's fiancée marries a third man, and a swindler (Ernie Kovacs) plots to steal everyone's gold.

Featured in the picture's "muddy street" brawl tangling with Wayne's double, Fred Graham, Loren threw a slippery stage punch which accidentally connected squarely with the stuntman's forehead, knocking off his hat and rattling the brains beneath. Continuing the exchange despite the shock, Graham retaliated with an improvised combination ending in an uppercut that caught Janes beneath the jaw, knocking him from his feet. Calling "Cut!," Hathaway exclaimed, "Now that's giving Fox its money's worth!" Viewed in dailies the following morning, Loren jokingly thanked Shamroy for his good camerawork, getting it in one take.

How the West Was Won, an epic five-segment western which began shooting in the spring of 1960, had multiple directors: John Ford covered "The Outlaws" and "The Civil War," Henry Hathaway "The Rivers" and "The Plains" and George Marshall "The Railroad." The film showcased 12,000 extras including 400 non–English-speaking Navajos, 2000 buffalo, 150 mules and several hundred horses (plus a score of wranglers from various ranches). The mega-western also required 5000 costumes, 77 sets, 40 covered wagons with full teams to pull them and one genuine steam-powered riverboat. Budget-wise it exceeded $15,000,000.

One of its 50 stuntmen, Loren handled everything stunt coordinator Richard Talmadge could dream up, from moving train leaps and wagon wrecks, to horse craft and dangerous doubling gags for Debbie Reynolds and Robert Preston. Filming took place in seven states including remote locations like Paducah County, Kentucky; Janes recalled an hour paddleboat ride followed by 14 miles of dirt roads to get there. Arriving at Lake Cumberland, the junction of the Ohio and Tennessee rivers, Loren and the stunt players were soon knee-deep in the rich silty deltas and spotting deadly snakes slinking across the water's surface. Dispatched to wrangle the serpents away before filming began, Janes and the guys caught 40 water moccasins in less than an hour. By the end of their stay, the stunters were waterskiing on Sundays, they were so accustomed to the danger.

Featuring James Stewart, John Wayne, Gregory Peck, Henry Fonda, Lee J. Cobb,

With a "long pole" in hand, Janes (left) watches *How the West Was Won* star Debbie Reynolds (sitting on the bow wearing hat and dress) as she takes direction from Henry Hathaway (on right in white hat).

Karl Malden, George Peppard, Walter Brennan, Robert Preston, Eli Wallach, Richard Widmark and Debbie Reynolds, the picture was a Who's Who of '60s Hollywood.

During the trading post robbery in the "Rivers" section, Loren stood in for bad-guy Karl Malden, cleaved in the back by an axe wielded by James Stewart. "Cutting edge" prop-craft of the day, a realistic rubber bit was used on a real hickory handle. Thrown by special effects guru Bob Overbeck, the specially balanced eight-pound axe struck with a heavy thud. Janes trusted Overbeck with life and limb (or headache, owing to bad aim). Fifty years later, the resulting shot remains compelling.

Loren was cast as a flatboat "poler" for rafting sequences shot on Oregon's Grants Pass River. Seven consecutive days of whitewater maneuvers left Loren's hands blistered. Guiding the heavy barge through the roiling river unaided by motor, he was thrown clear of the launch several times and struck submerged boulders.

Shifting from Ohio River poler to cowboy, Loren found familiar ground in the sweeping grasslands of Montrose, Colorado, during the film's "Plains" segment. Costumed in a dress and bonnet (with padding where needed) doubling Debbie Reynolds, he did a fall from a racing buckboard amid a horse stampede. The scene included 112 horses ridden by native extras from the Four Corners reservation who spoke little English—and headed straight for them, as the scene required that the heroine be nearly trampled. Janes avoided the panicked herd before doing a leap-mount onto

5. When the World Wasn't Padded 29

In the Alabama Hills of Lone Pine, *How the West Was Won* stuntman Janes doubled Debbie Reynolds in the segment "The Plains," as seen in these three frames (cropped and enlarged) as he approaches, mounts and then shares a ride with stunter Jack Williams.

In *How the West Was Won*'s segment "The Plains," Janes (center of image, white pants) portrays a settler shot with pursuing Indians' arrows, falling from the back of a covered wagon. He hit the hard ground at 30 MPH, rolling to a stop with prop arrows still attached. His instruction then was to lie prone as the braves overtook his position, their horses leaping over him.

the back of a passing horse. Describing the bareback lunge as anticipatory timing, the stuntman underlined the importance of his gymnastics training in making such a move look easy: "Launch too soon and you get kicked in the head. Not high enough, you can get trampled. You have to spring, then grab some mane and swing down onto the horse."

Working in *How the West Was Won*'s "Plains" segment under the second unit direction of Yakima Canutt, Janes (center of photo) ducks between galloping horses. There were just inches between his head and the charging animals' hooves.

In his lady wardrobe, Janes was kidded by real ranch hands drafted to work on the stampede scene. He was the object of many catcalls, hand-smooches and lewd invitations from the ranks. Offered a fist-full of wild daisies by his pal Jack Williams during lunch, Loren chased him down and forced one into his mouth following a judo throw and wrestling match. When fellow stuntmen kid around, distant locations become a little less lonely for the guys.

Working more of the picture's Indian attacks, Janes doubled Robert Preston for wagon train action. He performed galloping horse-falls controlled by rider-affected trip-rigs, then rose and ran off in continuous action. A good day's work meant not being rolled on by a horse. At the start of the attack scene, a near wagon-to-wagon collision at galloping speed (owing to unrehearsed Teamsters) forced Janes, playing a "good guy" settler, to reverse his team's direction so violently that his front wheels shredded to the hub. He narrowly avoided an approaching camera car; impact could have been injurious for man and beast alike.

Arrows felled him from a speeding covered wagon in the next sequence; a secondary tumble to the ground with horses running him over ended the shot. Janes: "Wearing the arrow rig requires you to fall on the top of your shoulders and sides of arms, to prevent ripping the harness out on impact. Landing square on 'em really hurts."

Doubling Preston as the fray progresses, Loren pulled off one of film history's least appreciated high-risk gags. Trapped aboard a runaway six-horse team with the wagon driver dead, he leaped between the first two animals (landing on the hidden running-board attached to the lower rigging) and worked his way forward until grasping the leads by the bridle (legs splayed over each animal's back), slowing them into a throng of other horses. Risky due to the chance of slipping and being trampled, the move has always required strength and athleticism to pull off.

Involved in another of the movie's more dramatic stunts, Loren piloted a crashing covered wagon as it tumbled 400 feet down a steep grade with a camera mounted in it to catch his every move. Filmed in Lone Pine's Alabama Hills, the Talmadge-designed rig involved 100 yards of pitched wood and steel track combined with bogey wheels. A six-horse cable-guided towline controlled the wagon's rapid downward movement, employing hilltop resets after each take.

Mounting the three-lens 400-pound Cinerama camera to a geared-rotating gimbal, grip Pete Papanickolas made d.p. Joseph LaShelle's vision a reality: filming a wagon rolling over violently *from within*, as contents including chairs, a table, bags of stores and a steamer trunk slammed into Loren each revolution.

Receiving $300 per shot, after three attempts, he was bruised, but far from beaten. Capping the roll with a gymnastic dismount perfected in floor exercise, he vertically leaped from the flipping buckboard and hit the ground with a side-hip somersault. Landing solidly just in time to dodge a real spear launched at him by a mounted brave, Janes

At Lone Pine, a cable-controlled enclosure was used to get *How the West Was Won*'s inside-a-rolling-wagon shot—with Janes being violently thrown around inside during the process shot.

dispatched him to the ground with a violent pluck from the charging horse. This required two days to prep and as many to shoot; down time was non-existent.

Drafted for Indian stunts as well, Loren did bareback flips at full gallop including a dangerous "whip around the neck" feature yanked from a horse. It was accomplished via reverse Pony Express mount, by which one catapults their body from the horse's back, jerking lower body, hips and thighs while using the horse's rising stride to lift cleanly away. Transitioning into a dragging, the scene continues as the whip is wrapped tightly by a mounted cowboy—pulling Janes along the ground for nearly 60 feet. It was necessary for Loren to place his palm between the leather whip and his throat; multiple takes left lasting abrasions on his neck and hand. "If the whip digs in too deep, it can crush your windpipe which is bye-bye time."

Janes did his best stuff on John Ford's "Outlaws" segment (shot in Superior, Arizona), where 38 miles of narrow-gauge rail track were found for the action. The legendary footage was shot by second unit director Talmadge despite Ford's reputation for wanting such scenes for himself. An antique steam engine was restored to full running order at MGM's expense. Capable of sustained speeds in excess of 40 MPH, it required a driver, tender and engineer to move its six cars. Taking part in the "running atop the train" sequences of the robbery, Janes worked as an outlaw galloping to the locomotive's rear. Transitioning from horse to train on the fly, he vaulted over the caboose railing onto its rear platform,

Pulling off one of stuntdom's greatest moments in *How the West Was Won*'s "Outlaws" chapter, Loren Janes leaps from a moving train onto a towering saguaro cactus.

all in one fluid move. On the train roof he bounded car to car across four-foot couplings, then engaged in a pistol battle that ended with him shot off the train.

Doing what was considered his greatest stunt, Janes sailed vertically through space at 40 MPH, face first, into a 30-foot-tall cactus, then rolled down a 20-foot ravine before coming to rest. Possessing deep knowledge of plant systems dating to high school, the ex-schoolteacher knew the saguaro had root stems equal to height. Hitting the huge cactus would be like hitting a rubber telephone pole; without taking precautions, he knew he'd bounce off its surface straight back into the moving train. Therefore, the cactus' massive roots were severed ten feet below surface.

Loren replaced the hard-packed dirt around it, and also removed razor-sharp quills from the impact areas with a propane blowtorch and pliers. Four takes and multiple puncture wounds later, he did the leap that had movie audiences cheering on their feet for two years. Janes was even in the center of the movie's poster.

Elsewhere in the movie, Mexican bandit Janes was on horseback in a shot where the horse galloped across railroad tracks. He rode over a buried camera and Plexiglas sheet—but the horse stumbled on the gravel-filled bed, catching its hind hooves under the rail tie. Panicked as the train approached, the animal fought violently to release itself. Effecting an instant correction, Janes threw his weight forward off the saddle, forcing the horse's neck down while allowing a half-turn to free the animal's back foot. Lurching off the bed, the horse bolted from the tracks within seconds of the train rumbling past. Loren got a chipped tooth and split lip in a collision with the animal's rearing head.

During the filming of George Marshall's section of *How the West Was Won*, "The Railroad," a lumber carrier stunt over an elevated trestle proved to be one of Janes' closest shaves. The action called for a high-fall expert, and veteran stunt pro Bob Morgan was the first to be assigned. But there was a failure of the chains securing massive timbers to a flat-top car while filming a swinging-log gag. Morgan's leg was crushed, and had to be amputated. Desperately wanting the shot, helmer Marshall requested a replacement. Talmadge chose Janes, who accepted. Rolling 40 MPH along narrow-gauge track on a log suspension bridge 90 feet in the air (over a rock-strewn gorge), Loren performed a two-hand hang from the end of a dislodged timber before plummeting 45 feet to a suspended safety net, 10 × 20 feet in diameter. Hinged upon timing and strength, his self-release by visual mark was imperative to landing in the catcher beneath the bridge. Failure would have resulted in hitting the frame or missing the target altogether, leading to a 90-foot drop to the rocks below. There was no wire safety around the wrist; Janes relied upon gymnastic hand strength. Considering inertia, forward momentum, centrifugal force and gravity, the calculus teacher let go at just the right moment. Seeing only swirling green water ten stories below with 50 knots combined wind in his face, Loren completed the stunt twice before Henry Hathaway was satisfied. Refusing to re-shoot closeups of Morgan's face (the stuntman was in the hospital), Talmadge persuaded producers to intercut pre-injury frames with the new sequence, providing his injured friend with some extra cash for the job. (Previous to the Stuntmen's Association, injury took money out of the pockets of the stunt players themselves. They got little reimbursement by the studios. Insurance for such an occupation was almost unheard of at that time. If a cowboy broke a leg, the production might pay the hospital bills, but he went to rehab on his own dime.)

Janes was also seen in *How the West Was Won* as a Mexican bandit, complete with large sombrero dwarfing a shaggy wig of blue-black hair, crisscrossed shell belts, droopy mustache and dark makeup. Crawling along the bottom of a railroad car at 30 MPH, he's

In *How the West Was Won*'s "Outlaws" segment, Janes hangs 90 feet from the ground on a log extending from a moving (40 MPH) train.

thrown clear of the undercarriage amid a gun battle and violent derailing of the train. There was minimal clearance between the narrow rails and antique wheel housings; hitting the step-bars would have spelled disaster. Cleanly making the move three times, Loren attributed his recitation of the Lord's Prayer while lubricating the bars before each attempt (as well as timing) as a key to his success.

6

The Misfits, Taras Bulba and *The Greatest Story Ever Told*

Director John Huston's *The Misfits* was shot in the late summer and early fall of 1960 in Dayton, Nevada. Loren Janes' live-action rodeo work added a gritty realism to the picture that only real cowboys could convey—strapped to the back of bucking horses or roping mustangs from speeding pickup trucks.

Brought in for second unit cinematographer Rex Wimpy's coverage, Janes was joined by saddle legends Corky Randall, Barlow Simpson, Jim Sherwood, Bob Davenport and Bruce Gailbraith. There were objections by the stunt crew (half of whom were solid cowboys) but for various reasons, the unflappable Huston insisted on dedicated rodeo players in those sequences. Footage of Billy Babcock, Chuck Roberson, J. Lewis Smith, John Daheim, Cole Palen, Teddy White, Jack N. Young (Gable's double) and Loren was first-rate and later used by the Pro Bull Riders Association as advertising. Featured in a steer-roping scene using a perfect lariat toss with the cow sprinting one direction and Janes' horse the other; his mustang reversed in midair as the line drew taut around the saddle pommel. One-handed roping with the trained response of a bovine partner, rider and mount moved in unison as the horn-hooked heifer slammed to the ground. Three bound legs and a blurred cowboy held frame before cutting.

Switching from cowboy tricks to "slapshtick," Janes was hired by Moe Howard to stunt-gaff 20th Century–Fox's big-budget *Snow White and the Three Stooges*. Helmed by Walter Lang and longtime Jerry Lewis cohort Frank Tashlin, the movie was a Technicolor marvel, and thus expensive for producer Charles Wick. The work for Janes was real: coordinating suit of armor–clad stair falls, swordfights, numerous horse gags, etc. Stooge leader Moe proved stubborn, insisting on doing stunts himself until shown the real danger involved; Loren donned a black bowl cut wig to take the tough falls for the aging vaudevillian despite the 62-year-old's objections. "He was very personal in his putdowns, often calling me the Golden Golem because of my blond hair."

In 1962, friend Steve McQueen offered him small assignments on very different war films, *The Great Escape* and *The War Lover*. The latter, made first, was shot in Kent, Cambridge and Hertfordshire, England; Janes did little more than ride shotgun with McQueen on freezing joyrides around Bovingdon's airfield when mechanical issues with John Crendon's B-17s slowed filming to a standstill. "I think Steve already knew he was going to do *The Great Escape* when he called," Loren said. "So getting me to Germany for *War Lover* was his way of shoehorning me in for the bigger show."

Free-tripping to Füssen, Bavaria, on *Great Escape,* Loren (doubling McQueen) handled a flying leg tackle—plucking a Waffen soldier from his BMW motorcycle moving

15 MPH. He was also utilized as a chase German pursuing "Hilts" on sidecar bikes. (McQueen played a Nazi while sporting a new '62 Triumph TR-6 Thunderbird motorcycle dressed as military.) The stuntman bowed to moto-master Bud Eakins when it came to the picture's climactic sequence of McQueen leaping pasture fences until crashing into barbed wire fencing. Portraying an air strip guard tackled by James Garner during the theft of the German Buckerbu 181 sequence, Loren remembered multiple takes ordered by director John Sturges—despite Garner's constantly aching knees. "That was a concrete tarmac," he revealed. "Every take, nine in all, hurt Jim like you can't believe. Yet," Janes continued, now slightly emotionally, "he *never* complained. We ultimately had him collapsing on me, to lessen impact. But the initial contact required force enough to sweep him off his feet, and you can't fake that. If you watch the sequence, you can see me get crushed and Garner really limp away in pain towards the aircraft."

His equestrian rep growing, Janes was drafted in mid–1962 for director J. Lee Thompson's saddle-and-sword historical biopic *Taras Bulba*. Second unit boss Cliff Lyons had him double Yul Brynner's riding and risky fighting parts. It was the first meeting of Brynner and Janes, and led to years of work for the latter. Employed in the picture's massive opening battle sequence (Turks vs. Poles, lensed by cinematographer Joe McDonald), Loren was slashed, speared, arrow-perforated and stabbed off horses, in both sides' wardrobe. Run through by a lance-wielding Pole from a sprinting horse, Janes was viciously knocked from his mount, utilizing a fitted chest pad beneath his tunic. The resulting impact was so good, the sound department recorded it for foley. Featured in the picture's many mounted charges and skirmishes using hundreds of riding extras (filmed at Disney's Golden Oaks Ranch), Janes did a spectacular horse-fall, mid-field between Pole and Turk lines. In a full-out gallop when the horse collapsed under him (courtesy of a flying-W rig); the resulting drop left much to be desired. Tripping the 1500-pound horse in full stride, he was nearly crushed as it landed in a heap. Forward momentum hurled Loren past the animal's neck; his quick butt-slide reaction and splayed legs kept the rolling horse beneath rather than on him.

Featured in saddle-work of his own design, Loren did underbelly gallops as a Cossack (hanging upside down from the horse, firing between its legs), as well as a dozen featured swordfight gags, costumed and made-up as Pole, Turk and Bulba's bunch. Knocked off horses by axe, arrow, staff and sword, he was stirrup-dragged, trampled and run through to the point of complaint by editor Folmar Blangsted, who lamented after dailies that Loren had been killed so many times, the audience was apt to believe him invincible. One person *not* invincible was star Brynner: He was accidentally socked during a fight scene with Tony Curtis (playing his son). The blow knocked Yul's hairpiece nearly from his scalp. Hanging like a skunk-tail, the toupee was hilarious, yet no one dared move. Curtis couldn't hold it in and fell to the ground laughing—ruining the take. Apologizing to Brynner (still rubbing his sore jaw from the errant punch), Curtis joked, "Maybe we need some more glue, Emil," referring to makeup man Emile LaVigne's attachment of Yul's thatch.

On *The Greatest Story Ever Told*, Janes was brought in by coordinators Paul Baxley and Henry Wills, who tasked him with toughening-up a thousand ROTC recruits cast as Roman soldiers (they replaced 550 Navajos bused to the Moab, Utah, location). The charming and affable Baxley, another Talmadge protégé, was a World War II Marine Scout sniper with multiple Bronze Stars, Purple Hearts and presidential citations for service on Saipan, Iwo Jima and Tinian. He watched as Loren trained recruits in full

6. The Misfits, Taras Bulba and The Greatest Story Ever Told   37

armor costume including shields, eight-pound metal helmets, tin chest pieces, phallus swords in birch scabbard, and leather sandals. Running laps, doing push-ups, practicing hand-to-hand combat and swordplay—he had them drilling every morning before the company reported for breakfast. A former Marine himself (decorated obstacle course participant), he knew how to put others in peak shape. And it was needed. While principal photography was slated for 90 shooting days, director George Stevens' multi-take style with dozens of set-ups bloated the schedule to nine months.

Filmed in the winter of '62 through August 1963 at MGM with extreme locations from Death Valley National Park to Nevada's Pyramid Lake Indian Reservation and

Doubling Eddie "Rochester" Anderson as an *It's a Mad Mad Mad Mad World* cabbie, Janes (top position on ladder) hangs in preparation for the sequence's finale when he gets tossed into the arms of a Lincoln statue.

Utah's Canyon Lands in Moab; strain on cast and crew alike was monumental. Exposing six million feet of Panavision 70 film through their cameras, d.p.s Loyal Griggs and William Mellor achieved the fourth most prodigious use of stock in moviemaking history. Including production costs and the actors' contractual overages due to missed projects, Stevens' film ran over $20,000,000 to make.

The action sequences showed every dollar. While shooting in Page, Arizona, Janes worked as a Roman soldier in a featured running horse-fall. Loren recalled hitting the rock-solid ground in full armor: "First the tin tunic would catch you under the chin. And then the helmet, which weighed like ten pounds, would whip your head forward, allowing only the ground's view before your knees would hit the gravel. It was rough, because Romans didn't wear pants. My knees were skinned to the bone by wrap."

Janes saw lead Max von Sydow in character with white robe, makeup and Jesus-like expressions, greeting all before a demanding horse collision, and queried Baxley as to the extent of danger requiring the Lord's son to "work the set": Loren was solemnly blessed by von Sydow (who was playing to the remark) and asked Baxley, "Just how dangerous are the gags today Paul?"

Following the serious *Greatest Story* with the most ridiculous action-comedy of its generation, Loren crewed Stanley Kramer's *It's a Mad, Mad, Mad, Mad World,* shot in the late winter of '62. Hired by Carey Loftin, he wore blackface makeup to double African-American Eddie "Rochester" Anderson as a money-chasing cabbie. The

Launched Superman-style 20 feet elevated off a double-angle trampoline, Janes performs his *It's a Mad, Mad, Mad, Mad World* gag.

6. The Misfits, Taras Bulba *and* The Greatest Story Ever Told

moviemakers had been unable to find anyone of color to perform the complicated and dangerous double trampoline launch required to land a grown man "baby-style" in the arms of a statue of Lincoln.

Janes was also the only candidate with aerial experience matching body size and shape. Flung from the raised hook and ladder top on location as it spasmodically cranked, Loren was propelled 15 feet horizontally, flying three yards off the ground, through a half-dozen painful takes. Hitting the bronze-painted plaster and steel statue with car wreck force, each attempt took a piece of Loren's shin, elbow or back flesh upon contact. As he was required to rebound backward (head and neck exposed during flight), his slightest miscalculation in landing could have been tragic. "It looked cartoonish," he said. "But being flung from 15 feet without padding, really smarts when you hit—no matter the frame-speed!"

Filling in as needed (the stuntman's path to residuals), Janes was cast as a Cadillac driver in the finale, forced into oncoming traffic on Long Beach Boulevard. Uttering the line "What the…!" he was allotted a small bump for speaking despite it being cut.

Janes was also in on the picture's most famous daredevil sequence, Frank Tallman's amazing twin engine airplane flight through Butler Aviation's hangar (door to door at 150 MPH—less than 23 feet of clearance from wing tips to walls and 15 feet to the ceiling). The shot eventually segued into the Beechcraft model C-18s touching down roughly, taxiing toward camera before crashing through the terminal's window. Janes played a restaurant patron fleeing for his life, the live-action shot allowing the aircraft's propellers and forward movement to tear through the mock-up hangar front, dressed as a restaurant. It was stopped by a steel cable attached to the rear wheel assembly. The turning props chewed through the aluminum and glass set-piece like butter, with Loren doing his "slippery step" running in place, four feet in front. Having set tape on the hangar floor marking the plane's supposed final position, Janes' situational awareness allowed for an instantaneous adjustment when the Beechcraft lunged two feet further than expected. If he'd been hit by the propellers, his chances for survival would have been zero.

Loren Janes was again tapped by pal McQueen to play cards and climb a few fences in director Ralph Nelson's '63 classic *Soldier in the Rain,* starring Jackie Gleason. Blake Edwards produced this bittersweet comedy of post–World War II stateside Army life. The stuntman had little to do on the picture but a few pratfalls and a fistfight. Loren moved on to a Doris Day project, *Move Over, Darling.* Day wanted to avoid injury no matter *what* her male double looked like in a skirt. Loren performed a slightly risky swan dive into the sea from a ship's top mast. With a vaulting spring-kick from the vertical tower, he sailed over the boat's listing decks below.

7

Western Classics: *McLintock!* and *The Sons of Katie Elder*

Presented with work more his personal taste, Loren was hired in '63 for John Wayne's two-fisted *McLintock!* co-starring Maureen O'Hara as his estranged spouse and helmed by Andrew McLaglen (son of actor Victor). The William Clothier–photographed Western had a famous fight scene revolving around a muddy hill. Directing second unit with Chuck Hayward, Loren gaffed the fisticuffs during the first week's filming of the brawl, shot during a frigid December in Old Tucson.

Mixing a drilling lubricant in the muck so that it stayed wet all day (real mud dries up rapidly); the slippery bentonite had the consistency of chocolate syrup, but hardly the taste. Swallowed, it went down oily and soon produced volumes of foul gas. Working the week of the brawl disguised in multiple costumes, Janes was batted, kicked, pushed or slid into down the 60-foot hill dozens of times.

Loren recalled the fight's opening as his proudest work on the picture. Hayward requested that he work out the landing point for Leo Gordon, who was to be sent down the embankment by McLintock's first punch. Janes knew "the Duke" disliked "pulling" his shots. Measuring the distance based on Gordon's height, Loren's set-up for the punch had the actor's body sail full-length before landing back-first on the embankment and sliding to the bottom of the clay bog. Janes appeared in the fracas as a prudish townie wardrobed in plaid suit and bowler. Wayne tossed him halfway down the slope.

Janes' next picture was another light-hearted spoof, the Civil War western *Advance to the Rear* with Glenn Ford as a displaced Union captain and Stella Stevens as his love interest, filmed at the Janss Conejo ranch. Loren was brought aboard courtesy of coordinator Chuck Roberson, who recalled Janes' heroics on *How the West Was Won*.

Gaffing a sequence with a dozen animals and riders simultaneously plunging 30 feet into water, break-away platforms were utilized to ensure that all the horses dropped safely at once. Doubling Ford, Loren did a rear saddle-flip into water, side-falls to the turf, and a comedic dragging sequence.

A dangerous "wagon drop" nearly sent Janes home in a box. Worked with a green-carpeted ramp, the action called for an eight-foot descent of the wagon (flying out of control over a grass embankment), with the driver barely holding on. He landed hard, the impact hurling him forward off the seat toward the churning back legs of the right-rear horse. Miraculously spared serious injury when his face smashed into the animal's hindquarter; the stuntman bounced clear, suffering only a split lip. It was lensed by Milton Krasner of *All About Eve*, *The Seven Year Itch* and *How the West Was Won*. A future stunt icon, Hal Needham, played a rebel soldier yanked off a horse by Janes.

7. Western Classics: McLintock! and The Sons of Katie Elder 41

Janes (flat on his back with feet in the air, lower right) mixes it up with other stunters in the comedic *Advance to the Rear*. He had been accidentally socked by Alan Hale, Jr., seconds earlier.

Warner Brothers' *Cheyenne Autumn* (1964) was Janes' second John Ford picture: He was tapped for stunt-planning duties while still shooting *Advance to the Rear* via Chuck Roberson, coordinator of both films. Doubling Richard Widmark as Captain Thomas Archer, Janes handled the star's riding gags, as well as doing featured bad-guy Indian sequences that saw him shot off and rolled on by horses. The stunter was abused to the point of exhaustion by schedule's end.

In a scene involving a rapid horseback descent of a 30-degree pitched shale embankment, there was a 60-foot drop on one side and jagged boulders on the other. "The d.p. William Clothier kept hollering for me to move toward camera," Janes said. "But [in that direction] was a bad drop-off, and my horse was skittish." Loren put blinders over the animal's eyes and shifted his weight to the rear to aid traction. By leaning far back on the saddle and guiding the horse down the embankment, he got the shot.

Janes was given numerous Cheyenne brave falls to do as well. He was blasted from a running horse at full speed. Completing a reverse dismount backflip from the mustang, and landing face-down on the hard canyon floor as planned, he tumble-rolled to a stop on the mark: 10 inches from the camera.

After doing one horse fall, Janes was nearly trampled by mounted extras following following too closely behind. (These amateur actors from Moab were bussed in for the work and buzzed on whiskey during the three-hour ride.) The rowdy bunch were reprimanded by their tribal leaders for playing too rough with the "make-believe Indians" from Hollywood.

Called upon for several "bad guy" Cheyenne aerial gags (his specialty), Janes did a 15-foot boulder dive, tackling a mounted trooper. Sailing Superman-style (face down, arms stretched forward, with ground-mounted coverage provided by a Super 70 camera looking up), he collided with the soldier like a mid-field Butkus tackle, taking him from the saddle to the ground and finishing him off by knife. Doing a high fall to end the sequence, Loren plunged head-first from a 20-foot cliff. He threw his Winchester rifle aside just before flipping to his back for a safe landing. Padding was provided by buried hay and blankets beneath pre-loosened dirt, but the impact was still enough to stun.

Loren spoke warmly of the Colorado River's majestic beauty and the comfort of Goulding's Lodge air conditioning after a long scorching day in Monument Valley. But not all his memories were as happy. "Sal Mineo was being ridden by Ford," Loren remembered. "Ford wanted him to play his character angrier. Getting away from the constant chafing between set-ups, Sal would hide out in the stuntmen's tents playing cards, smoking, and drinking the occasional snort of rye, as long days permitted. Protective on screen, stunt-folk tend to look out for actors off screen as well."

20th Century–Fox's *John Goldfarb, Please Come Home* was a Cold War spoof of a directionally challenged college footballer (Richard Crenna) turned pilot who crash-lands in the tiny kingdom of Fawzia (can you say Arab Emirates?). He is forced to coach the king's team after his (the king's) son is cut from UCLA. A CIA-rigged game is set up with hilarious consequence. It was a playful jaunt by a serious director, J. Lee Thompson (*The Guns of Navarone, Cape Fear*).

When not taking Crenna's falls, Janes again doubled for Shirley MacLaine. He was gang-tackled by the *faux* Notre Dame defensive line comprised of massive stunt-stock like Red West (Elvis' bodyguard), Guy Way, Louie Elias, John Strong, Kip Behar (a muscleman from Mae West's Vegas stage show), and the original horse whisperer, Glenn R. Wilder of *Ben-Hur* fame. Twelve takes were needed before second unit helmer Richard Talmadge (who hired Janes) was satisfied. "I got sacked by Elias and Red one take, then double-teamed by John Strong and Kip, who threw me on my head. Feeling a little abused, I went to Talmadge and asked what he was doing. I was told to shut up as *each* take paid 200 bucks. I was nailed ten more times without a peep!"

Goldfarb also featured Peter Ustinov (as King Fawz), Jim Backus, Harry Morgan, Charles Lane and budding actors Teri Garr (harem girl), Kent McCord and James Brolin (Notre Dame players). Telly Savalas, uncredited, played Macmuid, the harem recruiter. Lensed by Leon Shamroy, it was no small effort amid Fox's busy production schedule. A comic twist on Gary Powers' flight of a U-2 spy plane into Soviet air space, the picture was filmed four years past the event, and only two since the American pilot's release from Moscow's Vladimir Central Prison in February '62.

Loren and Kirk Douglas had stayed in touch after *Spartacus*, and in October '63 Janes doubled for Douglas on the World War II epic *In Harm's Way*. The perfectionist actor wanted his doppelganger for the picture's big scene, a Honolulu bar brawl, complete with closeups of Douglas breaking chairs and getting knocked over a table. The film was director Otto Preminger's look at the U.S. Navy from Pearl Harbor to the Battle of Midway, and the dramatic lives of a few of its gallant men and women. But with Preminger at the helm, it was no love fest. Loren recalled the Hungarian-accented director hollering at actor Tom Tryon one afternoon to the point of cruelty. Following six takes of a tender bedroom scene with Paula Prentiss, the notoriously gruff taskmaster bellowed that he couldn't understand Tryon's muttered lines. Tiptoeing behind him, Preminger shouted "*Relax*!" from two inches away. The actor was reduced to a quivering mass of discontent. Friends like Loren dissuaded Tryon from walking off the Paramount lot or quitting the movie biz altogether.

Playing a practical joke, Elvis Presley (his accent muted, pretending to be a studio talent scout) phoned Janes and asked him to audition for his new picture, *Tickle Me*. Janes informed the "scout" that he was already working on the film by virtue of director Norman Taurog; the singer thanked him and hung up. Loren didn't get the gag until filming a horse-breaking sequence a week later. While Janes doubled Presley (playing a rodeo rider) through a sequence of bucks, rides and falls, Elvis again did his fake scout voice, thanking him at the end of each bone-jarring take. From hard "ass-first" landings to real roping and bull riding, Janes made Lonnie Beale's Panhandle Kid character believable.

In the film's club fight sequence, Loren also doubled Elvis. Caught by a wild punch accidentally landed by character actor Bert Stevens (playing a club patron), Janes was sent reeling. Watching the movie, one can tell that it was solid contact.

Janes remembered Presley filming behind-the-scenes footage with a miracle device called a Sony video camera (a gift from Taurog), capable of instant playback. Loren said it was amazing to see what was shot, without delay. "While [d.p.] Loyal Griggs considered it a toy, Presley was serious and told all who'd listen that the Japanese camera was going to change moviemaking forever."

Featherbedding again in December '64 (via Pal McQueen), Loren was hired via a midnight call by the actor to double him in *The Cincinnati Kid*. He reported to location at Redondo Beach's Roadhouse Junction before dawn the following morning. Despite *lack* of danger in a fight scene, McQueen (starring as an anti-hero card player) insisted that his stuntman be used in the scuffle, claiming everything from pulled groin muscles to tonsillitis during two days of coverage. The Philip Lathrop–photographed picture looked good but played to half-filled theaters amid bland reviews.

Henry Hathaway's western *The Sons of Katie Elder* was Paramount's 1965 tentpole picture. Starring John Wayne, Dean Martin, Earl Holliman, James Gregory, George Kennedy, Dennis Hopper and Michael Anderson, it featured journeyman actors John Doucette and Strother Martin and was also cowboy-cast with stunt pros (like Loren) that Wayne enjoyed having on set. Saddle icons Joe Yrigoyen, Chuck Roberson, Red Morgan, Chuck Hayward, Henry Wills and Jack Williams all knew their way around a horse, to say the least.

Janes flew to Chupaderos, Mexico, in January '65 to double Michael Anderson. Anderson replaced Tommy Kirk, who was busted for marijuana and fired from the picture. Kirk was outed as gay when that was injurious to one's career. The weed charge didn't stick but his home studio Disney canned him nonetheless.

When Loren exited the shabby DC-3 at Durango Airport behind Wayne and others, a Mexican honor guard in ancient uniforms played a wobbly version of "The Star-Spangled Banner" until the badly hung-over actor cursed via perfect Spanish for the band to stop or he'd have them all shot.

Hired for the film's trail drive montage, Janes called on his real cowboy chops to single-handedly herd 200 horses in a majestic crane shot. He was also drafted at the last moment to perform the movie's dramatic water-dragging stunt after Chuck Roberson (subbing for George Kennedy) suffered a broken wrist when axe-handle-hit by Wayne. Loren scooped up the speaking part of Ned Reese as part of the deal.

Although Wayne did preliminary scenes rigged behind a horse in the cold river (attesting to the rumors the actor did the drag himself), recent lung removal kept his physical involvement minimal. The rigors of location shooting had him bordering on walking pneumonia with only half his respiratory system intact. The actor did not want his public to think he was through as an action star. When Lucien Ballard's footage was edited by Warren Low, his clever cuts were so good that audiences never realized it was two different men (Wayne and Janes).

In the picture's climactic shoot-out, Loren doubled Wayne's head-first leap into the river, handcuffed to Martin. (Wayne's regular stunt double Chuck Roberson was still suffering from his wrist injury.) Closeups and medium shots were intercut with coverage of Wayne in the water. As Dean Martin, at 48 years old, did little stunt work himself, Janes was tasked with underwater duty for the film's finale, and swallowed gutfuls of river over a dozen takes and 90 minutes.

Taking a punch from Wayne in the "brothers' brawl" (doubling Michael Anderson as Bud Elder), he received a right cross from Wayne that knocked him off his feet. He crashed back-first into a hanging rack of pans; the sound of impact was so loud that director Henry Hathaway cut the scene—screaming for repairs before Janes hit the floor. Multiple takes following, Loren received several socks to the jaw before all were satisfied.

Janes with the rest of the *Sons of Katie Elder* stunt crew. Hatless, he's kneeling in the bottom row left. John Wayne's stunt double Chuck Roberson is in the top row on the right. The others are unidentified.

Still doubling for Anderson, Janes was tossed into the river in a comedic moment by Wayne and Martin. He was doused via one-two-three swinging launches 11 times before Hathaway was happy. Suddenly the helmer's favorite, Janes was chosen for a saddle-jerk off a horse during a night exterior. Subbing for Paul Fix as Sheriff Billy Wilson, he was blasted off a horse by baddie James Gregory. A "cable jerk" was used to violently wrench him through space by way of "invisible" aircraft wire attached to a harness beneath his costume. Rearward horizontal flight carried him back as though cannon-blasted. Cutting-edge stunt technology of its time, the jerk-rig adds believability to bullet impacts to this day. Janes did the stunt a half dozen times before the perfectionist director called it a print.

Finishing the picture's shootout beneath the bridge trestle, Loren (doubling Anderson) was mortar-launched 12 feet skyward by a controlled explosion mimicking dynamite. Set by legendary industry "powder man" A.D. Flowers, the "boom" left Janes bell-rung for hours and concussed for several days.

8

G-Men, *Camelot* and More

By 1965, Loren Janes was a person of interest to producers, a stuntman much in demand. One money man who heard what Loren could do for an action TV series was Quinn Martin, producer of *The F.B.I.* with Efrem Zimbalist, Jr. Janes was his sole choice for the job of stunt coordinator. With the production promising to be action-driven each episode, Loren took the position—his first stunt coordinator title—and he was suddenly earning over $1000 a week while hiring all the guys he could find.

At Malibu State Park, *FBI* stunter Janes performs a 22-foot aerial leap (with a six-story fall if it went wrong). His specially prepped launch ramp (consisting of spring-boards and carpet) was attached to the cliff edge behind him; his flight path allowed a feet-first safe landing on the other side of the gorge.

8. G-Men, Camelot and More 47

Each episode required that fresh "heavies" be tackled, shot and/or run over; stunt pros Bill Catching, Gene LeBell, Jesse Wayne, Paul Williams, Dean Smith, Dick Warlock, Rick Sawaya, David Sharpe and Regina Parton gave the show its true-to-life look. Loren often did the scripts' most dangerous stunts himself.

One gag, that no one else would dare, was a 22-foot vertical leap from boulder to rock, over jagged granite. Hurtling through space from the higher formation to the lower, Janes "cheated" his landing towards the near surface of the giant curved rock to avoid tumbling forward. He "stuck" the fall like a gymnast's dismount. A hidden mini trampoline was utilized for takeoff, its angled position producing the needed arc and distance to clear the gap. He dropped one foot for every two flown horizontally, so cautious figuring was required to escape short-landing injuries. "Without the trampoline," Loren revealed, "I might have made it halfway before falling like a rock!"

When not risking life and limb, Janes was studying the differences between episodic television's demands vs. features. From back-up plans to budgeting, Loren used his time in the trenches learning to think like a producer. Perfecting stunt-craft along the way, including airbag landings, car crashes, fights, falls and protection of talent, his real education was deal-making with directors for proper payment. With the Stuntmen's Association still formalizing its deals around Hollywood in '65, each gag (jump, punch, prod or

Action coordinator for *The F.B.I.*, Janes (bending) is seen here with series star Efrem Zimbalist, Jr., and episode guest star Earl Holliman at Malibu State Park. In this episode, Janes plays a convict frantically fleeing an F.B.I. helicopter.

plane crash) had to be individually bargained by the coordinator for "his guys." Knowing the inside track, Janes handled negotiations, making his hires (and himself) more dough. Aiding producer savings by virtue of quick stunts to tell the action, Loren's ability to "understand the bigger picture" remained a bartering chip his entire career.

Producer Pandro Berman had Janes stunt-gaff *A Patch of Blue*, MGM's study of '60s racism starring Sidney Poitier and Elizabeth Hartman. Then Janes returned to Henry Hathaway for *Nevada Smith*, which reunited him with Steve McQueen. It was produced by Joseph E. Levine, lensed by Lucien Ballard and based on a character (Nevada Smith) from the Harold Robbins novel *The Carpetbaggers*. The story of a mixed Apache-white man avenging his parents' murder, it resonated at the box office.

The picture's water-dragging scene was shot in June '65 amid Inyo National Forest's Hot Creek area, Loren was semi-drowned for three days behind a running horse in two feet of frigid water. Already known for his river-drag sub for John Wayne in *Sons of Katie Elder*, Janes was regarded in the industry buzz as one of the best horse-drag guys around.

The scene required more than ten "runs" per afternoon to get all the necessary footage, and Hathaway had Janes pulled by the wrists at full gallop on every take. Ribs, arms, shins, elbows and knees were bruised and abraded from hitting rocks along the shallow river bottom. Forced swallowing of water induced coughing fits lasting several minutes. "Hathaway expected real," Janes said. "Giving him less would only result in more puking."

Janes (in white circle) stays low as steers with three-foot horns and crushing hooves surge past. According to Janes, Hathaway wanted even more takes than what he got.

In Inyo National Forest in Bishop, California, *Nevada Smith* helmer Henry Hathaway (right, Cuban cigar burning in his left hand) discusses body position with McQueen (left) as Brian Keith (center) approaches.

Shifting to knife-fights, Loren choreographed the film's cattle corral mix-up, between McQueen's character and Martin Landau's uber-sadist bad guy Jesse Cole. Recalling his Marine training, Janes taught McQueen the essentials of handling an edged weapon, then worked with Hathaway and Ballard to get the best angles while shooting the sequences. Landau lookalike Victor Romito (a World War II Bronze Star recipient and stunt actor) also knew his way around a knife. According to Janes:

> We really went at it. Victor was fast and had great balance. The bit where we fight on the fence tops was scripted, but really figured the night of. He would try and catch me with the knife, and I would hop at the last second. With the railing flexing and dimly lit exterior in the steer-filled corral, the shot was very compelling when cut.

The cattle, trucked in from a nearby working ranch, were not camera-savvy. After breaking through the pen as part of a planned gag, the Texas longhorns became excited

On location with the *Nevada Smith* troupe at Convict Lake, Janes (with lighting cables behind him) in costume as a menacing prisoner.

when avoiding the lighting gear and camera platform before them and darting in odd directions. At times they came close to trampling Loren, who rolled out of harm's way as the steers swarmed about.

In addition to doubling McQueen, Janes was cast as the Aberdeen Hotel cowboy role and a heavy in the Convict Lake work camp. He again got wet as McQueen's double paddling the heavy dugout canoe through the swamps of Krotz Springs, Louisiana, with the fleeing Pilar (Suzanne Pleshette) in tow. Janes said, "The trainer used harmless snakes for the biting sequence, and had a bunch in a plastic bucket. But the bigger local ones kept eating them. Before long, it was like bait. That's why the insert shot of the slithering moccasin was only three seconds. Any longer and they became lunch."

Loren traveled to China in November '66 for McQueen's next project, 20th Century–Fox's *The Sand Pebbles*. McQueen hired him directly, as stunt double and a second unit director. He also got another minor speaking role: McQueen's shipmate Coleman, an American sailor. The action was set in the revolution-ripped China of the 1920s, the era of Chiang Kai-shek's battles with local warlords along the Yangtze River.

One scene defined the fervor of violence and danger to U.S. gunboat crews during the time: the siege of the bamboo barrier by the Sand Pebbles. Shot amid the rugged hill-lined waters of China's Sai-Kung River, it was packed with stunt action including close-quarters fighting with fire axes, automatic rifles, sabers, machetes, bayonets and pistols. Janes' deadly realism gave the sequences an urgent feel that many war pictures miss.

Loren gaffed what was perhaps the film's most dramatic shot, the axe-hit to the belly of the student political leader. He coached the Taiwanese actor to double over as the

In *The Sand Pebbles*, Janes (left) stands in sailor garb, rifle at the ready, while Richard Crenna barks orders to the *San Pablo* crew.

Standing next to Steve McQueen, Janes (right) plays seaman first class Coleman in multiple *Sand Pebbles* sequences. The movie's boat mock-up was based on the actual boat (the USS *Texas*) that sailed up the Yangtze River in 1926 as the Revolution gripped China.

rubber blade hit, to better sell the impact. There were two months of construction for 30 shooting days of battle coverage. Loren injected other ideas like Ford Rainey wielding a Browning automatic rifle while exposed on deck, dying after killing several Nationals. Wounded multiple times while valiantly holding off the enemy, he's fatally shot before flipping over the boat's railing and falling to the sea. Accomplished with padded mattresses rigged behind the bulkhead, the gag induced a moan of sympathy in dailies.

One of the realistic touches Janes brought to director Robert Wise's picture was Richard Crenna's use of the saber. Practiced in swordsmanship via Olympic Pentathlon trials, Loren had expertise that he passed along to Crenna, whose cutlass-handling gained much from the lessons.

Other action benefiting from Loren's military past was the shoot-out at picture's end (McQueen vs. Chinese troops). In this sequence, Fox's Mission Ranch was seen as the China Light Mission School. Also notable: the mob scene where Po-Han (Mako) is flayed open by student-rebels on the dock.

Doubling McQueen in the scene, he needed to sprint across a flagstone courtyard. This called for hours of full-tilt running for Loren, automatic rifle in hand. The double's face was cleverly hidden in shadow and movement by Old School master Joseph MacDonald (*The Young Lions, Viva Zapata!*). The stuntman recalled the weapon growing heavy as the number of takes piled up. "That was a real B.A.R.," Loren said, "After three nights of filming, my arms felt like rubber. Between the humidity and running, Steve and I were drained. We were both in good shape, but when you see him fighting for wind during some takes that was no act!"

Equally realistic, the mob scene involved an actor (Mako) suspended for long periods of time in an uncomfortable position; his arms roped open from the sides between two mooring posts. Fitting a hidden support behind him, Janes made the gag physically possible. Employing rigged breakaway ropes for the actor's final rifle-shot impact.

Loren met Jackie Chan, then a teenager cast as a tough who attacks McQueen. He remembered the young man's sense of humor and his quickness: "I stood in for Steve when blocking the scene, and every time I tried to deflect Jackie as dictated, he would slip my grasp or snake under with blinding aversion. We had no idea of his real abilities until years later."

Having not missed a morning's swim for 20 years, Janes needed to settle for Taiwan's Keelung River. It teemed with toothed fish and writhing snakes (not to mention garbage) but he felt compelled to swim regardless of the locals' warnings. Enjoying the exercise, he was nearing the workout's end when he was stung on the right hand by what turned out to be a bamboo viper. Janes reported to the set the following morning; unaware of the toxins that were flooding his brain, he walked and talked like he was smashed. Glenn R. Wilder figured out that it was snakebite, not booze, causing his teetotalling pal's lurching walk and slurred speech. When he was raced to a hospital for the antidote, doctors were amazed at his recovery; most victims die within hours of a bite. He dropped ten pounds because of the incident.

Janes started 1967 stunt-coordinating a humorously bad Civil War farce, *The Fastest Guitar Alive*. (Roy Orbison starred after Elvis backed out.) Industry steady W. Wallace Kelley shot the action-spy film, with secret weapons saving the South. Director Michael Moore's hope was a San Francisco to El Paso gold heist gone wrong. Other than John Doucette and Iron Eyes Cody, the picture has little to warrant watching. Although laced with comedic horse galloping, wagon chases and leaps off low rocks (shot upward to

8. G-Men, Camelot and More 53

project danger), the movie was taken seriously by Janes, who presided over production like a mother hen. There were no stunt injuries on his watch.

On Universal's swashbuckler comedy *The King's Pirate* (1967), Janes showcased his acrobatic, gymnastic and juggling skills as never before. Don Weis directed it as a slapstick stunt platform meagerly disguised as a pirate flick. Janes was cast as the mute acrobat part of Zucco's (Kurt Kasznar) troupe. Hired by coordinator Ronnie Rondel, Jr., Loren

The stars (and stuntmen) of *The King's Pirate*: Holding up Doug McClure are stuntman Chuck Couch on right and Charlie Picerni on left. Behind them are stuntmen Bob Terhune and Louis Elias and actor Kurt Kasznar. In the back, with a blond shock of hair, is Janes.

The *King's Pirate* stuntmen comprising Zucco's troop practice their "human ladder" gag: The three on the ground are Bob Terhune, Chuck Couch and Bill Couch. The pair on their shoulders are Hank Monzetto and William Snyder. Danny Rees is on *their* shoulders and Janes on top.

8. G-Men, Camelot and More 55

was among Hollywood's agile elite including Bob Terhune and Chuck and Bill Couch, with Charlie Picerni adding a buffoon pirate to the mix. Performing live-action circus tricks like being launched six feet into the air via springboard actuated by a dropping tumbler from an eight-foot tower, Loren landed on the shoulders of a man standing across from him. He was also part of a human ladder gag with troupe members stacked three levels high. Janes climbed up the guys, gaining access to an open second story

Perched atop a 12-foot boulder, Janes (left) prepares to guide an unidentified stuntman in a fall onto fight choreographer Ralph Faulkner (white shirt on ground punching Morry Ogden). Clifford Stine (plaid shirt, photo left), photographs the *King's Pirate* action.

window. Taught to scale the arms and knees like ladder rungs (while off-camera help panted below to shove him up), star Doug McClure did his end of the stunt, with Loren doubling the stretch through the window.

Another nod to medieval tumbling arts was the use of a juggler's cradle. A small platform was mounted atop a 15-foot-high pole, its bottom held fast to the ground by one man. A second fellow, straddling the perch above, performs a handstand. Able to actually do it, Janes did the "feet in the air" master shots while McClure required an elaborate suspended overhead wire support to stay airborne for his closeups. Once established at the window's edge, the actor was substituted for Loren in the shot, "accidentally" seeing the inside of Jill St. John's apartment with the intention to rob it.

Janes tutored McClure through acrobatic basics like front rolls, handstands and springing leaps. One bit of real gymnastics was beyond Loren's ability to teach *any* amateur athlete: a palm-to-palm body-lift where one standing fellow (face to face) clasps another and raises him up on his shoulders in one fluid motion. It was a matter of leg spring by the lifted party with continuing launch by the bottom. Upward momentum was a must to gain the required height to land on the standing guy's shoulders, feet first.

Shooting subsequent "Going to Take the Fort" sequences, Janes (subbing McClure) led double trampoline catapult gags, sailing 20 feet through the air, ten feet from the

Propelled skyward off a double trampoline, *King's Pirate* stuntman Janes flies 12 feet through space as part of the fort attack sequence. Note the bales of foam rubber landing nets below and the safety catchers and grips standing by just in case.

8. G-Men, Camelot and More 57

Dropping 25 feet from the scaffolding, Janes bounces back up from an angled trampoline while rehearsing a somersault full-body flip for *The King's Pirate*.

ground. Filmed amid Catalina Island's woods, the shots utilized neutral density filters to render day to night. A gorge was superimposed below them as flight landings were managed by trapeze nets temporarily rigged to massive trees.

Aerial gags abounded for Janes and the other gymnasts; somersaults and high flips were integrated into the cannon destruction scenes of the pirate fort attack. There were hidden mini-trampolines and special effects mortars producing fiery explosions. Rondel's stunt crew, including Loren, suffered burns with eyelashes, brows, and sideburns scorched. Owing to the stunt folks' close proximity to cannons and excessive blasting powder used, playing the pirate guards left all without hearing for hours. "If you watch that scene," Loren quipped, "you'll notice none of us can see straight, or hear. After four hours of point-blank explosions, Ronnie had to tap us on the shoulder at take's end 'cause we were all lip-reading."

Purging the fort abutments presented another perfect gymnastic opportunity made to order for Janes. Powered by springboard catapult over the high wall via dropped stuntman from a ten-foot boulder, he pulled a back flip midair, hitting the ground on his feet. Cut into the frame, the result elicited wild applause in theaters. While impressive, little in the picture compared to Loren's work in the finale, the taking of the pirate ship.

A full-size frigate with rigging and masts was built on a stage. A second "floating boat backlot" was constructed at the studio's Universal Falls; the third was an authentic

In *The King's Pirate*, Zucco's troupe entertains in the pirate city. Chuck Couch (bottom) steadies the trapeze pole as brother Bill revolves midair above. Janes (hands above his head) drops onto a springboard, sending Danny Rees airborne into a back-flip. Bob Terhune (right) tosses flaming pins to William Snyder. Doug McClure (center of frame wearing hooded robe) makes his way through the crowd in disguise.

tall ship anchored off Catalina's leeward side. For initial siege coverage of the ship, Loren and the other stunt players did grappling hook climbs and swinging rope landings clambering up the vessel's side. They went indoors for reverse coverage on a "flooded stage" amid mock-daylight. Opposition to the boarding erupted into a free-for-all fight as

A dangerous airborne take for *King's Pirate* stunt double Loren Janes (top center) as he is catapulted eight feet by springboard. Note the real boulders and trees surrounding the action.

invaders landed. Featured in multiple high falls or over ships' railings as either a pirate or one of Zucco's men, Loren also doubled Kasznar (padded heavier and wigged) performing an over-the-bow plunge into Universal's artificial sea. He used his extraordinary diving ability (head first most times) and cat-like agility to set up the fall. Even in this picture, his work is obviously better than the usual fare.

Enjoying a nod to his mentor Richard Talmadge (Errol Flynn's double), Janes was given a swashbuckler standard: a swift rope swing from the masts across a crowded lower deck—clearing it feet first. Filmed on stage aboard the mock-up (whose sails topped 50 feet), Loren's flawless execution during 11 takes of two-footed impacts, near misses and "home runs" sent stunt players hurtling overboard. Ending the scene with a final homage to Flynn, helmer Weis had Loren leap the poop deck stairs with a flourish when landing, colliding with a trio of heavies in the process. Turning up the fantasy aspect of the melee, Weis captured Loren doing springboard-launched horizontal-flying kicks to pirates. "The trick" was holding one's body in flight, to ensure accuracy of landings. Paid per take vs. a flat rate (before the Stuntmen's Association bargained), Rondell and Janes rolled through Universal's gates by Cadillac limousine each morning, clad only in bath robes, earning in excess of $200 a day. This was on par with lawyers' salaries of the time.

Loren Janes was among a handful of stuntmen to do Joshua Logan's *Camelot*. Signed

The King's Pirate: Superb balance employed, Charlie Picerni stands atop the human pyramid. He's standing on the shoulders of Janes and Bob Terhune while they stand atop Bill Couch, Hank Monzetto and Chuck Couch. The dancing girls are Ami Luce and Tanya LeMani while Danny Rees (left) tosses pins to partner William Snyder.

by Yakima Canutt's sons Tap and Joe, he handled archery and swordfighting coordination, including personal instruction for Richard Harris and Franco Nero. Harkening back to Olympic fencing days, as well as many sword-and-sandal pictures, Janes knew the material well. He actually made the bulls-eye arrow shot during the archery competition, doubling Nero's Lancelot.

Janes was next hired for *The Dirty Dozen* by producer Kenneth Hyman from MGM casting books (photographic compilations of thousands of "actors" used to narrow down hiring calls for specific looks), and matched with Richard Jaeckel who played Bowren. With his sand-blond mane, blue eyes and height, he was a close second to the slightly stockier actor in line at breakfast, but perfect for camera, helmeted and in uniform.

Doubling Jaeckel, he made an arduous rope ascent, scaling the castle tower. The 40-foot climb was made tougher by the 14-pound MP-40 grease-gun slung across his chest and ten pounds of helmet, web belt and boots ill-suited to the task. Janes recalled,

> It was about ten o'clock at night and cold. [Director Robert] Altman's A.D. insisted I not wear gloves while climbing, as no one else had them and it would look funny. I voted for gloves. He said no way! "Sorta" pals with Altman from *Attack* back in '56, he asked me if it was necessary. "Only if I want to use my hands for the rest of the picture," I joked.
>
> I got to use gloves, but after six takes, it still tore me up inside 'em, not to mention my arms so sore I couldn't hold up a cup of coffee for an hour afterward.

Recalling camaraderie on the picture, Loren was in a push-up competition one afternoon with legendary footballer Jim Brown. While the crew cheered them, he finished just ten behind the massively built fullback (90 push-ups to Brown's 100 in 60 seconds). The loser's penalty, downing a glass of milk, was about as risqué as Loren liked.

Janes was rewarded by Altman for the rope sequence with "featured bits" like playing a German soldier machine-gunned from the bridge during the climax. His tumble to the moat below was no picnic. It was pitch black and cold, and he hit the water head-first, his helmet crushing his nose so that he was unable to breathe after surfacing. A medic checked and confirmed that the snout was broken. Janes was relegated to relatively easy work thereafter; for instance, he was seen as a wounded German up to his neck in the moat when the armored truck crosses the bridge.

Built on the MGM British backlot, the William Hutchinson–designed chateau set was steel girder assembled five stories high with a practical roof and balconies, measuring 250 feet across. And so well constructed, its destruction at picture's climax proved impossible. The multiple plastic explosive charges throughout its structure were set off but all attempts to demolish it failed. This forced producers to blow up a cork and plaster double, during reshoots weeks later. As a final gift, Altman cast Loren as a Nazi officer shot point-blank by Lee Marvin and Charles Bronson. Janes considered it fair payment for enduring a week of cold, wet nights. Janes: "I had Lee look in my eyes and pull the trigger, while Bronson jammed the gun, and still struggled to fire it."

Returning home from Great Britain, Loren landed at LAX on a Sunday, and by Monday afternoon he was doubling William Shatner in a new outer space series called *Star Trek*. No longer relegated to second calls, spur-of-the-moment fill-ins or luck, Janes was hired directly by stunt gaffer Paul Baxley. With each episode of producer Gene Roddenberry's series came two Captain Kirk fights and one alien battle with folks thrown around the *Enterprise*'s deck, making for consistent need of stuntmen.

Mirroring Shatner with tan hair, athletic build and matching height, Loren was one of five doubling for the rough stuff: The others were Dick Dial, Gary Combs, Chuck Couch and Baxley himself. Leaving no room for illusion owing to pull-over blouses and tightknit pants as wardrobe, physical subs for the star were difficult to find. When Janes doubled Shatner during hand-to-hand combat exercises aboard the *Enterprise* in the series' second episode "Charlie X" (airing September 15, 1966), his Marine training provided perfect judo throws as the captain.

Filling in later for actor Richard Tarto on the November 3, 1967, episode, "I, Mudd" (when his Norman character was crushed by falling boulders), Janes was brained by gunite-covered effect rocks, zealously hurled by a large prop man. They weighed nearly 60 pounds and were several feet in diameter, with batten stock and chicken-wire frame beneath. The blow to his skull produced dizziness and falling, without a stuntman's fakery.

9

From Apes to Frank Bullitt and Beyond

Moving on, Loren landed in another iconic picture: Mike Nichols' *The Graduate*. He was brought in by Dustin Hoffman's double Lee Faulkner, to coordinate the wedding fight, shot in United Methodist Church in La Vern, California. Loren's input began with the best man's family attempting to grab Benjamin on the modern staircase and finished with the violent use of a six-foot cross to ward off attackers. It was finally wedged between the handles of the glass chapel doors, sealing them against intervention as the hero runs off with the bride.

The third week of May '67, Janes reported to a sizable stunt call at 20th Century–Fox for Franklin J. Schaffner's *Planet of the Apes*. He watched as 40 of his closest pals donned 30-pound gorilla suits before reporting to wardrobe for another 15 pounds of leather costume over them. Selected by stunt boss Joe Canutt for a featured gag as a captured "human" victim hunted by horse-riding apes in the frenetic round-up sequence, he was to be wearing little more than a loincloth and wig when he was plucked from the ground by a nylon trapping net stretched between two riders at full gallop; the gap dividing the horses was less than five feet. Both animals needed to run straight without hesitation upon gaining the strain of the trapped person; stuntmen in ape suits then muscled the 170-pound captive aloft, while continuing to control their horses. Failure of either could have caused serious injury.

Janes said he found running at constant speed (without anticipation or looking back) to be best for the horse overtake and netting, as well as proper placement of heels at net's edge, allowing a smoother transition. "When two galloping horses ridden by apes runs up on ya," Loren said matter-of-factly, ",basic instinct is to turn first, then run. In this case, you just sprint, allowing the net to overtake you, then collapse once lifted to avoid sliding into the horse's churning legs or falling over the rear."

Loren joined the gorillas: He was fitted for the trappings of a primate on horseback. It was the same weighty costume that he saw his peers wearing in May, and his four weeks in costume (June and August 1967) took a toll. He became badly dehydrated from the latex facial prosthesis glued from chin to forehead (and bulky fur suit covering all else). Calabasas temperatures topping 104 degrees combined with perspiration pooling in the eye sockets reduced his vision to painful squints. He collided with another gorilla soldier on horseback and was thrown headfirst to the ground. Used in the film, the footage was more than producer Arthur Jacobs ever bargained for.

Charlton Heston's attempted escape from Ape City was filmed in Malibu amid man-made rock formation structures (utilized by art director William Creber as imagined from Spanish architect Antoni Gaudi's Goreme Valley works). Loren was kicked backwards down a steep set of stairs. Nine takes were required. He equated the work to carrying bags of cement up a ladder. "After two goes," he said, "the weight of the gorilla suit, and the form used to back-fall without cracking your head, really takes a toll. By the time we wrapped, I was so drained they had to help me to the trailers."

Janes was drafted in the early fall of '67 by old boss Paul Baxley as part of a small stunt ensemble on NBC's *The Man from U.N.C.L.E.* Joining pros Charlie Picerni, Frank Babich, Lee Faulkner and Steve Burnett for the spy series with a twist; the episodic used real locations like back-plant MGM tunnel complexes for everything from Iron Curtain prisons to nuclear submarine interiors. Cast due to broad ethnic possibility from German to Czechoslovakian or Soviet), Loren's buff-colored hair, narrow features and ice blue eyes meant he was a bad-guy guard garroted, karate-chopped or bludgeoned in every episode.

Janes recalled his most risky *U.N.C.L.E.* stunt, leaping from a moving train in a marshaling yard, working amid Union Station's crowded tracks on a busy day (the only deal producers could make). Even the use of flagmen with radios failed to make Loren's task safer as he was required to execute a running landing after leaping from a four-foot-high box car door (traveling 30 MPH). A secondary front-roll to his feet culminated with a sprint up the tracks until he was shot. Without warning, close proximity to an inbound express nearly sucked him into its path. There was a vacuum effect between trains moving fast in opposite directions; Janes' ability to "keep his feet" helped him to survive. Adrenalin and balance kept him moving up the track without being drawn into the approaching locomotive. "With trains and elephants," Loren offered sagaciously, "you never take *anything* for granted. Both of 'em take a while to stop."

Loren was freed from *Man from U.N.C.L.E.*'s casting mold by Steve McQueen for producer-director Norman Jewison's *The Thomas Crown Affair,* beginning in October '67 during New England's beautiful autumn change. He doubled McQueen in the polo matches and driving scenes. Hogging motoring time in his modified Meyers Manx dune buggy, McQueen topped 100 MPH along Ipswich's Crane Beach, slicing through morning's low surf and firm sand. Janes recalled, "The dune buggy was in my hands less than an hour the entire three days."

Earning his rate handling full-bore polo sequences filmed at South Hampton's Myopia Hunt Club, Loren did charges, bumps, collisions and sprints through crowds of other riders. Photographed by brilliant newcomer Haskell Wexler, the footage possessed a ballet-like flow of speed, power and violence that Janes' saddle skills enhanced. There were three successive mornings of full-out matches with scoring and defensive bits built around Steve. Once again the fact that Janes was a McQueen lookalike made him invaluable. Loren also worked opposing player gags for Wexler's multiple set-up coverage. He rode ten polo ponies per day to make it work. Seen on both teams through reverse shots, he can be spotted by the sharp viewer in almost every frame as a chucker, on various mounts.

Sticking with Paul Baxley, Loren worked Universal's *Coogan's Bluff* in November '67. Starring Clint Eastwood, the film featured a "cowboy cop in New York" storyline and was helmed by hardcore action freak Don Siegel (*The Killers, Two Mules for Sister Sara*, the *Dirty Harry* stuff); the picture possessed a gritty realism of violence particular to its director.

Showcased in the film's poolroom fight (Eastwood is jumped by several bad guys), Janes was tossed headfirst out a window by him. Hitting the glass hands-out (vs. smashing through with his skull as it appears) would ensure that only small slivers of the broken pane would lodge in his knit cap. But he was launched a tad too high and struck the reinforced window frame with his forehead as he went through. Thinking Janes was joking by lying still after take's end, Siegel asked if he needed a special invitation to get up. Checking, Baxley informed all that Loren was out cold.

Entering a prolonged phase of doubling Steve McQueen, Loren's first endeavor was his least known, but possibly most dangerous: *Bullitt*, which started in May of '68. Hired directly by the actor, Janes with his uncanny resemblance to McQueen was put to use in the picture's famous car chase sequence.

There were high-speed runs over San Francisco's pitched streets in the Max Balchowsky–built Mustang. (Bud Eakins and Carey Loftin switched with McQueen depending upon murky insurance parameters.) The stunt trio remained invisible by way of rear-view mirror positioning that blocked their faces. When McQueen was driving, the back seat mounted camera saw him in the mirror.

Lasting barely ten minutes on screen, the William Fraker–shot sequence showcased Bill Hickman (driving the pursuing black Charger), with a climactic motorcycle slide more dangerous than people know. Completing a high-speed skid in one direction as the automobiles veer into his lane from the other, Bud Eakins laid the bike down at 35 MPH with Janes driving the approaching car at 60—and they came within a foot of colliding. Steering a transverse course to "cheat camera," the move looked like inches when cut and edited. Choreographed with multiple vehicles (and background stunt drivers), Loftin's masterpiece required the exact timing of 20 people, all supporting Eakins' moment.

Loren Janes (left) and Steve McQueen go over last-minute details for the *Bullitt* finale, a shootout at San Francisco International Airport on a frigid "Bay weather" night in June 1968. Doubling McQueen in one of his most dangerous stunts, Janes did a sequence of running shots dodging a taxiing 707 jet—just ten feet away—rolling at 80 MPH.

Running less than ten feet from the moving 707's wheel assembly, Janes dashes beneath the huge Boeing. The dance with the 707 was his masterpiece of planning, execution and athleticism.

Wardrobed as Mexican bandits on *The Great Bank Robbery*, Janes (grasping left side of upper smokestack) and Carey Loftin (back to camera) brace upon explosive impact. Cliff Lyons stands safely atop rear. Multiple takes from different angles were required. Loren and the guys earned their $800 day rates on the balloon crash the hard way: repetition.

Laying the bike down *toward* incoming traffic, Bud risked life and limb as the slightest error would have resulted in a head-on collision. Janes: "Driving the swerving car that triggers the stunt, I had to get the timing right. If I screwed up, Eakins could have been badly hurt or killed."

Challenged with one of the more hazardous stunts of his career, Janes did the finale's airport foot chase across a tarmac of taxiing aircraft. An off-duty freight pilot— one agreeable to driving a 707 down a dark runway with actors running in front of the plane—was bribed to operate one of the Boeings. Sprinting directly in a jet's path (doubling McQueen), Loren was so close that engine blast singed his face during multiple takes; he lost eyelashes, brows and a sideburn for his efforts.

At MGM, Janes worked on *Ice Station Zebra* for a few days in June 1967. Hired by John Sturges (the director remembered him from *The Magnificent Seven*), Loren was cast as a Marine gallantly manning a .50 caliber machine gun vs. Russian paratroopers. Photographed by Daniel Fapp in Super 70 format on soundstages and beneath the waters surrounding Point Loma, the picture contained first-ever coverage of a complete submarine dive and breach. Incorporating a high-pressure camera housing operated by second unit d.p. John Stephens, it allowed full focus, zoom and aperture control vital to recording the image at depths up to 300 feet.

In *The Great Bank Robbery* balloonists race the horse-drawn wagon to the crest of the hill. With unpredictable wind shear, the stunt players and Teamsters had their hands full just to get close to targeted impact.

Warner Brothers' *The Great Bank Robbery* was a Hy Averback–helmed dud in the *Cat Ballou* vein, minus Lee Marvin. Loaded with comedic stunts, the "western" starred Zero Mostel, Kim Novak and Clint Walker and was stunt-gaffed by solid Janes connection Paul Baxley. Janes was brought in for a series of railroad crashes, wagon riffs and hot-air balloon gags; one of particular danger was a 20-foot jump from gondola to moving train. It was difficult owing to crosswinds, shifting balloon position and timing to intercept a train moving 40 MPH in the opposite direction. Landing feet-first on the roof without bouncing off required extreme physical control and focus. "Bicycling" his legs in descent (running in place upon impact), Loren negated the train's forward momentum.

Elsewhere in the same sequence, Janes piloted a balloon crash, slamming the gondola against the engine at nearly 35 MPH. Challenged by swirling winds, balloon-buffeting, gondola-sway and varying train speeds, Janes' anticipatory timing and last-second shift of the basket produced one of the picture's best stunts, instead of a missed wreck.

Loren and the boys (Hal Needham, Carey Loftin and Cliff Lyons) also played Mexican bandits made-up and wardrobed with sombreros, mustaches and bullet belts, hurled off the moving train car upon explosive impact with the gondola. There was a soft-landing zone of burlap bags (stuffed with foam padding buried beneath the soil). It required a dozen takes. Challenges over balloon reset and gondola P.O.V. shots were solved by Loren's outside-the-box thinking. He had chopper pilot J. David Jones "prop-chase" the

In this *Great Bank Robbery* scene, the gondola hangs from a 90-foot crane as it knocks bandits from the train roof. One of more than two dozen stunt players used in the gag, Janes can be spotted just under the gondola, his hand grabbing it.

Great Bank Robbery star Kim Novak (her back to us) chats with stunt coordinator Paul Baxley as effects technicians fill the massive balloon from a special liquid propane mixture pumped into the large open end. It was advertised as the world's largest balloon.

On *The Great Bank Robbery*, four mini-rocket engine propane gas burners were used to power the largest passenger-carrying hot-air balloon in the world to date (1968). A five-man labor tech crew set the pitch of the burners and readied the rig for inflation.

inflatable to its starting position for each take (as towing was too dangerous and flying against the wind time-critical); he instead grabbed gondola coverage by suspending it from a 90-foot construction crane with a camera rigged overhead looking down, the balloon removed. A workable, safe solution to achieve the "swaying gondola effect," the platform provided ample room for an operator, focus puller, second assistant director and massive Super 70 camera, thus avoiding catastrophic overloading of an untethered balloon.

More *Great Bank Robbery* action. Note the close proximity of the gondola and balloon to the debris of the church steeple explosion.

Using the crane for insert shots of the bandits "blown" from the train roof upon impact, Janes went one step further: He launched himself a dozen feet skyward by mini trampoline. He was caught by a 12-foot-square camouflaged net strung beneath the bridge trestle. Margin for error was minimal, with 30 feet to the rocky ground in the event of a miss.

The sequence continued with a cut-in of Loren and the Mexicans landing on the lumber car. A tumbling log flourish threw the stunt-players clear. They had to "ride" the rolling three-ton pine-tapers as the restraining chain-rig was loosed; inability to remain atop the falling load would have resulted in catastrophic injury. Doubling balloon captain Paul Edward Yost for tight coverage of the train-to-gondola collision, Janes endured close-quarter explosions that sent pulp-wood and paint flakes flying 30 feet with each blast. "Each take felt like a slap in the head. After the sixth, I couldn't focus my eyes."

One stunt set-up was particularly challenging to pull off: a horse-drawn wagon cresting a hill at full gallop, safely crossing train tracks inches before an approaching locomotive—only to be hit by a low-flying balloon. This was hazardous owing to shifting winds and other factors; exact placement of the balloon was essential to make it all work. Mastering "hot-air" piloting, Loren was able to align the gondola while engaging a swooping drop. He timed train speed and horses with triangular focus until the moment of collision.

To eliminate risk to animals, a horseless wagon launch was devised by Loren and Glenn R. Randall; both were bumped up to stunt-Teamsters, their final days on the film. Tasked with sending a 600-pound wagon ten feet through space, then splashing into water below, a wire-control assembly was devised with pullies, cable, wooden track and off-camera horses to rapidly move the load. Providing more than the required thrust, in one take it sent the half-ton rig sailing clear of the tracks into the water—20 feet beyond.

10

Tentpoles and Bogdanovich's Masterpiece Plus Custer's Last Stand

Coming up for air the end of June 1968, Loren traveled to Baker, Oregon, then Big Bear Lake, California, for Paramount's *Paint Your Wagon*. Directed by Joshua Logan, the William Fraker–shot comedic western (featuring songs by Lee Marvin and Clint Eastwood) contained much stunt fodder for the crack crew of 30 cowboys wrangled for the picture. Among them: Richard Farnsworth, Bob Herron, the Hudkins clan, Davey Sharpe, Boyd Cabeen (doubling Marvin), Buddy Van Horn (doubling Eastwood), Joe Yrigoyen, Fred Waugh and Lee Faulkner. Loren survived stirrup drags in effects–made mud, a saloon brawl tossed through a window, and a galloping horse-fall (reverse saddle somersault).

On the boot heels of *Paint Your Wagon*, Janes did Burt Kennedy's *The Good Guys and the Bad Guys*, a flop with Robert Mitchum, George Kennedy and Tina Louise. Its script was so bad, folks forgot to laugh. Janes was hired by coordinator Joe Canutt to double actor John Davis Chandler's Deuce character. Blasted from behind (off horseback), Loren picked up $250 a day for his trouble—with unspent per diem making his wallet seven hundred bucks fuller.

Getting calls throughout '68, Janes was one of a dozen very qualified "go-to" guys, able to stunt with the industry's best. Plucked by director Gene Kelly for *Hello, Dolly!*, he doubled Michael Crawford (both were 5'10", sandy haired and athletically built) during the "polka contest" melee on the Harmonia Gardens Restaurant set. Loren recalled the sequence as a choreographed slap fight wearing mittens. "Crawford was no soft actor," he said. "He did gymnastics and stage combat since Shakespearean plays in his early days."

After another middle-of-the-night call from Steve McQueen, Loren hopped a DC-3 redeye out of Burbank, then bused to Greenwood, Mississippi, for Mark Rydell's 1969 film *The Reivers*. Arriving at the location (an unkempt farm road 30 miles from town), he noticed a mud pit being filled by a water truck, with a replica of a 1904 Winton Flyer automobile parked nearby. According to production manager Jack Reddish, Loren was to drive the priceless car through the bog without damage (or face total loss if steered into the muck). Loren called McQueen to find out why he wasn't doing the stunt himself and learned that the car was slated for McQueen's collection at shoot's end (and that Relyea's insurance deal prohibited the star behind the wheel). Janes knew that McQueen was throwing him a bone, while safeguarding an investment.

Laying 2 × 12-inch planking with one foot plywood sides beneath the visible mud

10. Tentpoles and Bogdanovich's Masterpiece Plus Custer's Last Stand

line, his wise (and dirty) preparation provided a safe roadway of travel while ensuring the valuable car avoided sinking. Doubling McQueen, he drove the Winton Flyer at high speeds on half the takes, while the star put the car through its paces along Mississippi's dry farm roads for all others.

Arthur Penn's 1969 production *Little Big Man* was another landmark picture for Janes. He was brought in by Hal Needham along with dozens of other stunt cowboys, including world-class players Mickey Gilbert, Glenn Randall, Jr., and Jeannie Epper for large-scale battle scenes. A troupe of 100 Native American extras (from the Crow and Cheyenne reservations of Billings and Lame Deer, Montana) played against an equal number of costumed cavalrymen.

Loren portrayed both brave and soldier; his horsemanship shone as he did rough riding gags in buckskins, loincloths and 16-button cavalry smocks. Performing a "continuous dismount" doubling Dustin Hoffman's frantic defense of family as mounted cavalry attacked the village, he yanked a trooper from his saddle while standing, then leapt on the slain man's horse in a single vault before galloping away.

He was also featured as a tomahawk-waving Pawnee plummeting down a steep ravine on a wounded horse. Loren said a relaxed posture with a slight backward lean (holding with his legs) helped him survive the shot: "If you fall, you bail to the side, instead of under the rear hooves."

Doing his patented horse drags, Janes laid down a textbook stirrup sequence (as a "bad guy" soldier) that remains unparalleled today. Shot in the chest by a succession of arrows (via frontal foam piece under the uniform), he is knocked from the saddle except

Playing a Cheyenne brave in *Little Big Man*'s final battle sequence, Janes (in buckskins) leaps on a cavalry soldier from behind before clubbing him from his horse. On the left, Richard Mulligan as Custer fires his pistol amidst the melee.

Buckskin-wearing brave Janes yanks down the wounded cavalry rider at a three-quarters gallop, taking the brunt of the impact with his legs while safely unsaddling his foe without injury to horse or man.

Finishing the running saddle fall and grab, Janes supports the cavalry stunt player as he sweeps him to the ground. Note the supporting hand and body position Janes uses to protect his stunt partner. And notice the two arrows stuck in the ground—marks for the stunt landing focus.

10. Tentpoles and Bogdanovich's Masterpiece Plus Custer's Last Stand 75

In *Little Big Man*, a Union cavalry officer (Janes) is heel-dragged with sword in hand after being swept from his horse. The stunter performed a picture-perfect stirrup-drag as the horse continued to run through the camp. His ankles are crossed for control.

Behind the scenes on Little Big Man: 33-year-old Dustin Hoffman, sitting astride a Kawasaki motorbike between set-ups, takes in the action shirtless on the 100-degree Thousand Oaks location.

***Little Big Man*'s winter exteriors were shot in Alberta, Canada. Heavy coats and a sense of humor kept Dustin Hoffman (left) and cinematographer Harry Stradling, Jr. (right) in the proper spirit between shots.**

one boot in a stirrup, then yanked along the ground behind the panicked horse as it gallops away. "Those Montana locations were rocky," he recalled. "If you cracked your skull doing a drag, it could bury you, much less put you outta work for a while."

Employing bareback techniques learned riding his boyhood horse Hah-ka-nah, Loren did painful gun-blast jerks in buckskins, hidden wire harnesses looped beneath his costume. A ten-foot lanyard line was "pulled" by two off-frame effects men, down-lit to reduce visibility. According to Janes, "You gallop forward, reins in hand, then your back-cable would be jerked-fast as the horse shoots from under you." He sold the bullet impact well. "If you didn't open your hips," he added, "you got hung up on the horse and gut-wrenched as the harness is suddenly engaged. That produces a punch in the stomach, that really hurt." Janes' face winced at the memory.

Loren subbed for Hoffman in a scene in which mounted Crow warriors pursue his buckboard across the prairie. He executed a horse-to-horse transfer at full stride, leapfrogging forward as Harry Stradling, Jr.'s, camera rolled. Galloping 35 MPH over uneven field, he made his move and cleared the heavy halter and bridle rigging. "You launch your pelvis and hips up and forward in one thrust. Momentum and gravitational pull takes care of the rest."

The movie was filmed in Montana with amateur Crow and Cheyenne "actors." Battle action turned real as day players ran their horses into cavalry actors on foot, removed rubber tips from arrows (Gary Combs lost an eye) and generally showed little interest for safety as the days wore on. They were angry over rate discrepancies with reservation bean counters handling extras' payroll (and not thrilled at the picture's subject matter). A few breakfasted on whiskey, taking out their resentment on any blue uniform for the day's remainder. Loren and the other stuntmen watched each other's backs. "Bodyguards" protected against equine and arrow mishaps.

A man of peace, ex–Marine Janes brokered a lasting truce through barter (covered by producer Stuart Miller), hoping to cut down additional stunt costs. Grateful locals gave him the Crow name E Gee La Ha Da Aeesh (man who gives many horses), Loren arranged for "rented" ponies to stay with the tribes as extra thanks. This amounted to $100 per animal; production saved thousands in stunt crew payroll and had peace of mind as they safely finished the picture.

Janes picked up saddle play and barroom scuffles on James Garner's *Support Your Local Sheriff*, shot in the summer of 1970 by Harry Stradling, Jr. He was among old friends with longtime Garner double Roydon Clark, Richard Farnsworth, Nick Dimitri, Jerry Gatlin and John Daheim on the Chuck Hayward–gaffed crew. The Durango, Colorado, summer location was hot and humid. Next came *Suppose They Gave a War and Nobody Came* in September '70. Hired by coordinator Paul Baxley, Loren nabbed a featured role (commandeering a tank during the theft sequence), as well as multiple stunts ranging from jumping off an overturned water tower to precision driving with Jeeps and 4 × 4 trucks. Then he "jumped ship" (or tank) for a lucrative television movie back in L.A., *Wild Women*; he was offered the stunt coordinator slot paying $1000 a week plus gags. The Aaron Spelling production starred Hugh O'Brian and Anne Francis. It finished in 22 shooting days, and the afternoon Loren unpacked his gear, he signed a deal memo with Peter Bogdanovich's company for *What's Up, Doc?*, a film that featured one of Hollywood's most elaborate (and expensive) car chases. The director's goal was to surpass the famous stunts in *Bullitt*, still playing in theaters two years after release. The chase lasted 11 minutes on screen while requiring 19 shooting days under the brilliant eye of d.p. Laszlo Kovacs, 32 stunt drivers and a cost of a million dollars. Released in August '71, it was the first Tinseltown picture to list full stunt player credits.

Hired by "crash genius" Paul Baxley, the massive sequence culminated in Loren (doubling Ryan O'Neal) making a 60 MPH launch from the rear of a Cadillac convertible as it plunged 25 feet off a pier into San Francisco Bay. Janes was "clotheslined" by a rigid banner catching him across the throat as the convertible careened off the landing.

A softer plastic-and-rope banner was supposed to have been installed, but there was a screw-up, and set decorators employed permanent line. It struck Janes with karate-chop force before growing taut and finally snapping. The impact took the breath from his lungs and he was unconscious as he hit the water. Thirty seconds of face-down floating followed, as Baxley dove into the Bay and came to his friend's aid.

The chase sequence was a true automotive ballet involving tandem bike, Chinese Dragon, pedestrians, ladders, glass sheets and precise acrobatic timing. Barbra Streisand stashes some sought-after valises in the storage box of a three-wheeled delivery bike and takes off down a steep street with Ryan O'Neal running behind. Sprinting to catch up, he leaps on the trike in full stride. Bad guys hail a cab to follow. A black Caddy convertible joins the pursuit as the bike picks up speed. Loren (doubling O'Neal) and Patty Elder (subbing for Streisand) are swept down a steep hill and execute a left turn through a small cross street. Trailed by additional players via an old Buick full of gangsters (followed by a taxi), the tandem bicycle zips down a steeper incline toward a large intersection; as two laborers carry a ten-foot-square sheet of plate glass across the street, passing in front of a 14-foot double-sided ladder with a man on top hanging a banner. Missing the glass by half a second, Janes and Elder threaded the speeding bike beneath the ladder legs as the Buick roars by to its left with inches to spare. The yellow cab suddenly rips past the ladder at 60 MPH, and the man atop is left clinging to the banner. The Cadillac convertible rockets through the open expanse of ladder legs with two inches to spare on each side.

Streisand and O'Neal are ascending a very steep grade when the bike falters and

In the *What's Up, Doc?* chase sequence, Janes goes airborne as the Cadillac convertible drives off a San Francisco Bay pier at 60 MPH. Behind the wheel is stunt legend Bill Hickman, who counterweighted the rear of the Caddy (600 pounds of ballast bolted into the trunk) to keep it from nosing down on launch. Note the oxygen mask over Hickman's face as he prepares to submerge in the car.

rolls backward. Now approaching the speeding posse of trailing vehicles, Loren weaved between incoming traffic, forcing the Buick to skid into a parked VW van. Careening around the same corner, the yellow cab also slides into the VW. The delivery bike closes in on the intersection and the glass guys. The trike blows through the ladder legs, then continues down the street. Last in line catching the others with a sliding turn culminating in side-impact, the Cadillac's final blow produced a visual gag of the van "keeling over dead" on its side—just as the oblivious owner approaches the driver's door to open it.

Following the other cars back through the intersection while skidding close (but missing the ladder by inches), the convertible spins out, striking the ladder and catapulting the worker atop the banner. When it rips under his weight, he grasps the line and swashbuckles through the air, swinging straight through the large glass panel—still held by the shocked workers. The timing to strike the glass seconds after the skid-outs had to be perfect.

The plate glass sequence was child's play compared to Janes' rip through the Dragon Parade. He blasts through the heavy double doors of the Shanghai Costume Company, hitting them in excess of 30 MPH feet first—and fracturing his right ankle. He refused to let doctors treat him until the chase was wrapped; it was five hours before the bone was set by a surgeon at San Francisco's City Hospital. Loren spent a week in traction.

11

Life as a Pro

Recovering in record time, Janes returned to the Bay Area in September '72 to double Michael Douglas for the new TV police series *The Streets of San Francisco*. Coordinator Al Wyatt Sr. hired him to work on the gritty Quinn Martin series which paired a young detective (Douglas) with an older one (Karl Malden). Janes was needed for the action-packed scripts. The series cashed in on the *French Connection-Dirty Harry-Bullitt* trend of plainclothes cops chasing bad guys across urban neighborhoods. There was plenty for Loren to do in the pilot season. When not doubling Douglas, he was cast as everything from a longshoreman to a bank robber; there was no shortage of gags for him to work as a bad guy through May '73. "They had me 'flee' in every episode," Janes recalled. "But always uphill, so Keller could tackle me."

The day of February 6, 1972, began with Janes learning in a phone call from Carey Loftin that Steve McQueen wanted him in El Paso, Texas, by noon the next day for a new Peckinpah picture, *The Getaway*. He doubled the star in various touchy gags like a second story building-to-building fire escape leap (on a set where no net or safety pad could be hidden) and a trash-truck compactor scene. Janes was slated to pilot the Orange VW driving past the bank after the robbery, but at the last moment he was replaced by actor James Garner, a longtime McQueen buddy visiting the set.

Janes returned through Warners' gates in early '73 to stunt-gaff the sci-fi series *Search* at the request of one of its stars, Doug McClure (from *The King's Pirate*). The 23-episode series from *Outer Limits* creator Leslie Stevens was well-done. It was lensed by John Stephens and starred Hugh O'Brian, and had capable support from Burgess Meredith. Janes was given a speaking part as a chauffeur along with stunt coordinating chores. He hired *his* usual employer, Paul Baxley, to double McClure. Janes signed buddies Terry Leonard, Dean Smith, Nick Dimitri and Jack Verbois to fill out the stunt crew; he was surrounded by pros while paying back those who had helped him. He gaffed the usual fights, car chases, etc. Despite good ratings and cool technology, *Search* was a turkey. It was jokingly dubbed *Lost*—by now unemployed crew members—after its cancellation.

Loren could pick up work checking his answering service or simply by bumping into a coordinator at the fights. Bouncing to Universal's low-budget *Godfather* ripoff *The Don Is Dead* (at the request of stunter George Sawaya), Loren was one of two dozen mob guys shot, garroted or run over by picture's end. Directed by A-lister Richard Fleischer and shot by wonder child Richard Kline, producer Hal Wallis' flop starred Anthony Quinn as the Don and featured spaghetti-cinema bankables Abe Vigoda, Joe Santos, Victor Argo, Val Bisoglio and Al Lettieri as his usual scary self. When an actor no-showed due to a drunk driving arrest, Janes got his role as a mechanic by virtue of being the right size for the original actor's wardrobe.

11. Life as a Pro

Janes became involved on *Papillon* when he was summoned by Steve McQueen over a scratchy phone line at three in the morning California time (mid-afternoon the next day in St. Laurent Du Maroni, French Guyana). His longtime buddy tasked him with romping through the jungle, headhunter extras in pursuit.

Landing in Cuyuni-Mazaruni at Bartica Airfield 16 hours later, Loren was ferried up the Essequibo River, then trucked through the interior to the remote location. His head spinning from the long flight, oppressive humidly and jet lag, Janes was hustled to the "set" by stunt boss Joe Canutt. They careened along twisting grades transitioning into tight jungle roads with overgrown vines and branches lashing the windshield at each bend. Loren laughed at the memory of Canutt pressing the surplus Jeep to its maximum abilities, wheels slipping and thudding over the mud and rock terrain: "The Jeep ride alone was worth the price of the flight," he said.

Janes was shown a 20-inch-wide corridor, a hundred feet long, hacked through the dense foliage. (The jungle would grow back in 24 hours if the corridor was not maintained.) He was informed that he would be doing a scene at first light. It required multiple 30-yard sprints through vines and whipping branches over a treacherous muddy trail; the stunt's payoff was a cliff plunge with headhunters in hot pursuit. There were superlative 60-foot dolly shots paralleling the sprinting actor, who was held in medium closeup; other shots of Loren from behind were later inserted. He plummeted from a five-story precipice with arms flailing and prop headhunters' darts glued to his neck for the finale. Janes' flawless technique enabled him to make a feet-first landing in the lagoon below without mishap. "As it turns out," he revealed, "the water was full of poisonous snakes, piranha and nasty snapping turtles that Steve wanted to avoid." Sixteen takes and three drops from the cliff were needed to make director Franklin J. Shaffner happy. "We skimmed the lagoon in a flat boat before the gag," he informed. "And must have relocated a dozen snakes before filming. Many of which were venomous, according to locals." Loren found himself back down the Essequibo and on a jet home before the water in his ears dissipated.

Janes is often wrongly credited with Dar Robinson's amazing cliff leap at picture's end (doubling McQueen as the aged Henri Charriere atop the bale of coconuts falling 80 feet into Maui Bay). Janes' response to those asking is humorous: "After the trip back and forth from Guyana, I wanted to sleep in my own bed ... so I *let* Dar do it."

Returning to Los Angeles 24 hours later, Loren reported to Warner Brothers for the Mel Brooks epic *Blazing Saddles* without unpacking his gear. The 80-strong stunt platoon drafted by coordinator Al Wyatt, Sr., was a veritable Who's Who of Tinseltown horse gods, including Mickey Gilbert, Hal Needham, Buddy Joe Hooker, Terry Leonard, Tom Steele, Joe Yrigoyen, Chuck Hayward, Glenn Randall, Jr., Richard Farnsworth and May Boss. These were the best stunt cowboys in the world, gathered in one place. Filmed in the summer of '73 all over the Warners back lot, Santa Clarita and Vasquez Rocks for the railroad sequences, the picture featured large fights, wagon chases, horse stunts and crowd work not seen in theaters since Westerns ruled the box office.

Selected for underwater work as one of the tuxedo-clad Busby Berkeley dancers in the picture's finale, Loren danced a rumba (ten feet deep in a tank) with no external air. Drafted by Brooks to play one of the mounted braves perched next to him during the "cop-a-walk" scene (following the free-slaves' confrontation), Loren recalled "keeping a straight face" as the most difficult part of the work. He was featured as a brawling cowboy during the picture's climax (the Old West crashing into a 1930s Hollywood musical).

Subsequent melee coverage between top-hatted studio actors saw Janes double-dipping as a waterlogged gent.

A brilliant sci-fi offering directed by Mike Hodges, *The Terminal Man,* found Janes doubling George Segal as a computer scientist with a microchip implant that causes violent brain seizures. Then Janes was retained by stunt boss Max Kleven for the John Frankenheimer–helmed mob flick *99 and 44/100% Dead!* An off-target entry in the organized crime genre, the picture had one asset, its title, despite its brilliant director. It was shot on the cheap in Florida swamps and under Los Angeles' Vincent Thomas Bridge. Janes and 30 "bad guys" including Gene LeBell, Nick Dimitri, Dick Durock and Bob Herron were blasted, blown-up, drowned, knifed, crashed or otherwise dispatched in every way producer Joe Wizan could afford. And he couldn't afford much.

Rebounding to network series' better pay rates, Loren became part of NBC's family offering *Little House on the Prairie,* in the autumn of '73. Part of a carefully chosen stunt ensemble collected by Jack Lilley, an old-school practitioner of horse gags from *Zorro* and *Rawhide* to *Cat Ballou* and *Bonanza*), Loren was used as an occasional heavy for river swims, saddle falls and wagon turn-overs. While hardly a violent series, the Michael Landon–led production saw great success when most other network offerings consisted

Walking Tall star Joe Don Baker (left) strikes Janes full force with a breakaway pool cue as stunt players Gil Perkins, Pepper Martin and Ed Call observe the action. They hold their marks without flinching during the action. Janes wore a thin protective pad beneath his shirt to reduce the sharpness of the blow.

of private eyes, talking cars, Texas oil dynasties or cruise ships with lonely people seeking love. Janes felt at home amongst Big Sky Ranch's Walnut Grove setting in Simi and the Red Hills locations in Sonora. When not needed on set, he enjoyed fishing the creeks, lazily riding horses and observing nature.

Returning to Universal for another "tentpole" destined for greatness, Janes teamed with 150 other risk-takers on *Earthquake* in May 1973. He joined coordinator John Daheim for high-fall sequences from office buildings into massive inflatable airbags (new to the industry). Possible full-frame coverage was expanded to nearly eight stories of roof to street free-fall—without cables, or killing the stuntman for the shot. Janes was paid $500 each take; by the sequence's completion, he earned $6000 for a week's work. Janes volunteered for a pedestrian gag (walking next to a car as a falling slab of concrete smashes it) that was nearly his last moment on Earth. The two-ton block was suspended 30 feet above the car by a construction crane outfitted with a quick release cable. No one considered the crane arm's "back-whip" when the massive weight was released, forward rotation of the block propelled it into Loren's safe zone. It missed the automobile by three feet and Janes by less than 20 inches. The slab's impact produced shock waves, lifting him a yard off the ground.

In another sequence, Loren portrayed a hapless smoker entering a gas-filled house. Blown up by way of stunt mortar as the building erupts in a ball of fire, he was unexpectedly over-launched by the air blast—straight through the set's ten-foot ceiling! He was also featured in a breakaway balcony stunt (plummeting three stories headfirst). The practical set piece (weighing a half-ton), employed a series of quick release bolts to "effect the dump." As it was released from electromagnetic hinges and fell to the ground four feet behind Loren, a last second rear flip into the airbag landed him safely out of harm's way.

Part of the "live action effects" era of big studio motion pictures, *Earthquake* led to *The Towering Inferno* for Loren and 75 other stunt pros. Filming from January through September of '74, the John Gullerman production saw Janes doubling Steve McQueen—who wished to do many of his own stunts, even if it meant unprotected exposure to real flames. The studio refused to allow McQueen near the flame rig, with Janes taking the heat instead. Because of Janes' uncanny resemblance to McQueen, the on-set insurance agent rushed the group of stuntmen dousing Loren and, thinking he was talking to McQueen, accused him of breaking the safety provision of his deal. He reeled in shock when the fire helmet was removed and Loren's dirty face was revealed.

"Even [when I was] in the silver suit," Janes recalled, "the flame blower could inflict serious burns." Effects masters A.D. Flowers and Logan Frazee's fire rig was capable of projecting six-foot flames, 40 inches in circumference. Working on the Malibu Fox Ranch, Janes, Dar Robinson, Bob Yerkes and others executed countless high-falls from a movable structure into airbags. Second unit helmer and stunt boss Paul Stader had hired them all.

Loren worked on *The Master Gunfighter* in late '74. The Jack Marta–lensed quickie combined old western quick-draw setups with samurai sword action. It was a veritable horse-fall, saddle-jerk, stirrup-dragging stunt fest; no fewer than 30 action players drew a salary from producer Phil Parsons. It starred Tom Laughlin and was directed by his older brother Frank. Janes was tapped for a featured bad-guy sword gag, being dispatched by Laughlin via a backward stab to the gut. Struck sharply in the side by the blunt but otherwise real katana, Loren suffered a fractured rib. "In wanting it to look real for the screen,"

In *The Master Gunfighter*, Tom Laughlin blasts a Mexican gunslinger (Janes) who was out to kill him. Janes performed a spinning back somersault from the six-foot stairwell as he revolved with the bullet's impact. He landed on the hard-packed dirt with stunt-pads buried beneath to break the fall.

he explained, "Laughlin went pretty hard. For stuntmen, that meant more lumps and bumps by day's end."

The Other Side of the Mountain was a picture perfect for Loren Janes: It was filmed in Mammoth and Bishop, California, amid 60-foot snow drifts in the early spring of 1975. The Larry Peerce–directed biopic of a champion skier's tragic mishap and her struggle for recovery, it starred Marilyn Hassett as Jill Kinmont, with Loren doubling her in ski sequences. Brought in by coordinator Max Kleven (aware of Janes' expertise gleaned during years as a teenage ski instructor), he performed a six-story vertical free-fall into a ten-foot-deep snowpack. Cardboard boxes were buried beneath the surface to reduce landing shock. Simulating skiing off a sheer cliff (as the real-life character accidentally did), he made a perfect landing, but it turned bad as Janes' ski tip pierced the upper cardboard boxes, instead of impacting flatly as planned. Driving his left knee into his right thigh, Loren was plunged into paralysis from the neck down, crumpling into the snow motionless upon impact. Revived by Kleven's cold hand brushing snow from his face, Janes experienced an excruciating "electric current" running through his mouth while a headache shut his eyes. He was in and out of consciousness as Kleven attempted a fix: Max grasped Loren's head with his fingers interlocking behind. He yanked the cervical expanse of neck with one swift motion, and a profusion of popping vertebrae elongated Janes' upper spine. As the hold was slowly released, Loren's paralysis evaporated as

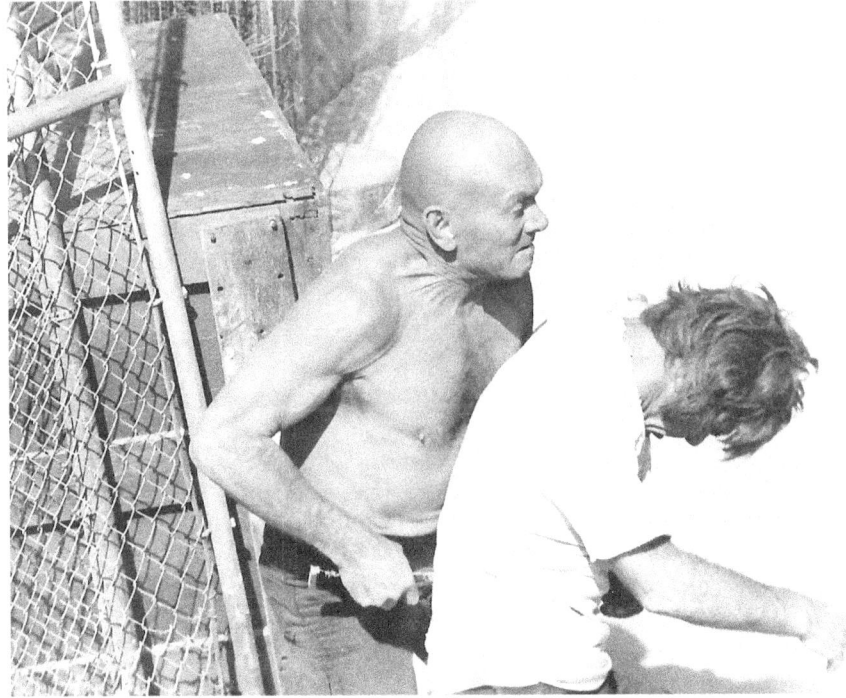

Top and above: Playing one of the heavies in *The Ultimate Warrior*, Janes (in bad wig) is held in a half-nelson as Yul Brynner prepares to finish him off with a knife (actually a collapsible prop knife). Note Janes' right arm and the massive forearm development—visual proof of his years as an acrobat and stunt player.

the electric buzz and battery taste in his mouth diminished. Walking within an hour, he stumbled from the Mammoth hotel's front desk to his upstairs room without help.

Advised by studio physicians to quit the picture, Janes returned to the slopes in less than two days. Skiing his way back to fitness (enduring the pain of a compression fractured disc), he finished the film with limited use of his back, and then rehabbed in Los Angeles. His spinal trauma was similar to that of Jill Kinmont (who remained wheelchair-bound for life), but Loren's problem proved temporary.

Janes fully healed and hung around Pima, California, with pal Steve McQueen through the summer of 1975; the star's personal woes and high acting fees found him unemployed after *The Towering Inferno* (not to mention his demands that his wife Ali MacGraw be included in *any* script offered). Blowing off steam as a motocross "extra" in Lee Frost's *Dixie Dynamite,* McQueen competed alongside friends Bud Eakins, Carey Loftin and Bud Davis in a 90-minute filmed race montage, passed off as a low-rent moonshine feature. Paid $50 a day (background rates), Loren rode at the bequest of coordinator Paul Knuckles to protect Steve. Gaining motocross skills (but little money for 11 days of shooting), Janes was glad when opportunity released him from his McQueen babysitting duties.

Following a late-night conversation with producer Elliott Krasner, Janes caught the next flight to Billings, Montana, for *The Missouri Breaks*. Jack Nicholson had been injured

Janes (left) donned yet another bad hairpiece to pass for a movie's star, in this case Jack Nicholson (right) of *The Missouri Breaks*.

when horse-thrown; Janes was signed to double the actor for the rest of the production. Also starring Marlon Brando, Randy Quaid, Frederic Forrest and Harry Dean Stanton, the Arthur Penn–directed post–Civil War western was ably shot by William Butler with an eye for realism. This carried over to the stunts. In one scene, Janes doubled Nicholson stealing a corral full of horses. Flanked by mounted stunters James Halty, Walter Scott and Jerry Young in the sequence, they wrangled the herd through narrow canyons in true cowhand form. Loren did 11 takes before Penn had his coverage.

Doubling Nicholson in the train stickup, Janes leapt from the vault-car with cash bags in hand. The train was straddling a 60-foot trestle. A sudden lurch dropped Janes between cars. He was left grasping a ladder rung, one-handed, to stay alive. Regaining his balance and continuing the shot, Loren descended the bridge's wooden trestles to "retrieve the loot" as scripted. The 60-foot move covered without calling for a cut.

There was a Three Stooges–like comedy moment: During the cabin rebuilding sequence, Loren hit a horse on the ass with a plank so that a guy using the animal's back as a ladder toppled face-first to the ground. Loren was up to his neck in the frigid Missouri River while shooting the horse-swimming sequences; six-knot currents made repeated takes exhausting.

12

A Hard Day's Night

Loren Janes jumped from western to sci-fi: On *Logan's Run,* he engineered one of the picture's most complex stunts. Featuring wire suspended stuntmen wearing hidden harnesses beneath costumes, the carousel was a ballet of timing, design, and coordination. Utilizing a 60-foot circular truss hung from the perms—culminating just above the set walls—initial runs had 30-odd stunt players dangling like puppets from a single source. As the carousel rotated in sync with the revolving stage floor, resulting entanglements proved impossible to avoid. Cables twisted and lines crossed, and fixes were time consuming. Placing each on separate chain-motors, the solution allowed all to rise and fall independently. Worked in conjunction to the revolving stage floor and overhead trusses clockwise rotation, the Calder like gimbal provided a natural flow of vertical movement, manifesting Ernest Laszlo's most memorable image in the film. The stunt players were provided with "momentary kill switches" wired to the chain motor; folks "in the shot" controlled their own movements while the cables remained unfouled owing to separate rigs for each. "After a week of the harnesses," Loren reminisced, "you got rubbed raw." "All of us were walking tenderly by picture's end," he laughed.

The Call of the Wild came Janes' way next. Drafted by producer Art Stoltz to run stunts and play a bad guy, Janes jetted to Jackson Hole, Wyoming, with the rest of the film company. One stunt: an attack scene with a 90-pound mixed Shepherd, Buck. Loren and trainer Frank Weatherwax readied the dog for the arm bite shot. Cameras rolling, Janes teased the animal, then turned away (as scripted). Pouncing *before* being cued, Buck leaped upon the shocked stuntman, biting his left arm with such ferocity that its teeth punctured Janes' thick leather shirt. Despite the shock, Loren threw the dog off, as rehearsed. Concealing his pain, he continued, and Buck suddenly charged again: the Shepherd chomped Janes' right ankle, jerking his head side to side. Janes kicked free while shoving Buck several feet back. As the action continued, no one was aware of Loren's danger. Remaining in character, he stood before the animal with arms stretched protectively when Buck lurched forward again. The dog's teeth punctured Loren's groin, searing pain giving way to fear as he froze in the dog's grasp. The crew moaned at the sight as the stuntman emitted a high-pitched "Hey Frank!" begging for the trainer's help. Rushing forward, Weatherwax pried the dog from Janes' scrotum with a wrenching of its lower jaw. Janes' testicles were punctured, and blood flowed. He was patched by a medic with clotting salve and butterfly bandages before returning to finish the fight sequence, despite his wounds. "I knew if I didn't get right back to it," Janes recalled, "the swelling would be too severe to walk. Plus the fear factor meant I had to show Buck who was boss." Completing the scene to director Jerry Jackson's delight, Loren handled Weatherwax's mutt with cautious control the remainder of the day: "Instead of anger, which the dog would

12. A Hard Day's Night

Sitting in a cage (top right), Janes donned a dark wig to double Robert Shaw in *Swashbuckler*'s dungeon escape sequence.

sense, I projected boredom, confusing him enough to get the rest of the shots. 'Twas less painful for us both." Hardly one to blame an animal, Janes' feeling on the bite issue was: Everybody makes mistakes. Even dogs. He hit the slopes the following day for an aerial skiing exhibition at Teton Village, performing 60-foot jumps, speed demonstrations, etc.; he had recovered sufficiently to execute a series of downhill somersaults that got standing ovations from the locals.

In the summer of '76, Loren was tapped for his diving and acrobatic work in James Goldstone's *Swashbuckler*. Starring Robert Shaw, James Earl Jones, Peter Boyle and Genevieve Bujold, the salty throwback was a three-masted pirate picture celebrating the Errol Flynn days. Setting this seafaring actioner apart was Janes' climactic 90-foot cliff plunge atop a horseless wagon into a bay. Janes, Pamela Bebermeyer and Jophery C. Brown doubled Shaw, Jones and Bujold, respectively. Buddy Van Horn figured out how to launch the buckboard off the cliff without harming horses: a 24-foot wooden ramp tapered skyward like a V-1 rocket launch.

Sand berms and jungle foliage obscured it from camera, and it was rigged with large pulleys and ropes threaded through guides connected to the wagon with quick release bolts; its team of horses went free while the wagon flew over the 16-foot crest of the cliff, plunging 90 feet toward the sea. Separating from the wagon via head-first dives seconds before impact, Loren and friends came through mostly unscathed.

On a pirate ship staged at Singapore Lake, practical, controlled stunts could be more

Above and opposite: One of Janes' most spectacular stunts: flying from a wagon plunging off a 90-foot Mexican cliff. Also airborne: Jophery C. Brown and Pamela Bebermeyer. All lived to spend their checks.

readily filmed. Constructed with 68-foot masts, full sails and rigging, it presented a gold mine of action possibilities. Featured doing a high-mast ship-to-ship transfer, Janes swooped downward, hitting 30 MPH by rope's end and landing perfectly on two feet with a pronounced upward flourish. Four out of five takes were printed. Leaving no pirate gag unmolested, Loren (subbing Shaw) took on two opponents with a back somersault and double sword-hilt punch, knocking both overboard.

12. A Hard Day's Night

Part of a comedic spoof during the boat siege joining "Peg-leg Bates" to vanquish the heavies, Janes fought back-to-back with Bob Morgan, who lost his real leg on *How the West Was Won* with Loren as a witness.

Continuing in the high-dive vein, Janes' next challenge was Paramount's *King Kong*. Hired by Bill Couch the first week of January 1976, Janes scouted Catalina's far side to double the Hawaiian locations previously established by Jeff Bridges and Jessica Lange for a cliff-leap into the ocean—escaping Kong's hot pursuit. Initially filmed in Kauai, the special effects employed a 20-foot practical leap of Bridges and Lange over a virtual cliff—-rear-projected on stage at M.G.M.—landing safely in pads below frame. Combined with

Approaching the surface of the Gulf of Mexico after a 90-foot descent, *Swashbuckler* stuntman Janes (right) makes his fall in a controlled frontal dive while Jophery C. Brown prepares to hit the surface ankles together. Pamela Bebermeyer didn't fare as well: She impacted back-first. It was some time before she worked again.

"running-dolly footage" through the jungle (amid glimpses of the impending cliff), a transition to an overhead insert of Loren to sell Bridges was used, supported by wardrobe, fake blond hair, and flowing beard with Lange doppelgänger Kelly Nichols by his side. The 60-foot vertical fall was seamlessly spliced into water's impact with the projected stuff—dissolving viewer doubt of the plunge's authenticity.

Fulfilling a fall requiring a gymnastic twist, Loren doubled a sailor (costumed in knit watch cap, backpack and with a high-powered rifle slung over a shoulder)—shaken

12. A Hard Day's Night

Another shot of the *Swashbuckler* plunge. Preparing to break the water's surface with his chin tucked to his chest, Janes was the only one of the trio unscathed by the jump.

off the "tree-log bridge," attacked by Kong. The second victim in the tracking party to plummet into the "bottomless gorge," Janes maintained a back-first fall transitioning to a somersault (dropping 60 feet from the perms), into an airbag. Precisely matted footage of Loren mated with forced perspective shots of the pit were intercut with the actual high-fall, creating the illusion of a fluid event. Performing multiple takes to satisfy John

Guillerman's coverage, Janes revealed his mindset of success for the stunt. "Transitioning in air from somersault to face first," he instructed, "requires torso control and spacial direction to set the dive's pitch. Otherwise, you flop or turn. You have to visualize the mechanics nano-seconds before you do 'em. Then focus on landing right at the end—so you don't break your neck!"

Janes voiced his concern about Lange's vulnerability during the sequence where she's floating in a rubber raft: He said that Catalina Island's south harbors teemed with sharks. Armed with high-powered spear guns, Loren and Gene LeBell stood watch a dozen feet away in a decrepit rowboat towed behind the camera barge. Fortunately, neither fish nor female were harmed.

Ted Post's *Good Guys Wear Black*, filmed between Thanksgiving and Christmas of '77 around Squaw Valley's snow country, was a notch above most Chuck Norris flicks. Loren was tapped by coordinator Hubie Kerns for a ski jump. Doubling a member of a Vietnam commando team dubbed Black Tigers, his character is sniper-shot while airborne. Constructing an inclined ramp 30 feet long, Janes froze the plywood base with water, compacting it with snow for smoothness. Towed down the ramp by skimobile at 40 MPH and then released, Loren flew 145 feet from launch to landing with each take. His target zone was padded with cardboard boxes buried beneath the snow. Reaching his arc height of 40 feet he activated a switch (secreted inside his wardrobe), firing off a "squib

In this stunt crew photo from *F.I.S.T.*, Janes (no hat) kneels in the front row, just before Sylvester Stallone and his high school diploma.

hit" rigged to his chest; it exploded a blood pack while shredding his ski jacket. The effect was perfectly timed by Janes, who waited until the last second to set it off. Encountering 35 MPH crosswinds during the shot, Loren feigned the bullet hit perfectly. Allowing his body to go limp, he dead-fell through space. Hitting the snow following the four-story drop, Janes' legs crumpled beneath him as the boxes broke the fall. He slid 60 feet over the snow head-first, stopping precisely on his mark for a final eyes-open closeup. Janes earned $1000 a day on the Bob Steadman–lensed action picture.

Janes accepted Max Kleven's invitation to work on United Artists' *F.I.S.T.* with Sylvester Stallone, Peter Boyle and Rod Steiger. The Norman Jewison action-drama was based on Jimmy Hoffa's start in 1930s labor, spanning allegations of Teamster mob control through the '50s and beyond. Working the picture's police-and-protestors skirmish scenes, Loren was seen as a trampled cop, bludgeoned union activist and a trucker run off the road.

Answering the phone at 8 a.m. the first Saturday in September 1977, Loren found himself talking to Jack Nicholson, requesting his services on a western to be directed by the actor. Nicholson promised Janes an experience that would be fun *and* financially rewarding. At best, he was half right.

In the first scene of *Goin' South*, Janes (doubling Nicholson) performed his signature horse-gallop down a steep slope. Loren revealed that the secret of such a stunt is to lean back in the saddle equal to the angle of descent. "Your tailbone floats on the leather, and your feet are locked straight in the stirrups. Use the horizon to guide the horse. Otherwise you pitch forward from looking down its neck."

Nicholson had to rely on Janes for all his horse work after being thrown from a mustang during the production's first week. (The horse tripped and rolled over the actor, nearly killing him.) Janes did a scene in which Nicholson's character, fleeing a posse on foot, is roped by multiple riders and taken into custody. A closeup shot of Nicholson, lassoes securely attached, was filmed to help "sell the scene."

Two weeks after *Goin' South* wrapped, Janes jetted to the U.K. for Michael Crichton's *The First Great Train Robbery*. Drafted to design and perform some of movie history's most dangerous train gags, he delivered while keeping the picture's star, Sean Connery, in one piece. The film featured an authentic coal-powered locomotive circa 1855. Its top speed hit 50 MPH on the narrow gauge track but felt more like 80 to those riding. Shooting the rooftop robbery sequences, Janes applied a gritted paint to the roof (to insure safe footing) and added handholds made from blackened pipe so that they would blend in. The stunt master gave Connery grasp-points that made the dangerous moves plausible for the 49-year-old star. This meant that lenser Geoffrey Unsworth could get clean shots of Connery *actually* doing the stunts; dynamic editing produced edge-of-your-seat action that viewers expected from the rugged actor. They shot in Ireland's Cork, Kent and Dublin stations, as well as the National Bank and Trinity College. This view of the continent left Loren wanting to see more.

Seated at the American consulate finalizing plans to return stateside, Loren spotted old friend Ali MacGraw, who was entering Britain to work on Robert Evans' tennis flick *Players*. She told him of the producer's difficulty finding a suitable stuntman who could hit a tennis ball. Knowing Janes to be a solid player, she made a quick phone call that got him the job. Extending his visitor visa with help from the Paramount and Wimbledon brass behind the film, he doubled the lead (Dean Paul Martin) for the entire movie. Doing court falls, lunges and running collisions in tennis attire, Janes was required to hit, bounce up, skid and land repeatedly in the same spot, take after take. Soon he was scraped raw from elbow to ankle. Heavy body makeup was applied to hide the abrasions. Janes quipped, "I never thought of tennis as physical until I doubled Dean." He was pitted against pros John McEnroe, Ilie Nastase and Guillermo Vilas. The court speeds proved brutal for Loren. "Trying to look solid against 120 MPH serves took every ounce of effort I had just to meet the ball."

Home in Los Angeles by mid–1978 after his extended overseas duty, Janes was shanghaied by producer Lew Grade for wet work on *Raise the Titanic*. Cast as a deep sea excavation diver, he spent 16 nights submerged at 1000 bucks a shift. Referring to the 55-foot-long *Titanic* "miniature," Janes said, "I saw the boat sink at Gilligan's Island" (at CBS Radford's backlot). Between the lagoon being too shallow and actor issues with director Jerry Jameson and Jason Robards, Loren recalled no one being very happy on that project. Except for him, each payday!

Loren next opted for some land-locked television assignments that offered challenge and dry shorts. Retained for his mastery of horse falls, drags and jumps, he stunt-gaffed *Roots: The Next Generation*. Designing shots with d.p. Joseph M. Wilcots, then consulting director Georg Stanford Brown on pace, Loren felt very much part of the creative process. His staging was historically accurate whether rolling a buggy or being blasted with a Kentucky long rifle. They filmed amid Savannah's lush plantations before going on-stage in Burbank.

Jumping from one episode to the next, Janes received *another* late-night call from a panicked producer, and agreed to take *The Rebels* without seeing a script. Set in Colonial times, the Russ Mayberry–helmed drama starred Don Johnson and included solid work from Richard Basehart, Forrest Tucker, Doug McClure and Guy Madison, with Jim Backus stealing every scene as John Hancock. Janes was required to hire a multitude of stunt folk capable of handling the weighty Brown Bess infantry rifles. British Redcoats took on buckskin-clad, raccoon hat–wearing Americans wielding long guns, tomahawks and flintlock pistols.

Casting began with an interesting test. Janes' knowledge of military history focused on details like stunt extras holding the guns properly while in battle. Putting fully wardrobed players under scrutiny, Loren would command each to "shoulder arms" and march a few steps. Any who failed the former Marine's tutorial were invited to hold the heavy guns before them, until muscle fatigue lowered their arms.

The work encompassed stunt basics one would see in any western, from horse falls and bullet hits to wagon turnovers and hand-to-hand combat. Loren's challenge became purely one of pulling off large-scale action on a television budget. His production value came from air rams and trampoline rigs depicting deadly explosions via hidden charges beneath the soil. Stuntmen were launched skyward a dozen feet with each take. "It takes a trained person to hit an air ram launch correctly," Loren said. "The budget only allowed us four pros to start. But we needed ten who could be run over or blown up by show's end."

Enlisting stunt friends in need of work (paying cash out of pocket), Janes assembled the team he required. "You can't teach this stuff to amateurs. Or even just good athletes. It's too dangerous. Failure to keep your feet together on launch from an air ram can really ruin one's day."

Returning to an all-out western, Janes signed to coordinate director Richard Lester's revisionist prequel *Butch and Sundance: The Early Days*. Lensed by Hollywood up-and-comer Laszlo Kovacs, this second try at box office lightning starred Tom Berenger as Butch and William Katt as Sundance. It was filmed amid New Mexico's majestic Toltec railway through Chama, and subsequent locations in Taos, the Eaves movie ranch and the Tent rocks of the Cochiti reservation in Pueblo. The company also traveled to Alamosa, Telluride and Colorado's rugged San Juan mountains.

Encompassing all that Loren knew about cowboy gags, the picture featured spirited horse work including high falls, trips, water crossings, steep grade descents and fast galloping. The film was an attempt to replicate the charm of George Roy Hill's '69 classic with Robert Redford and Paul Newman, but only Jeff Corey's Sherriff Bledsoe and amazing stunts made it watchable. The project lacked the writing and rhythm the two great stars had in the original.

Janes was happy hiring a dozen top-notch cowboy-stunters. Surrounding himself with pros like Larry Holt and the Walker brothers, Greg and Rock, he also got saddle royalty Dick Durock and Walter Robles. The film contained rooftop plunges and blasts through second floor windows (using airbags and hidden pads); the nature of the action required Loren's constant attention. Doing a balcony fall into an airbag after being shot, Durock was nearly undone when a Teamster's wagon mark was two feet off. Performing a railing flip and back somersault, he had to rotate in midair to avoid striking the buckboard's tailgate.

Janes returned to Hollywood for Irwin Allen's *The Swarm* in the spring of '78, a film underwritten by Warner Bros. studios in a massive deal with sequel options. No expense was spared employing cinematographer Fred Koenekamp to film bees attacking cast members Richard Widmark, Michael Caine, Richard Chamberlain, Ben Johnson, Slim Pickens, Bradford Dillman, Cameron Mitchell and Henry Fonda. Fred MacMurray buzzed around as a mayor.

Stunt coordinated by Paul Stader, the action was to rival Hitchcock's *The Birds* with lots of "nature gone wrong" crowd panic sequences, including trampling, car crashes, jumps from high buildings and schoolyard attacks. They used nearly a million domestic honey bees wrangled by an army of apiculturists. In refrigerated rooms, the poor creatures had their stingers removed by teams of technicians armed with jewelers' loupes and tweezers, rendering them impotent. Despite extraordinary stunts pulled off by Tinseltown's most able including John Moio's bathing suit–clad fall through a plate glass window, and Larry Holt's high-speed run through a trailer on a Triumph motorcycle, the picture failed to impress paying audiences. Executing a 35-foot bee-covered fall from a billboard, Loren was severely stung upon landing in his airbag. Bees with stingers (not *all* were removed for stunts by that time as "supplies" ran out) were trapped throughout his wardrobe, attacking upon impact. Suffering toxic response to venom, Janes' ankles swelled. Respiratory failure choking him as severe pain from multiple stings electrified exposed skin, he crawled from airbag to ground without recollection. "When I finally focused," Janes recounted, "a couple of my stunt buddies were messaging my legs, and one slapping me. My cheeks ballooned like a trumpet player. And it was several hours before my legs returned to normal." Sixty-five shooting days later, it was simply another story for the stuntman to tell. "All in a day's work!" he graciously concluded.

13

McQueen's Best and Last

Requiring 247 shooting days (and a million feet of film), Columbia's *1941* was a stunt bonanza combining thrills with comedic timing. A Steven Spielberg take on the West Coast's post–Pearl Harbor "invasion paranoia," it was ably shot by William Fraker in Santa Monica and Malibu and on beaches in Oregon. Stars included John Belushi, Dan Aykroyd, Mickey Rourke, Treat Williams and John Candy; the stunt side was comprised of Terry Leonard, May Boss, Bud Eakins and Jack Gill, all legends.

Filling in for multiple camera angles to cheat small crowd scenes into bigger ones (without additional paid extras), Loren was swapping out sailor suits, civilian duds and Army uniforms while in the U.S.O. riot fight. Featured taking a sock in the jaw, he was also used as a white-helmeted, nude M.P. tossed through a plate glass window and a curious bystander trampled by the surging crowd. Tapped for his high diving expertise for the picture's Ferris wheel stunt, Janes executed a risky burn fall on Warner Brothers' Stage 16. He plunged six stories before green-screen backing into 15 feet of water. Janes relied on Burn Jell, a gelatinous flame retardant developed by the Air Force and adopted by the stunt community. "The idea was for me to windmill my arms as much as possible on the way down to sell the height," Loren recalled. "The fanning action whipped away the goo on my arms, and flames burned the eyebrows right off my face before I hit the water."

By the spring of '79, Janes was at the height of his career's golden arc. A master of high falls and cliff-diving, he was also expert in swordplay, trampoline work, gymnastics and stage combat, plus western staples like fistfights, knife and gun handling, bareback riding, saddle jerks, roping, stirrup drags, wagon rollovers and moving-train jumps.

In February 1979, Janes was roped in as Steve McQueen's double in Warners' comeback *Tom Horn*. The throwback western was full of gags at which Janes excelled. Returning to the star's side via longtime pal Gary Combs coordinating the picture, Loren began with roping sequences as McQueen (playing the title role), in creative partnership with cinematographer John Alonzo and helmer William Wiard. Doing McQueen's riding for all but simple closeups, Janes did a difficult galloping stint over rugged terrain while in pursuit of the first group of rustlers. Firing a Winchester .45-70 rifle one-armed (subbing for Horn's actual .30-30), Loren clutched the speeding horse's reins in his other hand; long and medium wide shots of the action blended well with inserts of the star in shorter runs. Fighting for breath because of respiratory trouble associated with cancer, McQueen needed Janes to do his mounted shots more than ever.

One illusion was Horn's trick-riding at the Cattle Association party. It was a complex exhibition of saddle work and dismounts from a galloping horse, including Pony Express one-foot transitions. McQueen's double was Jim Medearis, a rodeo star in his own right.

His footage was intercut with coverage of the actor doing simple moves in medium and wide closeups; only Medearis' mother could tell them apart on screen. Likewise for the bronco-busting sequences. Medium-wide coverage of Janes in the saddle combined with low-angle closeups of McQueen being jostled sell the moment's reality to viewers.

Horn has his horse blasted from beneath him during the slaughterhouse showdown against the final group of rustlers. Following the trained gelding to the ground with legs sprung in anticipation of impact while firing his rifle as the animal collapses in a heap, Janes' medium-shot was jump-cut to McQueen's closeup as he kills the rustler who shot his favorite horse.

In the scene where Horn attempts to escape from the jail, Loren stood in for McQueen and was savagely lasso-whipped to the ground. Despite rubber prop ropes, the blows produced welts across Janes' face and neck. Various montages of McQueen as Horn, riding at breakneck speed across prairie and plains in pursuit of rustlers, were Janes as well. He was so physically similar to the star that crew members mistook the two from behind in wardrobe. Never one to turn down work, Loren played rustlers as well.

One gag Loren declined was the picture's last, where Horn is hung by the Julian water–weighted gallows (named for its inventor, James Julian). Lacking practical mechanisms to operate the rig supporting "on-camera" believability, the knot-trick was live, requiring careful operation. Gary Combs doubled McQueen when the noose's "Peter Pan" safety jammed, inflicting rope burns on the coordinator's neck before he could pull the breakaway release and save himself.

Hired by stunt boss Craig Baxley, Janes grabbed ten weeks on Gary Weis' shoulda-been-funnier flop *Wholly Moses!* He was a Roman soldier one moment and a Hebrew slave the next. Running around Southern California's Mojave Desert through Lancaster and Palmdale (plus practical sets in Burbank), Janes was one of 20 stunt players at cinematographer Frank Stanley's mercy. "It was really cold in the morning with nothing but a cotton thing and sandals," Janes laughed. "And hotter than Hades by lunch!"

Among the movie's comedic stars, Dudley Moore stood out for Janes. He played piano between set-ups no matter day or night. "One minute he would be playing Beethoven's 'Midnight Sonata,'" Loren recalled. "Then he would joke with a rank punchline about Gary [director Weis], or the producer Freddie Fields." The movie was plagued with many production problems (including a near no-show by Richard Pryor as Pharaoh), and it failed in its attempt to reach the Monty Python audience.

In February '79, Loren was challenged by McQueen to pull off his most dangerous stunts yet. He was flown to Chicago for *The Hunter*, a fact-based bio of bounty collector Ralph "Papa" Thorson. Directed by action pro Buzz Kulik, it was scripted with a myriad of stunt opportunities. The second unit was helmed by friend Gary Combs. McQueen's health was failing and *The Hunter* was his swan song; Janes handled much of the star's physical action.

Early in the film, McQueen is pitted against a psychotic giant in a lakeside shack; Loren subbed McQueen for throws against walls, through a window and being crushed by king-sized Karl Schueneman. Kicking down the door on top of McQueen, Schueneman was seamlessly intercut with the star in closeups. Schueneman snatched McQueen from the floor and hefted him like a rag doll; then Janes doubled McQueen in a long shot, being dropped five feet onto the specially padded carpet. Janes also got pitched through the shack window. It's a dangerous gag (owing to breakaway glass and wood shards), and adrenalin, inexperience or bad aim can hospitalize the guy thrown. "Karl was pumped,"

Grabbed by the scruff of his neck and belt, Steve McQueen's stunt double Loren Janes is manhandled by 6'6", 320-pound Karl Schueneman in *The Hunter*.

Loren recalled. "By the time we did the window work, he was eager to toss me through it." He hurled Janes with enough force that Janes momentarily blacked out on impact.

The bounty hunter next tracked the Branch Brothers to a farm. The siblings began by lobbing dynamite. McQueen was seen in a medium shot, then inserts of Janes for the big blasts. Employing buried air rams with supplemental charges to blow up dirt and sod, effects pro Phil Cory spared no powder. Flipping into a back somersault as the charges blow, Loren (in medium shot) rotated as though lifted by the blasts; then a cut back to McQueen going down in closeup (so folks would believe it was him). Ramping up the action, the brothers attempted to hit him with the car after the failed explosions. A closeup of McQueen sitting on the ground stunned, then Janes (doubling) rolls clear to avoid being run over.

A wheat combine was commandeered for an aerial ballet between car and thresher. Chopper jockey Ross Reynolds provided the bird's-eye coverage that made the dance work. Through-the-windshield P.O.V.s of McQueen alternated with medium stuff of Janes for the cat-and-mouse head-ons with Bobby Bass driving the Trans Am; the corn field pursuit was difficult to fake. Owing to the tractors' lower speeds, spin-outs and rear-end thrashing near-misses, communication (and ensuing steering adjustments in the high corn) were rendered nearly impossible by lack of visibility. Because of the radio link to Reynolds' helicopter, several close calls were nothing more. Production moved to downtown Chicago for the picture's latter half and its most dangerous stunts. March of '79 was as lucrative for Loren as it was sad. Informed that old pal McQueen was ill with cancer, he received more and more marginal doubling assignments—along with the highly adjusted big stunts.

One "action blast" was perhaps the film's best: the capture of Tony Bernardo,

13. McQueen's Best and Last

***Hunter* stunter Janes' feet are up and arms out from his sides after being struck at 20 MPH.**

played by Tommy Rosales, Jr. A heart-pumping chase across roofs, down multi-storied stair landings and racing atop elevated train cars ends with a carjacking and Bernardo's ten-story plunge from a parking structure. The sequence included dangling 30 feet up from an elevated train's maintenance ladder (traveling 50 MPH), as well as two-story roof-to-roof leaps spanning ten feet between buildings without a net. Location-shot with Housing Authority approval, the chase's start with fire escapes and roof leaps was slated for uninhabited structures. No nets or airbags could be used because in wide shots, the camera sees all.

Actor Tommy Rosales tackled his own stunts in the hair-raising run, leaping a ten-foot roof span. He was followed in medium coverage by Loren (as McQueen), who effected a rolling paratrooper landing to absorb impact. Then a return to the star in three-quarter closeup (dropping off a six-foot-high scaffolding into pads rather than the roof); ingenious framing of buildings and skyline made the drop appear genuine without the risk. Cutting to Janes landing in full frame, the chase continues to a second city-scape more challenging than the first.

An ancient brick wall was used; its 18-foot span to the next structure meant a risky jump. Loren sprinted ten yards toward the precipice; a mini-trampoline provided vertical

Doubling *The Hunter*'s Steve McQueen, Janes makes a building-to-building leap in pursuit of a perp. (Photo courtesy Dave Friedman).

launch, with Loren's tremendous upper-body strength doing the rest. Ascending six feet a second (falling two feet for each traveled horizontally), Janes plummeted before catching the roof edge. Inserts of McQueen waist-up (standing on a hidden platform, struggling to pull himself atop the roof) were framed in closeup. This illustrated the physical fatigue of the "older turtle chasing the younger hare."

Then down back stairwells to the subway station, with McQueen seen in facial close-ups and Janes in medium coverage from behind. The chase's final leg is on a moving train. Pulling from the platform with Thorson trailing Bernardo through crowded cars (shooting people who "got in the way"), McQueen clambers out the train window to flank him. Coverage of Loren (in long shot) struggling to his feet on the rapidly moving train were jump-cut to McQueen crouching. Establishing interiors of Bernardo aiming his gun upward then firing; exterior train P.O.V.s held McQueen in closeup, flinching as random shots penetrated the roof around him. Bullet hits swing a service ladder into Thorson (sweeping Janes off the elevated train roof); the stuntman did a single-hand grab onto the ladder's steel rail, 30 feet above the street—with no safety cable, nets or provision for falling. Transitioning into a two-handed trapeze grip, fingers wrapped around the bar, palms facing out, Loren hung for 60 seconds per take, the train hurtling down the elevated track at over 50 MPH. Using only his own strength, Janes made a dozen runs without mishap. Loren (in long shot) struggles to swing himself onto the train roof (hanging slack-armed from the ladder in exhaustion), while tight intercuts of McQueen

13. McQueen's Best and Last   103

On *The Hunter*, Loren Janes (doubling Steve McQueen) holds onto a bar extending from the top of a Chicago elevated train with a single over-hand grip. Thirty feet from the ground, he is traveling 50 MPH. His only guarantees of survival were his extraordinary hand strength and gymnastic experience.

Another look at *Hunter* stuntman Janes as he dangles from the elevated train. Note the expression of physical strain on the stuntman's face: As in the film, Janes—*and* McQueen—are older men in battle against the young.

sell the danger. With a series of tunnels looming ahead. Janes (in wide coverage) finally gets a perch with one foot and returns to the roof's safety with great effort. Medium shots of McQueen refastening the ladder (then collapsing on his back to catch his breath) were seamlessly integrated. There were ten inches of clearance between opening and train, a tight frame of McQueen's face underlining Thorson's realization of impending death.

Steve McQueen poses atop the elevated train while shooting his last motion picture, *The Hunter*. The actor (playing real-life bounty hunter Ralph Thorson) looks ready for action despite being in the advanced stages of his illness.

13. McQueen's Best and Last

Then flash to Loren (in medium and long master shots). Pancaked to the train roof, he made his body flat as possible. Blasting through the tunnel opening at 60 MPH, Janes calmly dodged low-hanging protrusions. As the train flies into the station, coverage shifts from platform to train interior as Bernardo pulls the emergency brake lever, bringing the speeding cars to a screeching halt.

Fleeing the train (running up a dark tunnel), Bernardo was again pursued by Thorson. Dropping 12 feet to the tracks below, Loren (intercut with McQueen landing squarely on both feet) continued the chase in step. Inducing lung-fatigue owing to the wind sprints, McQueen required long breathers after each take to continue. Stoically toughing it out with a concerned Janes by his side, the actor refused to quit regardless of pain.

The chase's finale has Bernardo legging it into the Marina City Parking Structure and hijacking a Pontiac Grand Am. Racing to the top of the multi-tiered round structure, he is followed by Thorson (McQueen in closeups), driving a commandeered wrecking truck with a towed vehicle attached. He scrapes, bangs and collides with so many cars during the vertical pursuit that there is little left when he finally shoves Bernardo's Pontiac off the parking structure's top floor. It crashes into the "lake" ten stories below. "The parking lot chase took three days," Janes recalled. "Between Steve and myself, we must have taken-out half a dozen more cars than slated."

One stunt far from laughable was the picture's last: a huge science lab explosion

The Hunter star Steve McQueen is hoisted high by Janes (right), stunt coordinator Gary Combs (center) and Bobby Bass (on the left in ball cap). It turned out to be the star's last picture. (Photo courtesy Dave Friedman)

while Thorson moves in on sicko Rocco Mason (Tracey Walker). Implementing Phil Corey "shape charges" and a springboard, Loren was catapulted a dozen feet doubling McQueen in the wide shot. Hit by the searing hot wave emitted from the gasoline's fireball utilized for the blast, Janes suffered blistering on his forehead and neck.

Earning in excess of $30,000 for *The Hunter*, Janes was at the physical and professional pinnacle of his career. Unfortunately, McQueen was not. Janes sensed that the man was not long for this world. Broken-hearted, he would never again swear allegiance to one star. Loren the master technician became a journeyman player in Tinseltown's ever-evolving stunt profession.

14

New Beginnings of a Journeyman Player

Aptly titled *The Big Brawl*, Jackie Chan's American debut vehicle was a two-fisted martial arts flick that shone brightest during fighting bits by pros Gene LeBell, Ox Baker, Jeep Swenson and Loren Janes. Directed by Robert Clouse and produced by Freddie Weintraub, Warners' low-budget quickie was lensed by Robert Jessup in late 1979. The hope was to turn Chan into the next Bruce Lee.

Set in 1930s America with Jackie the underdog in a mob-controlled fighting competition, the film provided Loren a memorable sequence at picture's end: Featured as a gray-suited mob tough attacking Chan in a movie theater; he hits him with a double fist punch to the back, knocking him over a row of seats, and follows by taking a swing at his adversary's head. But he is beaten to impact by Jackie's kick to his midsection; Janes' grab at the martial artist's shirt earns him an open-palm strike in the forehead. After Janes misses with another punch, Chan delivers a series of rapid chain-punch blows, punctuated by a final right cross that sends him over two rows of seats. Loren rises on wobbly legs and gets a lightning-fast front snap-kick that takes him off his feet. Struck in mid-chest, Janes did a backflip to accentuate the impact, off a balcony and down into the seats below. (Loren landed in an off-camera airbag.) This theater fight had audiences cheering.

Loren leapt to stunt-coordinate an all-female cast in *Lovely But Deadly*. Giving America its first and last look at Lucinda Dooling as a leading lady, the David Shelden picture was cartoonish fun, more comic-book than feature film: An undercover cheerleader attempts to expose the drug ring behind her brother's murder. The stunts ran the gamut from drugged driving and fistfights to violent girls. Janes hired old mentors Max Kleven and Dick Warlock for double work.

Loren jumped ship within hours of production's wrap: Booked by Warlock for a month of nights at $500 per day, he was on a plane to St. Louis without so much as the picture's title. The job turned out to be John Carpenters' *Escape from New York,* an apocalyptic vision of America's future after the crash of Air Force One into the island prison of New York, and one man's mission to free the president. Starring Kurt Russell as Snake Pliskin, Lee Van Cleef, Isaac Hayes, Harry Dean Stanton, Donald Pleasence and Adrienne Barbeau, the film also had Ernest Borgnine as a scene-stealing cabbie.

Filming during 1980 in East St. Louis' urban wasteland required three months of night exteriors from August's stagnant humidity to November's frigid cold. Janes was involved with roving gang scenes and high-fall gags, until machine-gunned off the wall at picture's end. "We had pads but no airbag money," the stunt legend remembered. "[Cinematographer Dean] Cundey's coverage had you falling, but never hitting the ground."

Janes coordinated a small Jack Fisk production in December '80, *Raggedy Man* with Eric Roberts, Sam Shepard and Sissy Spacek. Loren did three weeks on the Universal feature (again, all nights), wrapping before Christmas. Designing and executing an elaborate violent sequence bordering on bloodlust, the stuntman desired a more profound expression of his craft.

Loren Janes was tired of constant travel, hotel beds, "milkman sleep schedules" and midnight wardrobe fittings. By the winter of '80, he was longing for good-paying episodic television, in town. As if created by the Fairy Godmother of unemployed stunt performers, Glen Larson's *The Fall Guy* was 20th Century–Fox's answer to Warners' *The Dukes of Hazzard*, a big hit the year earlier. Employing the services of every fast-driving, high-falling, motorcycle-riding, fistfighting, horse-breaking, plane-leaping stunt player with a SAG card in Los Angeles, the Lee Majors–starring action-fest was a collection of the finest risk talent in the world performing a weekly "show within a show" episodic spotlighting of a Hollywood stuntman who's also a part-time private eye. Featuring a Who's Who of Tinseltown's most talented stunt players: Terry Leonard, Dar Robinson, Andy Gill, Larry Holt, Chuck Hicks, Gene LeBell, May Boss and 60 others; each week, the challenge was topping what came before. Working dozens of episodes during *The Fall Guy*'s five-year run, Loren did everything from platform dives and high falls to car hits, horse work and stage combat on a daily basis, often cast as a victim in harm's way or a heavy. One of his favorite stunts was a backflip over a railing, followed by a two-story plunge through a plate glass atrium. "The space between my airbag and window was less than ten feet," Loren remembered. "We all thought up challenging sequences, but never at the expense of each other's safety."

Returning to features after *The Fall Guy*'s second season, Loren (and half the crew from Larson's money machine), were drafted for Richard Washington's *The Sword and the Sorcerer*. Launching Majors' pal Lee Horsley, the picture was an independently produced magic-and-robes action flick, more camp than credible. Directed by Albert Pyun and lensed by Joseph Mangine, it was visited by tragedy in its first stunt: Jack Tyree was killed leaping from a 60-foot cliff. Lateral air gusts pulled him from the canyon face and the stuntman missed the airbag. Saddened, sobered yet determined, the other stunt players chose to proceed, despite the gravity of the loss.

Cast as a good guy complete with white stallion, Loren was "ripped" from the saddle by a bad guy (on foot), wielding a huge sword. Performing a reverse-somersault over the animal's rump to accentuate the blow and landing on his back on the ground, Janes "foot-flips" the Black Knight over him. Then, with a magic sword, he zaps his foe with an "energy-blast." Audience laughter drowned out his subsequent dialogue.

Loren spoke of playing one of three red-costumed heavies (complete with turban and face wraps) swordfighting with Lee Horsley on the steep castle stairs. Struck by Horsley's scripted haymaker, Janes collided with his cohorts, knocking all three down. But he failed to relax his hips upon impact. Combined weight pinning him against the bottom landing, Loren suffered a fractured coccyx. Delaying medical attention until wrapping the film, Janes had extreme lower-back discomfort for many days following.

Showcased in the picture's final skirmish, Loren was again a hooded and veiled bad guy dispatched by Horsley: He was grabbed by the larger man (Horsley was 6'3") and thrown through the air head over heels. "Lee got excited," Loren laughed. "He's strong and nearly tossed me clear of the pad."

Laughing at movie stunts' occasional miscalculations, Loren recalled friends Gene

LeBell and Chuck Hicks doing an early morning swimming sequence in the cold waters of Pyramid Lake. "When they yelled *rolling*, both stuntmen splashed into the lake, full leather chest armor, boots and broad swords with belts; breast stroking with earnest." Instructed to keep swimming, the duo struggled past camera, 10, 20, 50 feet away. Suddenly laboring under the weight of the real tack, the seasoned pros exchanged looks of panic before they frantically shed their costumes, the lake swallowing them whole. Valuable swords, tunics, helmets, belt and boots followed; at 100 feet from camera, they surfaced and motioned wildly to gain the second assistant director's attention. Perched atop an apple box on the shore, he waved back like a tourist—unaware of the stuntmen's danger as they dramatically disappeared beneath the water's surface once again.

"They realized no one would comprehend they were *really* drowning," Janes remarked. "Seeing two stuntmen hamming it up ... the camera department ignored what came next." Switching to survival mode and disregarding the scripted direction of surface-swimming into the distance until cut, they made it to the far shore via dogpaddle and five-second underwater sprints. Collapsing on the banks like two beached walruses and still gasping for breath some minutes after, LeBell and Hicks were amazed when producer Mark Rosen ordered them back into the drink for the swords. Loren remarked, "The real museum pieces were retrieved after a 40-minute search."

Loren worked nights on a Dick Durock show, *Halloween III: Season of the Witch*. Killed five times in the horror picture, from cleaving to being crushed by a stone slab, Janes regarded the Lee Wallace–directed scare show as "kid stuff." He credited the picture's silver masks and Dean Cundey's photography for making "a lot of nothing" look pretty scary.

Janes' reputation as a fencing pro landed him top of the heap to coordinate *Fire and Ice* in early 1983. He was hired by helmer Ralph Bakski to handle the myriad of fights involving swords plus broad-axes, spears and clubs; Francis Grumman shot live-action black-and-white rotoscope, with animation cells combined with each frame for the "cartoon look." More than 1,000 oils, based on the fantastical paintings of Frank Frazetta, were created and used as backgrounds, while muscle-bound fighters, subhuman henchmen and voluptuous women proceeded through a world of battle in daily filming. This took months of grueling hand-to-hand sequences with heavy (blunt) weapons. Injuries included dislodged teeth, a fractured jaw, several broken fingers and multiple dislocated shoulders. Actors hefted 20-pound wooden shields, lances, broadswords and massive axes (rubber and steel); errant smacks did damage. Filming around L.A.'s Bronson Canyon and Great Sand Dunes National Monument in Colorado, Loren and crewmates Bill Ryusaki, Jeff Imada and Melvin Jones worked diligently to avoid mishap during the daily ballet of putting the storyboarded violence onto film.

The performers rehearsed sequences into muscle memory, including blade-strikes and blocks (then utilized exact placement for 10 to 20 takes per shot), and overlaid animation allowed seamless edits with live action. "We set up a gladiator school," Janes said about teaching the finer skills of sword and club.

> Despite the weapons' dulled edges, getting whacked with a 20-pound rubber axe will definitely ruin your morning. By picture's end, we were *all* bruised and sore-ribbed to the point of *really* fighting for one's self-protection. Guys like Jimmy Bridges and Douglas Payton, playing subhumans, had it even worse. Between [artist Frank] Frazetta and Bakski posing everyone to match storyboards, and the hours of rotoscope needed for the individual action sequences, they took a licking.

Swinging back to swashbuckler work after *Fire and Ice* fizzled, Janes did a Monty Python-ish comedy, *Yellowbeard*. "The idea of doing a full-on pirate movie appealed to me, after the restraints of the Frazetta stuff," Loren shared. It was directed by Mel Damski and featured Graham Chapman, John Cleese, Eric Idle, Peter Boyle, Tommy Chong and James Mason, the latter doing a Capt. Bligh send-up. The trailer promised laughs but the movie delivered few despite its talented cast. Tasked with basic training for swordplay, once again Loren used his Marine and Olympics breeding to assist coordinator Buddy Van Horn to keep everyone realistic but safe.

Janes executed a 30-foot sweeping plunge from upper rigging to deck in one fluid take (doubling a sailor's rapid rope-descent from the crow's nest); the move, he said, was

> all in the wrists, once you measure the rope to avoid plowing into the deck or sailing past your mark into studio lights. The stunt required a rigid swing while holding through the bottom of the arc—where the gravitational pull was the greatest. Releasing with accented upswing, I was doing "Errol Flynn" landings all day.

Executing a backflip somersault in one sequence, Loren performed the gymnastics a dozen feet above the ship's deck from a mast-arm without net, landing flush on his feet each time. Failing to excite audiences, *Yellowbeard* was poorly attended and quickly forgotten.

The end of '83 found Janes and Carey Loftin on *The Dead Zone*. Paramount's psychic detective story was directed by David Cronenberg, underwritten by Dino De Laurentiis, and starred Christopher Walken as a crash victim suddenly out of a coma with the ability to foresee future events.

Janes appears as a soldier in a night-time battle sequence during Poland's fall in the Second World War. Envisioned as a defeated cavalry officer succumbing to modern German armor, Loren did a stirrup-drag along muddy ground with saber in hand. The doctor's P.O.V. growing ever more spectacular (witnessed by his violent clutching of Walken's hand), a large ground explosion erupts, hurling Janes (as foot soldier) ten feet through the air. Leaping up and over into a waist-high half flip (via buried mini-trampoline), his extra effort to sell the blast came with costs. Closer to the explosive effects mortar than desired, Janes scorched a layer of facial skin while losing eyelashes and brows. "With air-blasted flying debris nailing you," Loren explained, "you always shut your eyes during mortar gags. In this case, it saved me!"

Signed to handle "stunt safety" by *Repo Man* stunt coordinators Brad Bovee and Eddie Hice, Janes also utilized his automotive skills for the driving segments of Bud and Otto (Harry Dean Stanton and Emilio Estevez) vs. Napo and Archie (Eddie Velez and Miguel Sandoval). Filming took place along East Los Angeles' storm washes, where the miles of cement passageways made for perfect stunt action. Off the street and safe by nature of their width, the washes proved a great location for automotive monkey-see, monkey-do antics. Using high-speed runs and curb-jumps, the duel between Ford and Chevy was low-budget camp; but cinematographer Robby Muller tweaked it to cool. Hidden mini ramps blasted cars over jumps as though launched. Muller's camera's "real speed" coverage of the action captured all four wheels off the ground in sustained flight.

Supervising a full-body burn done by Bob Ellis, Janes was responsible for "pulling the plug" if anything went wrong. He stood by with a powerful dry extinguisher as Ellis strolled towards camera, engulfed from head to toe. Fourteen seconds of "burn time" left him warm but otherwise unscathed at take's finish.

14. New Beginnings of a Journeyman Player

Moving to Paramount in 1984, Loren and 30 of his closest stunt pals crewed Martin Brest's *Beverly Hills Cop,* a "Detroit meets L.A." Eddie Murphy comedy including tons of stunts produced by the Bruckheimer-Simpson team. Coordinator Gary McLarty assembled a first-rate crew; Vince Deadrick and Eddie Donno led a bunch of drivers, all vying for featured gags. Grabbing the audience's attention, the opening sequence was a wild truck chase with undercover cop Eddie hanging on to the trailer for dear life as the driver flees. Piloting a gold Buick station wagon in the action, Janes did a near–head-on collision at 30 MPH; the imminent crash was prevented when the truck suddenly swerved and braked hard, sending it into a jack-knife. Cheating injury one moment while paying the piper the next, Loren was T-boned at 40 MPH while driving an old pick-up truck in the chase's finale and was knocked unconscious on impact. "The rig hit slightly off-center," Loren said, "and I was thinking how happy the transpo guy [Jay Fuller] was going to be, if production had to buy the truck."

Returning for the final shoot-out at Victor Maitland's mansion (actually the Jaglom estate on L.A.'s Channel Road, Los Angeles), Loren can be spotted on a balcony firing an Uzi as police reinforcements swarm the place. "While much of what you do is *really* stunt work," Loren joked, "sometimes you just stand there and fire a machine-gun until they yell cut."

Loren Janes' next job was another one-man-against-the-machine reboot, *Rambo: First Blood Part II.* Brought in by Richard Farnsworth to coordinate the second unit aerials from June through August 1984, Janes planned and orchestrated all the chopper work (including Rambo's rescue) employing multiple aircraft. Photographed by second unit d.p. Peter MacDonald, the fly team consisting of pilots Tom Gehrke, Harry Hauss, Ross Reynolds and Karl Wickman pushed their helicopters to their limits. Coverage required hours of filming with countless passes over three separate valleys—including multiple refuels to get the shot. Responsible for all phases of the sequence including staging tanker trucks on the edges of Mexico's dense Tecoanapa jungle, Loren found cash incentives to the fueler-drivers the only way to keep the Hueys airborne.

The stunt folks were challenged with storyboards full of anti-aircraft fire, ground explosions and strafing runs with M-60s. Filming safe passes over Viet bad guys manning gun emplacements was no simple matter, requiring coordination of air, ground and stunt personnel. Janes used direct, multi-link communication, allowing *all* to hear their cues, embark on stops and starts at marks, and adjust mortar fire to reflect real-time explosions as the choppers roared past. Buried charges used by Mexican special effects chief Fredrico Farfan simulated ground explosions; dozens were ignited owing to variations in framing, airspeed and desired fireball sizes. Too close to the explosions, stuntman Clifford Wenger, Jr., sadly died playing an attacking Viet Cong.

Resuming production soon after, Loren was tasked with more aerial coverage using Russian "Hind-24" helicopters, chasing Rambo through dense jungle. French Aerospatiale SA330s were cast as Soviet birds; pilots flew perilous runs despite poor visibility, rapidly changing weather, and forest canopy blending into skyline at high speeds under failing afternoon light. After having suffered a fatality on the picture, even the simple stuff required extra attention. Shooting pre-dawn B-roll of Soviets bustling to join the chase required every costumed extra producer Buzz Feitstans could find awake. A low chopper pass blew over lights along the tarmac. As they crashed down with bulbs exploding, Loren watched background players scatter off the set in panic.

Filming Stallone (on foot) with Russian helicopters dogging him through a river channel boxed in by canyon walls, Loren's juggling act of direction included ground-to-air communication, flying and stunt cues. As the pursuit intensified, Loren Janes coordinated a scripted grudge between Rambo and Sgt. Yushin (Voyo Goric), starting with a large bomb stunt. A fireball mushroomed 60 feet skyward while Rambo remained safe beneath the water's surface. Coaching Stallone double Mark DeAlessandro for a vertical leap from the river into the open chopper door, Janes used mechanical advantage to make it possible. Rigged to the river's bottom six feet beneath the surface, a powerful springboard launched the player's body right though the open door. This was later intercut with a shot of a sopping wet Stallone entering the helicopter.

Taking the brawl from static to airborne, Janes directed the hand-to-hand battle between Yushin and Rambo at 500 feet above the jungle doing 75 knots. Filming from a second chopper "platform" (with stage-rigged green screen inserts completing the toughest action), Loren and camera ace Tom Gehrke had their hands full. They shared the dangers of the shot as pilot Harry Hauss held the Aerospatiale steady, through open cockpit air-buffeting and cosmetic fuselage add-ons that plagued flying. Wires around the actors' ankles insured their safety. Yushin attempted to force Rambo out the hatch as the ground raced by below; getting the upper hand, Rambo dispatched the larger man, flipping him out the door.

The fall, covered in long shot chopper to chopper, featured high diver Harry Mok (doubling Goric) executing a perfect front tuck and somersault six stories into an airbag. It was an amazing high-fall considering wind shear, hover instability and down-blast from the helicopter prop.

Embracing the technology of his time, calculus wiz Janes triangulated ground stunts and aerial interplay with piloting and human courage manifested by a ballet of action filming. Years ahead of its time, the "talk-now" model became the industry standard for action pictures.

Going from blood and guts to goofy sci-fi, Janes returned to the States as a stunt player for coordinator Walter Scott on Robert Zemeckis' *Back to the Future*. Driving the DeLorean for the chase with a Libyan terrorist in the mall parking lot, Loren manned the silver car as McFly delivering 50 MPH swerves over wet asphalt. Side-to-side jinking maneuvers were used to avoid exploding squibs hidden in the road's surface. By the end of the night, Janes had done 16 takes, the effects department expending 1100 rounds of blanks in the process. In the film's most iconic moment, Loren drove the DeLorean picture car for the "time barrier" break, pushing it in excess of 100 MPH. He also recovered the vehicle after a 70-foot sideward slide, owing to oil residue on the lot. Sand covered the oil in subsequent runs, to increase traction.

Wrapping *Back to the Future* in April '85, Loren shifted to UCLA's Culver campus for Tom Holland's *Fright Night*, then joined 75 of Hollywood's best for the biggest stunt picture to hit town in years, *To Live and Die in L.A*. By this time, 1986, Janes was earning in excess of $200,000 a year, plus S.A.G. residuals.

Janes was hired for *Live and Die* by Buddy Joe Hooker for the mind-blowing car chase against freeway traffic, which required six weeks for the "wrong way" work alone. On a par with *Bullitt* and *The French Connection*, the gag on *Live and Die* was one of artistic complexity. Beginning on East Sixth Street crossing Mateo (entering San Pedro's Harbor Freeway against off-ramp traffic), the sequence utilized more than 100 stunt drivers. Featured in a near head-on, Loren cut left in a silver sedan while the bad guy's tan Chevy dogged right to avoid collision. A montage of moving metal, the shot involved more than 60 vehicles requiring 30 minutes to reset each take. "Cranking the wheel right to clear the Chevy," Loren said, "I had to gauge his speed [45 MPH], then anticipate any changes before the last second. Jumping two lanes, the other stunt drivers were on *my* cue, to slip over too. With multiple cars approaching head-on, if I hesitated, the combined 90 mile an hour impact could easily be fatal."

Returning to horse work, wagon turn-overs and trampoline blasts, Janes moved over to Disney's Civil War episodic *North and South*. Brought in by stunt honcho Fred Lerner for the summertime pilot, military consultant Billy "Butch" Frank was tapped for accuracy in depicting cannon explosions, arms of the day and wounds. Janes' acumen with buried springboards and hidden mini tramps provided action for first-rate coverage by cinematographer Steven Larner. Janes was shot, blown up or otherwise dispatched 26 times during as many days of filming; at one point, he was blasted a dozen feet higher than planned by an exploding ammunition tender. "The effects guy liked his job a little too much!" Loren laughed.

Utilizing thirty stunt players and scores of action extras, battle sequences employed 200 re-enactors with stunts and combat bits throughout. "I was a Confederate officer shot off a horse in one scene," Loren recalled, "then Yankee cavalry being dragged dead in the next." Featured in a mounted saber engagement as a Union captain against three Rebels, Loren was pulled from the saddle as his horse collapsed to the ground on top of him. "The timing was a bit off," he said. "The guys accidentally forced down my mustang's flank onto my lower right calf and ankle, trapping it." His foot was hairline-fractured, but he worked the remainder of the schedule, trainer's tape and surgical foam padding seeing him through.

15

Cold, Cold, Cold Around the Heart

Hired in February '85 as stunt coordinator for Golan Globus' *Runaway Train*, Loren was responsible for stunts including moving locomotive gags, high falls and prison yard riots with dozens of guards and convicts mixing it up. Using real trains on miles of snow-covered tracks (with multiple helicopters as filming platforms), the picture is large-scope due to director Andrey Konchalovsky and cinematographer Alan Hume. Janes needed to plan everything to the second.

Challenged by complexities of air velocity affecting choppers (including wind shear, downdrafts, and thin mountain atmosphere), the mathematics instructor equated engine speed vectors accounting for head winds and track pitch to figure stunts safely. *Runaway Train* became one of Janes' finest accomplishments as stunt boss, as he assumed second unit director duties beside old friend Max Kleven. Starring Jon Voight and Eric Roberts vs. John P. Ryan, it was a dark look into security prison life under a sadist's warped rules of penal rehabilitation—and astronomical risks taken by those seeking to escape.

Tasked with staging a large-scale boxing scene between inmates, Janes gave the old-school movie gimmick a new twist: real training. A packed brawl featuring Roberts against Danny Trejo culminated in a flurry of punches with a right-cross resulting in a face-first fall by the heavy. Janes allowed Trejo to work with Roberts as fight coach (by way of helmer Andrey Konchalovsky's personal offer of $320 a day upon seeing the real ex-con visit the set); by picture's start, the actor had gained impressive stamina and solid boxing skills. Born in Los Angeles' tough Echo Park area in '44, the weather-beaten Trejo earned his boxing bones in San Quentin beginning in 1965 while serving time for armed robbery and drug possession. He won light and welterweight divisions in the prison by '68 before transferring to Soledad in 1969, 12-stepping his way out of the pokey and ultimately into the movie biz. Transferring storyboards to action, Loren directed a knife bit for the sequence that left audiences gasping. Upon Manny being released into general population at the fight's conclusion, a violent disturbance ensues. Fending off a hitman (Tony Epper, Jr.) armed with a large shiv, Manny (now Voight's stunt double Russell Solberg) is impaled through the hand. Using glue, photographic trickery and prop-making excellence by Robin Miller, the illusion incorporated a collapsing knife mechanism for initial thrust (with inserts of an artificial arm and palm pierced with blood squirting out), and finished with a blade affixed to the back of Voight's hand. Voight smashes his assailant across the face with a corner stool; a follow-up stabbing of the failed hitman (by stunter Chuck Hicks, cast as an inmate) took the phrase "the guy had guts" to a new level. Eviscerating Epper like a slaughtered pig, Hicks ran an effects blade the breadth of his stomach, dropping prop intestines from a gaping horrific gut wound. As Epper collapses knee-first to the ground, Voight delivers a final kick to his face, with cheated angle closeness. Janes exhibited his faculty for a sizable combat sequence as baton-wielding helmeted guards swatted prisoners to the deck. Rubber mock-up clubs aside, grunts and groans from stunt extras were real, as Konchalovsky directed all to go full tilt. Especially the corrections officers.

Upping the stunt ante as the picture shifts to the prison escape sequence, the helmer's order for Janes was one of his specialties: a high fall. Manny and Buck would drop from the ice-caked sewer pipe into the frigid rapids (protected by plastic wrap and Vaseline). A 12-foot plunge by the actors from an off-stage parallel was combined via quick cut and forced camera perspective (high to low) selling the perilous look. Shift to inserts of doubles Terry Jackson and Russell Solberg actually impacting the roiling waters of Placer Creek in Whittier, Alaska. The near freezing river had the capacity to sweep a man under in seconds. Deployed in rescue boats beyond frame should mishap occur, Loren and Kleven lifeguarded the entire proceeding.

Janes' next challenge: a full-scale locomotive collision, two trains approaching each other over icy rails. As one rounds a gradual curve, the second closes on a parallel cross-track switch—but it's too long to avoid impact. Staging the wreck by way of the second train engine striking the first's caboose mid-flanks, Janes knew an actual speed of 15 MPH was required for the pinpoint collision. (The footage was sped up in post along with intercut miniatures to complete the look.) Complicating the shot, a stunt player leaps from the caboose just before impact. The target for his landing was a snowdrift-covered airbag with only a small branch stuck in the bank marking the safe impact zone.

Filmed amid blizzard conditions, ensuing footage of Manny and Buck on the train engine as it hits was beautiful. Yet, between helicopter coverage's variable danger factor and a speeding train's 60 MPH slide over icy sections of track without the ability to stop, two shooting days were needed for the crash alone, with hours of repositioning for subsequent angles. "We had scale models of both trains," Loren explained, "and used a stopwatch to approximate the window of collision in rehearsal." Relying on his faculty for mathematical precision, Janes utilized the "variable speed equation" of two objects traveling on intersecting planes to plot the shot. "Hitting the train too soon was a real problem. We only had *one* mocked-up caboose for the gag. Keeping the primary engine at a constant speed was imperative to the timing of the crash." The stunt folks were unable to adjust for iced tracks or velocity once moving; the gag required precise communication between Janes and the two trains' motormen to hold uniform acceleration and constant rate for a smooth interaction. Traveling 6600 feet to reach 57 MPH for impact, his "ultimate crash" was accomplished in one take as planned.

Raising the stunt team's peril one notch further, Konchalovsky charged Janes with the disconnection of a speeding engine from its boxcars, by hand. Lensed along Portage, Alaska's, snowbound western provinces, the series of daylight exteriors were accomplished during white-out conditions including 40-knot crosswind gusts, all while hurtling down frozen tracks at 80 MPH. Wind-chill factors dropped temps to 20 below. Initial set-ups of Manny and Buck (crawling along the engine platform's lower stairs to disable the train) froze cameras in place.

First they filmed Solberg and Jackson for Voight and Roberts, respectively: Medium and long shots showed the stuntmen struggling to keep their feet against buffeting blasts of wind, bent forward like ski jumpers as they proceeded. Intercut with closeups of Voight and Roberts' upper bodies, the combination of controlled stunt and real stars worked well. But not without cost. As they shot the "around the waist" sequence (Voight and Roberts attempting to cut the motor's power, hovering inches above the track), wind and wet snow made the ploy extremely hazardous for their doubles. With metal surfaces slippery with ice, hands numb from cold and grip questionable, Solberg labored to smash the electrical cable while Jackson held him. "Safetying" the guys, Janes used hidden ankle wires bolted to the engine; the scene had theatergoers biting their nails. Hours of cold work were required of Loren as the trains repositioned, coverage was decided upon, multiple cameras placed. There was communication via multi-link radios with railroad coordinator Ted Hewitt and second unit d.p. Don Burgess (and chopper jockeys Soren Jensen and old pal Harry Hauss). Extraordinary overhead passing shots in medium and long lens showed the survivors in heavy snow and wind, standing on the engine platform as the train roared along. Snow flew from the blanketed tracks like a Freddie Young master shot from *Dr. Zhivago*; the moment was memorable.

Reminicent of Buster Keaton's 1926 classic *The General*, this picture's dangers hit new heights. The gag was extended with Jackson doubling Roberts in an attempt to climb the train engine's roof. Unintended swaying movement produced a near-fall from the ladder's top rung. Clinging in medium closeup with two-handed strain, the stuntman is clearly seen through blizzard conditions—wind-driven snow buffeting his face—as telephone poles zipped past close behind him. Following a quick cut to a closeup of Roberts struggling to catch himself, Burgess' second camera covers Jackson in full frame, saving himself by gathering his feet beneath and holding fast.

As the complexity and danger increased, Konchalovsky's vision transitioned to an aerial chase for the runaway locomotive, including the 40-foot rope ladder descent of a deputy (traveling 80 MPH through a snowstorm) suspended from a police helicopter and attempting to land on the train in motion.

Janes created new levels of aerial anxiety. He coordinated multiple choppers, a fast-moving train with actors standing on its ice-covered engine, and a stunt player clinging to a ladder strung beneath a helicopter—and all occurring during blizzard conditions. When power lines loomed, pilot Harry Hauss had to be quick on the stick to avert tragedy. Chopper-to-chopper coverage (in medium closeup) framed the stunt player's slow descent. A wide shot followed, revealing the train he is pursuing. Then an overhead shot encompassed the copter with the deputy tethered to the ladder, twisting and struggling to hang on, and the train below. It all culminates with the helicopter swooping down on the train, flying parallel at 85 MPH. Attempting a feet-first Superman landing, but misjudging speed and placement, the deputy was suddenly seized by wind and forward momentum, then launched through the engine compartment's upper windshield. An insert shot showed audiences that he was dead upon impact.

Continuing the chopper-mounted shot of the train and trailing helicopter with ladder extended, John P. Ryan's stunt double John Casino exited the cockpit and stood on the skids preparing to descend. He got on the ladder and instantly began descending. Then an overhead down-view encompasses the speeding train and helicopter above. The stuntman continued to climb down, the ladder whipping in the frigid air. A tunnel suddenly looms in the distance, and a shot zooms in to reveal a rapidly approaching suspension bridge. One step from the bottom, Casino clung to the ladder, clearing the bridge header by inches.

15. Cold, Cold, Cold Around the Heart

Instilling more drama, Konchalovsky inserted Buck (Eric Roberts) failing to reach the engine's control room. Doubling the actor, Terry Jackson served Janes' vision of the brave but defeated escapee. "Terry had athletic ability that far exceeded Roberts," Loren revealed. "It was so cold on that steel deck. I give him credit for reducing his natural coordination to that of Buck's—all just inches from falling off an ice-encrusted speeding train."

Filmed with a combination of half-speed location inserts and 80 MPH full-bore runs, Manny's attempt at breaching the gap to the motorman's station was truly breathtaking, covered in medium closeups using Voight and Roberts at reduced speeds and then repeated with stunt players taking the high-speed risks. Intercut set-ups blended seamlessly.

Continuing to raise the stunt ante, Kleven and Janes designed an old-fashioned cliffhanger that became one of the picture's finest action sequences. Moving swiftly forward on the engine by way of a ten-inch steel catwalk, Solberg (doubling Voight) did a flip-fall over the front of the train (presumably to his death). Cut to Voight with arms stretched above his head rising from the apron (hands clawing at the ice-coated steel), his feet slid to the track below as he hung on for life. Insert shots of Manny's legs dragging beneath the engine, bouncing inches from the huge steel wheels, were filmed at 15 MPH on a closed section of rail in Butte, Montana. A second pass was done of Russell Solberg's legs and torso at twice that speed. It took a dozen takes, but the resulting footage produced fine results.

Cutting back to Warden Rankin perched at the ladder's base on the train, a quick-pan to Manny (Voight) shows him "cliff-crawling" his way onto the moving train deck, minus fingertips on his left hand. A fight ensues ending with the warden handcuffed to the motor room, the train roaring towards a dead end at terminal velocity. Ryan's "touchdown" was so dangerous, Janes refused to allow any stunt player to actually attempt it; the possibility of slipping off the engine to the tracks below was too great.

The scene culminates with the 90 MPH smash-up of a full-sized locomotive into a dead-end terminal nearing. The massive impact was covered by trackside cameras as human operation was deemed suicidal. Yet the shot was nothing short of film perfection as the train roared through the tunnel entrance, colliding with the real stone landing just before Manny disconnects the trailing cars. Leaning stoically forward like Washington in Leutze's *Crossing the Delaware*, the image was cinematographer Alan Hume's loveliest of the picture. Employing brilliantly cut interim coverage of Russell Solberg (doubling Voight) standing free on the engine as it races toward destruction, the Don Burgess second unit footage was spellbindingly beautiful. Utilizing medium to long lens chopper coverage for Voight's 60 MPH stroll along the moving train, an insert followed Manny (Solberg) uncoupling the trains before cutting back to a cowboy closeup of Voight (thighs to head) climbing atop the engine as it toboggans down the tracks.

Then a transition to long shots of Manny enveloped in actual blizzard conditions at full speed (Solberg again). The stunt player leaned forward like a ski jumper through 15 seconds of film that was the crystalline vehicle of Konchalovsky's intent. The final image: Voight riding the engine in medium frame slowly zooming to tight closeup, ready to meet his fate, life or death. The actor's serene facial expression said no more prison, either way. The picture ends with the train disappearing into a total whiteout, Manny's arms raised in victory.

This was the most challenging stunt coordination of Janes' career, involving mathematical timing, moving trains, blizzards, altitude and multiple helicopters. The fact that there were no serious injuries was a result of Janes' meticulous planning and effective leadership under trying circumstances. A film of its type today would certainly involve CGI, miniatures and months of shooting in cavernous warehouses to lesser effect.

16

Master of the Tinseltown Universe

Loren took a late-night call in June '85 from coordinator Walter Scott, and was invited to Astoria, Oregon, to work a low-budget action-comedy called *Short Circuit*. He departed Los Angeles in a 1970 Porsche 911 Targa, the 1000-mile drive taking the stuntman 12 hours flat. Used for everything from a featured thug to hapless target of Number 5's boundless powers, he was one of a dozen stunt folks on the upbeat feature. He doubled Fisher Stevens in dark makeup and black wig performing pratfall gags from the Bonneville Dam sequence to the car chase over the Columbia River gorge. "They had trouble getting that robot to run," Loren said of the gas station sequences filmed along Astoria's Highway 202. "The hotter it got, the slower that prop rolled. Finally, they cheated a tow line below frame and pulled the thing from its front wheels."

John Irwin's *Raw Deal* was a stunt vehicle attached to an Arnold Schwarzenegger platform if ever there was one. Drafted by horse whisperer Glenn Randall, Jr., for utility crew, Loren knew the gags would be plenty, physical and risky: explosions, machine-gunning, beatings and car crashes, one after the other. Dispatched by a brutal burst of Schwarzenegger gunfire early in the movie, Loren was body-yanked via steel cable through a wood-paneled door, impacted a dozen times via wired squibs beneath his wardrobe; the effect was disturbingly realistic.

Performing a car-hit stunt, Janes had to roll off the windshield traveling 30 MPH while back-flipping over the roof and landing flat on the pavement behind. "If you mis-time the vertical jump, you'll fail to roll *up the hood*, or worse, get hit by the front grill and probably injured. What's more, your momentum has to accelerate you up and over the automobile at the same speed the vehicle's traveling in the opposite direction. Otherwise, you go *through* the windshield, instead of over it!"

In another Walter Scott picture, *Ruthless People*, Danny DeVito was pitted against Bette Midler in an over-the-top hate-fest. Janes worked on the slapstick picture for two weeks through January 1986. Performing driving stunts during the kidnap sequence, he executed one of his patented spin-hits off the front of a moving auto. Intercut with *his own* driving, Loren was struck (via editing) by himself—a fact not lost on his sense of humor. "Who else can say they ran themselves over and kept driving?" he quipped.

That March he was called by Steven Bochco for his new series pilot *L.A. Law*. Janes' uncanny resemblance to Corbin Bernsen ensured his place in Ray Lykins' stunt stable with their first meeting. Cast in a small, featured bit as Norman Chaney in the Greg Holblit–directed episode, Loren turned down the series long-term despite aspirations of acting that ran deep. Returning to the bread and butter of westerns, he was gladly dragged, thrown, shot and pulled from moving horses on John Landis' comeback picture *Three Amigos!* And that was just the audition.

Starring stand-up comic turned actor Steve Martin, *Saturday Night Live* mumbler Chevy Chase and real-deal comedic talent Martin Short of Second City fame, the Lorne Michaels–produced romp through '20s Hollywood was a moneymaker for studio and stuntmen alike. Doubling Short's Ned Nederlander character, Loren was seen executing a 30-foot rope swing to avoid Goldstone Studios security guards. On Universal's Mediterranean Square backlot, Janes rigged and measured the line before attaching it to the "perms" of the outdoor structure for his second-story landing. "The swashbuckler stuff is straight ahead," the ex–calculus teacher lectured. "The issue becomes speed and gravitational pull drawing you off the line. Launching your swing smoothly, then holding through the lower apex of the inverted parabolic arch. As the g force doubles the swinging weight, upper body strength and coordination make the move possible."

Again doubling Short, Loren joined Bob Herron and Johnny Hock (Steve Martin and Chevy Chase's doubles) for the crashing of El Guapo's birthday party sequence. Cranes were employed as swing platforms; a transition cut of the actual building with actors poised to leap gave way to the stunt pros gliding through space and dismounting. Finishing with static closeups of the Amigos (actors) dropping from short parallels above, the look was first-rate if not old-school camp.

In March of 1986, Janes and 39 other crew members boarded a Qantas Airlines 747 at LAX three minutes past four in the morning to go to New Zealand to make *White Water Summer.* Janes received strange looks when checking his safety gear with customs officers, from a ten-inch Bowie knife with strap-on scabbard to cold water wetsuits, steel cables, line cutters, carabiners, pitons, rock hammers, wire wedges, climbing line, flare guns and more. They would be shooting amid the rapids of New Zealand's Rangitaiki and Wairoa rivers.

Janes was one of two stunt coordinators on the water-soaked feature. In day after day of filming with expert canoeist Phil Dove and Gary La Hood merged with rafters Paul Van Der Kaag and Hamish McCrostie for camera platforms, Peter Bell's whitewater unit (including Ken Lake's jet boat), made possible shooting the impossible. "The jet boat allowed for upstream and cross-current coverage, that no other mount would provide," Janes said. It handled everything from grip support (capturing dynamic circular shots of the canoes racing through white water) to hauling box lunches upriver for lunch. According to Janes, "Trying to photograph in white water, you're at the mercy of the river. From using underwater parachute anchors to rigging steel cable beneath boulders along rapids to pull the boats, we spent the entire show keeping camera platforms in place and canoes on mark. The actual tip-over stuff became simpler by virtue of finding proper location spots where we could safely control the action."

Janes returned home five weeks later, minus the knife which he gave to a Kiwi counterpart, Steven Davidson. He was suffering from water on the ear (owing to flying immediately following weeks of wet work). Despite temporary deafness caused by the condition, he stunt-coordinated for ten relaxing days in Cromberg in California's Sierra Nevada Mountains to wrap the show.

Producers Yoran Globus and Menahem Golan arrived at Janes' front gates at sun-up to convince him to do their kiddie flick *Masters of the Universe.* Having seen Frazetta's *Fire and Ice* with its amazing swordplay, they courted Loren for the project's vital choreographer role. He and his stunt crew were paid above-scale rates; Loren earned in excess of $1500 a day as boss. The movie starred Dolph Lundgren, Billy Barty, Jon Cypher and Anthony De Longis performing as Blade. The Gary Goddard film was ably lensed by Hanania Baer around Malibu Creek State Park, Whittier's boride mines and Aqua Dulce's Vasquez Rocks. Tapping Loren's expertise for everything from horse falls to mounted combat and standing battle (including broad axe, clubs, long swords and daggers), Walter Scott coordinated camera coverage and background stunts while Janes constructed and gaffed the individual swordfights, interactions and multiple skirmishes. Loren recalled, "Dolph was so strong, his blows with a half-weight shield nearly knocked out Kent Jordan, while his swordplay in others was slowed down owing to the power in his six-foot-five-inch frame." The stunt work was first-rate. Ticket and toy sales boomed.

Janes next worked on what proved one of Hollywood's worst late '80s buddy films (think *Beverly Hills Cop* meets the Walking Dead). Mark Goldblatt's *Dead Heat* was so bad, it was nearly unwatchable. Filmed in Van Nuys' Japanese Gardens at Woodley Park (and the not-so-lovely Tillman water reclamation plant nearby), the low-budgeter featured a muscle-bound Joe Piscopo at his least humorous (thanks to scribe Terry Black and producer David Helpern—who let the thing go camp) and Treat Williams in a constant state of angst. Seen in support, Vincent Price, Keye Luke and Darren McGavin nearly made the thing passable. Well, almost.

Loren was one of a throng of 20 stunt players who got eviscerated, tossed about, shot, run over or chased in cars. Signed by coordinator Dan Bradley especially for his air ram skills, the stunter was thrown a dozen feet via pneumatic launch into walls and trees, over cars and into a moving bus; by picture's wrap, he and mates Andy Gill, Gene LeBell and May Boss had earned their paychecks.

By decade's end, expansion of cable networks like HBO and Showtime saw the thinnest scripts shot for profit in Hollywood history. Action-horror was a winning combo for producers; even master stunt coordinators like Janes were tempted by easy money. Loren's reality was about paying his bills by keeping his air rams on rental. The new stuff was wafer-thin, but rich in stunt action.

Nearly as bad as *Dead Heat* (but getting better box office results), the camp classic *Weekend at Bernie's* was shot in the spring of 1988 on North Carolina's Figure Eight and Bald Head Islands and along Wrightsville Beach. Ted Kotcheff's dark comedy focused on two hapless losers who find an accounting error. Their crooked boss Bernie plans to have the boys murdered at his beach house, but instead winds up whacked by his own hitman.

Loren was tapped for a high fall with the boys taking their corpse Bernie off a high dive into a pool. Janes: "That diving board sequence was tricky owing to three folks required to fall evenly. Matched by weight, we locked elbows and leaned slightly forward, falling all together to effect the perfect impact into the water."

Janes was back to zombie fare for David Irving's horror reboot *C.H.U.D. II* in May '88. Hired for his acrobatic air ram craft, Loren was used by coordinator Hubie Kerns, Jr., for the picture's second unit gags, set against Veluzat Ranch's dark hollows and broken-down western buildings. The place was thought to be haunted by movie folks. Then came the bad luck. Several misfire launches on Loren's air rams (usually perfect) caused ankle injury to stunt players. Janes replaced failed units with others, but more problems arose. "We got to the point that we ran everything at half-power tests, until convinced the replacement rigs were okay." Loren was pulled beneath the ground, attacked, mauled and dispatched in a multitude of fashions by C.H.U.D. (six-footer Bud Oliver).

Other stunt gags revolved around severed limbs, fountains of blood squirting from those severed limbs, decapitations, and a few guys getting face-munched for good measure. The makeup effects were by Doug White, Allan Apone and John Fifer.

Descending from teenage horror to sea-bottoms in August '88, Janes was enlisted by coordinator Dick Warlock for 20th Century–Fox's *The Abyss*, directed by James Cameron. Location-filmed near Gaffney, South Carolina, in an unfinished Cherokee nuclear power plant, the $700 million write-off included a 7.5-million-gallon tank 55 feet deep by 209 feet across. The largest freshwater tank in existence, its basis of lighting control beat out the Bahamas and Malta hands down. With six modules making up the deep-core rig, it took five days to fill the underwater set anchored to a 90-ton column. Gradating light, D.P. Mikael Salomon and Al Gittings floated layers of plastic beads on the water's surface; Cameron brought resources to the diving masks worn by actors, allowing for clear speech and individual lights within to better see faces. Loren dealt with long hours of safety diver duties backing up stunt double Jon Epstein. He heard the crew's gripes consisting of nicknames for the director and his film like *Son of a Bitch, Son of Abyss* and *The Abyuse*. Janes said "due to the subdued lighting, depth of the tank, and practical difficulty of shooting underwater for five-hour stretches, it was physically one of the toughest pictures I ever worked." Viewing dailies through a portal in a decompression tank while normalizing blood levels, Loren often fell asleep owing to exhaustion. With 40 percent of the picture's live action photography filmed underwater, Janes suffered fluid on the ear. In the key role, Loren recalled that star Ed Harris nearly drowned while shooting the fluid-breathing sequence: The tinted saline solution used for the liquid lung trick dilated Harris' nostrils, swelling his eyes to the point of blinding pain. He blacked out from loss of oxygen and a quick-thinking camera operator saved him. "Between the horrible visibility from blooming algae materializing every few hours, chlorine burning off body hair and stinging eyes, then hanging half-unconscious from the side of the tank huffing pure oxygen at days end, I have never been *so tired* in my life," Janes recalled. "And that made taking care of others beneath the surface much harder. Losing focus from exhaustion and submersion disorientation, we had to monitor talent *and* ourselves every second."

In all careers, there's a classic or two. In Loren Janes' case, the number is closer to a dozen. One such gem was David Lynch's *Wild at Heart*. Signed to the cult flick by coordinator Jeff Smolek, he worked locations like Palmdale, Colton, Pasadena's Green Castle apartments and the downtown artist colony in Santa Fe South. Featured as a driver-victim of Willem Dafoe's character Bobby Peru, Loren labored a week behind the wheel.

Blue Desert and *Write to Kill* (both 1991) were little more than ten days' employment for Janes; he was hired by stunt bosses Dan Bradley and Mike Filoon respectively. By then part of Hollywood stunt royalty, Janes was often brought in by an admiring new generation of coordinators who appreciated having a living legend around who could "one-take" the tough stuff. Gifted with a speaking role as a cop, Loren executed everything from a stair fall to a gunfight in *Blue Desert* before moving on.

Now at a place in career and personal wealth one might call comfortable, Janes continued to work because he loved what he was doing. It was part pride of expertise, part that he had a bit of kid left. He was enjoying himself as a premier stuntman, and as long as his phone rang with decent offers, he gladly saddled up and took 'em.

Crewing what was perhaps Steven Spielberg's least appreciated but funniest films, Loren started *Hook* in February of '91 through 116 shooting days ending in June. Brought to the massive undertaking by coordinator Gary Hymes for his gymnastic and tumbling abilities, Janes was one of over a hundred stunt players on the project. Occupying nine Sony sound stages including the lot's largest, on which a full-size pirate ship was constructed, the picture was also shot on locations including Griffith Park (the baseball game) and London Harbor. Showcasing Robin Williams, Bob Hoskins, Julia Roberts and Dustin Hoffman in the title role, *Hook* was a much-criticized masterpiece of epic proportions. The bits were also classic. Among the stunt elite who worked the picture: Jophery Brown, Bobby Burns, Garry Epper, Henry Kingi, R.A. Rondell, Jim Arnett, Bob Yerkes, Conrad Palmisano and Gene LeBell: all were first rate in their respective fields.

Featured as one of *Hook*'s random shooting victims, Loren did a 25-foot fall from the bleachers into the drink, putting the Janes twist on the gag by adding a half gainer as he entered the water. Tapped for comedic swordplay, Janes designed the picture's big swashbuckler mix-up. Attacked by bad guys, Jack (Williams) flips a heavy over his back. Jack picks up another pirate and spins him, smacking Loren with the guy's feet, sending him into the harbor. Janes hit the water back first, a difficult move given the fall's angle of trajectory. A seesaw catapult sent four pirates airborne courtesy of kids leaping down from above. Loren performed a neat back tuck upon entry into the water. Requiring perfect timing, it took several takes to get right, but it provided a slapstick flourish the director loved.

20th Century–Fox's *Jack the Bear*, shot in the summer of '91, starred Danny DeVito as a grieving TV kiddie clown and Gary Sinise as the heavy. Loren took on coordinator duties following a last-minute pullout of another big-name stunt boss, Terry Leonard. He was responsible for designing a vicious Doberman attack on Sinise. "I've been nailed by trained 'attack dogs,'" he said, referring to his *Call of the Wild* groin chomp. "So exposing Bobby Porter [Sinise's double] to *three* animals really presented its challenges." There were separate handlers for each Doberman just inches out of frame; orders to break any take and grab the dogs were in effect if action became too heated. "Even with trainers," Loren interjected, "I was ready to jump if Bobby needed help."

Following an hour-long phone negotiation with Jack Nicholson, Janes agreed to coordinate *Man Trouble*. For coordination alone, his weekly rate was $10,000, plus any on-camera work. One of Nicholson's least appreciated ventures, the Stephen Burum–lensed dark comedy contained enough slapstick antics to make it farcical. Janes said, "Nicholson liked my work from *Missouri Breaks* on."

Wolfgang Peterson's *In the Line of Fire* was an action-packed rollercoaster of a movie sprinkled with ingenious stunts. Hired by long-time Clint Eastwood action boss Buddy Van Horn, Loren (not to mention a crew of nearly 30 specialized stuntmen including the Gill brothers, Larry Holt and Orwin Harvey) played it full out. The rooftop sequence with Eastwood and Dylan McDermott pursuing John Malkovich was perhaps the picture's highlight. Used primarily for driving and street-crowd stunts, Loren was running circles around younger actors despite being old enough to have fathered many of them.

Robin Hood: Men in Tights came Loren's way in early January 1993. Grabbed ostensibly for his swashbuckling chops and a special thatched roof fall, Loren was featured in a fight scene with Dave Chapelle as one of six guards beating him up. (Janes recalled Chapelle as side-splittingly funny, each take presenting the stand-up comic with material.) Performing a bump routine on stairs during the big Locksley vs. the Sherriff of Nottingham fight, Loren was booted from one guard to the next in a roving joke. He was ultimately kicked through a thatched roof, landing back-first on the timber floor below. The impact jarred the stunt player's teeth each time he did it. "[Stunt coordinator] Brian

Burrows got me three takes," Janes says, referring to the requests for additional coverage. "At a thousand per go, I was up to three grand by lunch." Janes was involved in one of the picture's trickier bits: He was one of 20 soldiers falling like dominos when punted by Robin Hood swinging from a chandelier. Taking two days of rehearsals to acquire proper timing and flow, Burrows' efforts had a physical pop that most comedic live-action vehicles lack: realism, with laughable physical gags, possessing a charming cartoon effect.

Following brief stints on Julie Corman's *Silence of the Hams* (a spoof of the neo-classic *The Silence of the Lambs*) and director Franco Amurri's *Monkey Trouble*, Loren did *Steal Big Steal Little* in 1994, a transitional year for Janes (and Hollywood). High fall experts were a dime a dozen and westerns non-existent; saddle jerks and stirrup drags had all become extinct things. Loren Janes was slowing down, but far from done. Like other physical processes, the erosion of a stuntman's physical abilities exacts a reverse osmosis. No longer capable of falling from a galloping horse or surviving the impact of a 40-foot airbag landing, precision driving and doubling "older actors" become one's employable talents. Bartering knowledge and experience against youth's unbridled energy, Loren used smarts rather than testosterone to continue in the younger man's world.

Janes suffered a serious stroke in late '93. It was a shock to all who knew the tough guy. At first he suffered total debilitation of motor and speech skills, yet the former Marine's recovery was nothing short of miraculous. He was written-off as oxygen-dependent and wheelchair-bound for life, but Loren resumed full ambulatory movement and basic speech (including unassisted breathing) in three months.

The stunt industry helps its own: Janes returned to its bosom when hired by coordinator Joel Kramer for horse-work on James Cameron's *True Lies* in December 1993. Playing the tuxedoed half of a refined couple sharing a glass-enclosed elevator (trapped by Arnold Schwarzenegger as secret agent Harry Tasker—riding a large horse), Loren was accompanied by his wife, Ginger. The culmination of the picture's exacting Washington, D.C., chase, actually utilized Los Angeles' Ambassador Hotel for the mounted lobby entrance, switching to the Bonaventure Westin for the action-elevator sequence. Requiring equine stunt double Billy Lucas for some of the approach shots, action star Arnold did much of the work himself, including threading the 1500-pound horse onto the lift without trampled feet or panicked steed.

"Joel knew I needed to work during recovery, to keep from going nuts," Loren Janes says of his *True Lies* chores. "I was barely able to walk 20 feet without holding on to something. Keeping myself between Ginger and the horse, the six takes Cameron needed went off without a hitch."

Loren Janes regained control and body strength over the next six months, seeking transitional assignments such as wheel work or low-budget coordinating while on the comeback trail. The occasional plum assignments were a nod of respect to a master, from his students. He spent two weeks driving donuts in the Vegas desert by invitation of coordinator Danial Barringer for Martin Scorsese's *Casino* in late '94. Then he returned to the Bonaventure Hotel's glass elevators for Rick Freiberg's comedic romp *Spy Hard*. Recreating *True Lies*' horse-boarding-elevator sequence (alongside his now ex-wife Ginger), they stood professionally as Leslie Nielsen rode into the car. "Ginger was afraid of horses," he said of his former spouse. "And Nielsen was hesitant and only slightly in control of the white mare he was riding." Thanks to double Bruce Barbour, cheating angles and clever editing, audiences bought the sleight of hand, laughing aloud at the scene.

Janes fully recovered but his pace slowed to just a few pictures a year by 1995.

Physically, he couldn't do more than coordinating or day player work for big stunt driving sequences and specific utility-player calls such as simple fights, police and fire fare. He took what jobs he could, to stay in the game. *Out to Sea* was a soft gig: Janes was hired by old friend Roydon Clark to double Jack Lemmon in this *Odd Couple*–ish rehash.

Best Men (1996), a romantic crime comedy starring Andy Dick, Luke Wilson, and Dean Cain, utilized Janes' precision driving skills (still fully intact). Also involved: Terry Leonard, Vince Deadrick, Sr., and wheel man Hal Burton. Days of saddle drags, bull bronco riding, high falls and car crashes had also taken their toll on these old pros. Completely capable of doing most of the automotive gags required, these old-schoolers also taught the new bunch some tricks of the trade. Loren said, "In cars, an old gladiator like me can still use his skills to effect a physical stunt, without leaving all the fun to the kids."

Acting bugs being the transitional tonic of many stunt players, Loren enjoyed the occasional closeup. Especially without being required to take a punch. Landing a featured player bit on David E. Kelley's *The Practice* in February '98, he was cast as a cop restraining a large gang banger. Growling the line, "You're comin' along, pal, 'cuz *we* say you're comin' along!," Loren was paid the Screen Actors Guild minimum but won bragging rights with the stunt players as director Dennis Gordon raved about his delivery.

He was hired to coordinate Frank Gilroy's *Money Play*, filmed in late spring of 1998 in Las Vegas and around the deserts of Wendover, Nevada, and Salt Lake City. The zany crime movie starred Roy Scheider and Sonia Braga as partners hiding a cash belt belonging to the mob. With few challenges but a running automobile chase, the Showtime production was a low-budget quickie that wrapped in six weeks with little fanfare before running on the cable network a month later. Then Loren worked in Tinseltown's biggest movie that year: He was hired with over 100 other stunt performers (including legends May Boss, Larry Holt and old friend Max Kleven), for Barry Sonnenfeld's *Wild Wild West*.

Assisting second unit director–stunt coordinator Terry Leonard on the picture's many wagon roll-overs, saddle jerks, stirrup drags, fights and high falls, Janes utilized his expertise at designing stunts rather than his faded physical skills. From the film's opening water tower fight (James West against a rowdy batch of Confederate soldiers), to the nitro gag on the runaway buckboard, to the train roof brawl with Indian Joe, the sequences had Loren's unmistakable imprint. Flourishes like backflips, multiple angle saddle jerks and galloping gunfights—the best of his repertoire—came back to the screen. For a minute the next day at dailies, the old soldier was again back in time at the sight and sounds of his visions, as crew members cheered at the screen.

Loren said, "Despite my ability to lay out major sequences for Terry, the physical strain of being present on set each day began to take a toll." Suffering a second stroke three weeks after wrapping *Wild West*, he was facing certain death had not a quick-thinking surgeon performed a quintuple bypass to save him. Again, on borrowed time, the unbreakable stunt legend was now anything but. Yet, like a phoenix rising from the ashes, Loren Janes once again recovered. Within two years, the tough ex–Marine was back under his own power. Amazingly, he again returned to stunt work.

America's Sweethearts, made in the spring of 2000, was the perfect medicine for Janes, as it required from him little more than basic bump-and-run driving. "I was so glad to be back on a set," Janes said quietly. "I wept like a kid when finally alone behind the wheel, waiting for the first take." Loren's amazing toughness and "never quit" disposition kept him in the driver's seat.

Taking one other call that year, Janes rose to the occasion on Brian Smith's *The Omega Code*. Hired by second unit boss Eddie Matthews (along with 50-plus other stuntmen), the old master was again utilized for his bigger vision. The picture featured multiple explosions; Loren helped with everything from placement of mortar ramps to selection of background players to play wounded and dying. He was only able to work the nearby Los Angeles locations (including Greystone Mansion and Santa Clarita). Within three weeks, he was exhausted and seriously planning full retirement. But not before his final bow.

Restored to life after months of comprehensive rehabilitation, including diet, exercise, and mental acuity work, Janes passed through Sony Studio's Overland gates on May 7, 2001, for his final curtain call, *Spiderman*. Arriving at Stage 27 as scheduled for his 4:15 a.m. makeup and wardrobe fitting, the tuxedo-clad gentleman looked upon the aged studio's catwalks and perms as old friends. Large, chained arbors amid gray faded I-beams arched over the massive sets like a primeval steel and lumber forest; it all brought him to a quiet place. The stage's musky scent of perspiration, dust and roscoe smoke filled his nostrils—a total sensory moment.

Brought in by coordinator Jeff Habberstad for a three-story balcony drop, Loren was playing one of the formally attired bigwigs dispatched by the Green Goblin's exploding grenades. According to Janes, "Standing there inspecting the catch nets was a surreal experience. It was like *no time* had passed at all since [the beginning days of his career]. But the cutting-edge pneumatic rigging of the balcony gag ensured me that I was indeed down the road a bit." Completing the sequences without mishap, Janes was rising to his feet after the final take when crew and cast gave him a standing ovation. All of the picture's stunt performers had been brought in to witness the moment; over 150 of Hollywood's best surrounded him and cheered. Tough guys Tony Brubaker and Bobby Burns teared up; others looked on in amazement. Loren Janes remembered: "On the final take of the last bit of the balcony fall, I laid against the net, peering high up into the O-Zones. The sting of sweat in my eyes and heart pounding…made me feel capable of doing anything!"

"For just one moment," he sighed, "I was young again."

PART II: MICKEY GILBERT

17

Birth of a Champion

Michael R. "Mickey" Gilbert was born April 17, 1936, to Jenavive and Fred, who made their own luck through backbone, good genes and a strong work ethic). Mickey's brother Freddy arrived in '38. Dad took the opportunity to ditch the lumberjack trade for another, giving the boys a permanent home and consistent education. "Mickey" (as grade school chums called him in Pasadena) was descended from first-rate athletes. Great-grandfather Frederick labored two years in Oregon's frigid Coos Bay (driving mule teams); 20 years later, his son Frank made the Olympic trials in pole vault, when not breaking high-speed motorboat records.

With World War II looming, Fred Sr. traded Pasadena's roses for fertile acres in Van Nuys: He found a spread with water for corn fields, chickens, hogs, milk cows, goats and horse barns. Soon their fields of alfalfa were bulldozed for military barracks and landing strips as tarmacs sprang up after Pearl Harbor. Mickey's childhood rapidly transitioned to one of toiling at men's jobs around the ranch. Growing up fast, he loved the responsibility, if not the blisters.

He rose before dawn for pre-school chores like pitchforking hay, replenishing water and filling feed cribs. Mickey attended school in Van Nuys all day, then rushed home for workouts with Dad—pole vault, shot put and otherwise running around the half size football field until it became too dark to see the makeshift chalk markings on the grass.

He was also involved in schoolboy misadventures (like fights) to burn off adolescent energy. Mickey was introduced to rodeo via the older brother of a past adversary. The boys made a bucking bull out of two barrels rigged with cables attached to telephone poles and "boy muscle" at each end yanking up and down to replicate erratic movement for the rider. Sneaking into nearby corrals behind the local tack shop late at night, Mickey and pals graduated to the real thing. Roping and riding horses, he and brother Fred avoided injury while getting their first bronc lessons.

The war was over by '45 and the "cluck business" was cracked by America's new-found appetite for steaks and hamburgers. Subdividing their large expanse of ranch property in 1948, the Gilberts once again survived. Hard-working brothers Mickey and Freddy helped too. They converted the ranch's 300-foot-long, 25-foot-wide chicken coops into covered stalls, and money was made boarding local horses. Corrals were built with scrap wood and reclaimed fence; the stables were soon filled to capacity. "Blind-riding" his horse Monty the Mustang through Panorama's pitch-black alfalfa fields to reach remote neighbors, newspaper delivery boy Mickey tossed papers onto the porches of the new tract homes along the sidewalk-less blocks. Mickey slept in the saddle while his horse instinctively headed home. Once home, Monty removed the mustang's saddle and gave him a brush down, water and feed, then (on his bike) made his final newspaper deliveries en route to school. Mickey delighted in vaulting the split ranch-style kitchen door when leaving, despite his mother's warnings of breaking his neck if he fell.

Mickey secretly rode his smallish horse to calf-roping events on the weekends. Boarding horses was fun for the fifth grader. He cinched bucking straps on customers' animals, and only luck kept the ten-year-olds from discovery while they enjoyed their private rodeos.

A famous old trick rider from the Buffalo Bill Wild West Show, Buff Brady, fell on rough times after the war, and he was put up by Mick's father. Since Mick was a child, Brady had taught him the intricate details of Pony Express running mounts and basic stunt riding, all things equestrian. And with mentoring, Mickey connected to horses, more than a grade schooler might. The aging cowboy lived amidst the remains of the ranch's bunkhouse (tending horses as part of his keep). It was Mickey's greatest reward to see Buff perform his famous "under the belly" move at full gallop.

"Even at 70 years old," Gilbert recalled, "Buff could rotate beneath a horse's stomach at full run (arms draped around the neck and feet locked over the saddle), without falling. Back then, I knew I wanted to do that!" And so he did. He competed in Van Nuys' Junior Rodeo at age 13. (The event was a big deal, and shown on the new medium of television, which was hungry for content). The youngster placed first or second in 11 events including calf-roping, bulldogging and bronc riding. Mickey: "All I could think about was doing the best I could. The cameras seemed okay and natural to me."

Graduating from Van Nuys High in 1954, Mickey attended Woodland Hills' Pierce College in the fall of '55. He was already studying with future Hall of Fame stunter Dar Robinson at his father's gymnastics school; the two were getting a ground-up course in stunt survival without knowing it. The school's trampoline and tumbling workouts improved their bareback riding technique for wrestling steers to the ground: grab the bull around the neck, forearms "full-nelson" over horns, fight for control with boot-heels digging into the ground seeking traction. The 150-pound kid was dragged by the 800-pound heifer a dozen feet before he brazenly muscled the creature to its knees after seven very long seconds.

Gilbert, 17, majored in agriculture but quickly gravitated towards the school's fledgling rodeo team, rapidly established himself by winning a National Collegiate Championship in bareback bronc-riding and calf-roping his freshman and sophomore years. Mick took second places in bareback bronc-riding and calf-roping at L.A.'s Olympic Coliseum in December '55, earning $1500 his first week as a pro.

Deferring to his father's knowledge of rising property values, Mickey used the prize check to make a down payment on a neighboring spread; he financed a deal through Dad at $116 a month for the rest.

Rodeo prize cash and boarding horses kept Mick flush as he toyed with the idea of transitioning to show biz. But something was missing. TV series such as *Tales of the Texas Rangers, Colt .45, Tombstone Territory, The Tall Man, Death Valley Days* and scores of others launched countless cowboys to careers long and prosperous. Unknowns *were* getting discovered, and Mickey wondered if destiny was passing him by. Weaned on Republic westerns and serials, Gilbert developed an appetite to be a cowboy hero too. But getting a shot at it was almost impossible. Patience was the key, and Mick had that in spades.

Mickey was trotting a neighbor's filly one morning when a Lincoln convertible quietly rolled up his packed-dirt drive. It was a Hollywood couple who were boarding a mare there, director Edward Dmytryk and his actress wife Jean Porter. Jean watched Mickey

17. Birth of a Champion

Mickey R. Gilbert, 18, works his mount with ease before 80,000 fans and secured a second place win in the 1955 World Rodeo Championships at the Olympic Coliseum. Note the fine form of his right toe pointing skyward while the left pulls down to remain control: gliding with the horse, rather than being bucked off.

handle the horse and said, "Edward, *look* at that guy, he can do anything. Why don't you use *him* in your movie?"

The film was *Warlock* starring Richard Widmark. And "anything" turned out to be a bit in a saloon where Mickey lassoes a whiskey bottle out of a bar patron's hand from a dozen feet away. He was paid as an extra; regardless of six perfect takes on the sequence, it ended up on the cutting room floor. Soured by his initial movie exposure but not enough to quit, Gilbert returned to the daily grind of horse ranching for sustenance. But not without longing for the "big time."

Still anxious for a stake in Hollywood's western gold mine, Mick caught a break. Following a phone chat with Jean Porter, he was mentored by Central Casting's George Light. He started getting steady extra work on *Rawhide* in '59, playing saloon patrons, sidewalk fillers and rowdy crowd types. Being on the Universal lot was exciting to Gilbert despite his low ranking. As he was hanging around chatting with "the cowboys" one afternoon, a gruff A.D. told him and another man to "get going" or be fired. Mickey told the 20-something clipboard carrier what he thought of threats and walked off the lot, swearing off extra work for good.

Mickey met a successful NBC script scribe named Mary Williams. She wanted to fix up her girlfriend Yvonne Yrigoyen with Mick but all efforts were ignored. Then fate intervened. When fast horses were needed for a new series, *Pony Express*, Mary suggested that they come from the Gilberts. Mickey also got the job of doing horse work for *Pony Express* lead Grant Sullivan. Some of the Gilberts' ponies were bought and trained under the young cowboy's watchful eye. The show's signature "running mounts" were perfectly worked out by Mickey along soft-sanded stretches of Iverson Ranch. On one occasion, Gilbert was required to sprint several strides alongside a bolting horse.

Gilbert doubled nearly all the Pony Express riders in the first dozen episodes. There were horse chases along spectacular ravines and sprawling valleys, and horses vaulted over fallen trees whenever possible. One exciting shot was of a rider overtaking and passing the mailbag off to the next galloping rider. The good guys intercepted payroll thieves, stagecoach bandits, rustlers and all the other "black hatters" the writers dreamed up.

Costumed as several different characters a shift, Gilbert rapidly earned a Screen Actors Guild card. Enjoying a monopoly on the design and execution of the show's signature move, he was paid every time he did it. Careful to keep his techniques secret, he taught specific ponies the running mounts, saddle vaults and special gags required for the show. After years of rodeo experience, Mickey could launch himself vertically from parallel running horses; flying from one saddle to the next with Velcro-like landings.

These stunts looked simple to producers and they soon refused to pay Gilbert for the horse work, mistakenly thinking any cowboy could do it. One morning he was informed by a snotty assistant director that he had been replaced by another wrangler. Gilbert watched 14 failed attempts the next morning; one man split his pants from crotch to knees. By lunchtime, Mick had been reinstated with full pay.

There was an awkward first meeting between Mick and Yvonne, but then came a barbecue thrown by Mick for *Pony Express*' cast and crew. At one point during a group horse ride, the line of riders waited for a freight train to pass; Yvonne's horse got spooked and bolted. Giving chase instantaneously, Gilbert saw her frightened colt racing toward a low hanging cable on the far end of a bridge trestle—and he was amazed when she leapt to the safe side of the track's rocks. This led to a courtship that became serious over time; they became man and wife two years later.

When *Pony Express* reached the end of its run, the newly married Gilbert rejected his new father-in-law's efforts to bring him into motion picture stunt work and instead returned to rodeo for a living. Fear of folks saying he married Yvonne to get the golden connection of Hollywood through her dad persisted. "Big Joe" didn't take no for an answer. Agreeing to practice equestrian stunt workouts at his ranch under his father-in-law's watchful eye (coupled with brother-in-law Joe, Jr.), Gilbert rapidly mastered the art of horse falls including drags beneath and behind. Combined with his extraordinary athleticism and acrobatic training, Mickey "The Kid" Gilbert was a natural waiting to happen.

A well-respected rancher tending 700 head of cattle amid Bob Hope's prime grazing land overlooking Malibu's Canyon Hills, Yrigoyen was a major force in Hollywood's spurs-and-saddle genre for two decades. If Joe liked your cowboy skills, you could earn a fine living on his projects, motion pictures or ranching.

Despite multiple invitations to "cowboy crew" the plethora of pictures using Big Joe's horses and riders, Mick still refused. (During this time, Mickey and Yvonne's first son Tim was born.) It wasn't until Mickey and Joe, Jr., were asked to perform their saddle falls on the movie *Alvarez Kelly* that Mickey decided to join the family business. He had been primed without realizing it by his father-in law to perform at showcase level, mastering the dangerous art of saddle jerks, shoot-offs, trips, transfers, stirrup drags and more. And it was about to pay dividends. Flown to Baton Rouge, the guys were hired for the show.

18

A Career Begins
Alvarez Kelly *and* Peckinpah

Starting director Edward Dmytryk's *Alvarez Kelly* in June 1965, Mickey played both Confederate and Union soldiers in fierce skirmishes. Stunts included mini-trampoline labor (cannonball explosion victims) and multiple 60-foot falls from trees and cliffs. Gilbert's backward somersaults from rearing horses in the midst of battle got him noticed. Brought in by coordinator "Poppa" Yrigoyen for his first big movie, Mickey was able to show some established stunters, including Hal Needham, Buddy Van Horn and John "Bear" Hudkins, how good he was.

Familiar with Dmytryk's penchant for realism from *Warlock*, Gilbert gave it his all. But not all went smoothly. During one of Mickey's stirrup drags, Gypsy, a trained falling mare (the favorite of Joe Yrigoyen's stable), was hurt. During a large stampede sequence employing 300 head of cattle, Mick was dragged the planned 40 feet through the herd. Then a longhorn veered in front of his horse. Gilbert's body was launched into the bull's hindquarters and Gypsy's right upper femur was instantly snapped as he landed on it. Mick was aware of his luck in escaping serious injury, yet had tearful memories of his father-in law's "favorite faller" for years following.

Mickey doubled Richard Widmark (wearing eyepatch and identical Confederate wardrobe) in many dangerous situations on the action film. Mickey would greet the actor each morning in his most pronounced Southern accent: "Good morning, sirrrr. What bit of deadly debauchery do you hold for me today, colonel?" He always got a laugh, but never really got to know the quiet leading man. But in '69 Widmark certainly remembered "his stuntman" and, on the movie *Death of a Gunfighter*, refused to work without him. "Get Mickey Gilbert or I'm out," the star demanded in the first production meeting.

Alvarez Kelly was shot in Louisiana's sweltering August humidity, with cast and crew harassed by squadrons of hungry mosquitos and venomous snakes. Repeating his old *Pony Express* trick of being in every scene he could (both Union and Confederate casualties), he invented new ways to "die." He showed his skills like never before, even in the smallest bits. Nailing six-foot back somersaults for cannon explosion hits, spinning airborne when shot off moving horses—Gilbert did it all to get on camera. Rather than just fall over when shot, Mickey instead used acrobatic control, imagination and skill to shine in his daily work.

Based upon the September 1864 Confederate "Beefsteak Raid" (led by Major General Wade Hampton III), Dmytryk's movie employed nearly 300 Texas longhorns to cover the real story's 2000 stolen from the Union Army. The deal was brokered by Yrigoyen (who also arranged for the use of 100 horses, and wranglers to ride them). An ambitious attempt on a large scale, *Alvarez Kelly* featured cinematographer Joe McDonald's cutting-edge sequences of the cattle drive through mangrove swamps (located in southern Louisiana's flood plain). Everything from rats and cottonmouths to stubborn steers made shooting difficult. The picture's ending involved an earthen bridge head over a river (with cattle stampeding through defending troops); explosions replicating Howitzer fire during the siege manifested more than the moviemakers expected. Fast-moving wagon teams were filled with stunt players firing rifles, riders blown from their mounts, and stampeding steers doing what they pleased.

"I did a galloping leap off the bridge as it blows up," Mickey said of the film's conclusion. The stunt required an elevated pommel-vault from the saddle of a sprinting horse (at a right tangent over the six-foot rail, then transitioning airborne into a clean dive before hitting the water). Every ten feet of bridge, sharp posts were sticking up, and it was crucial that Gilbert clear them. He got constant speed from the horse and timed his launch perfectly to avert the hazards. "Is there *anything* he can't do?" Needham asked Yrigoyen on the plane ride back to Burbank following the picture's wrap.

Thoroughly impressed with Joe's find, Needham phoned Gilbert a week later to offer him employment on *Beau Geste*. Derived from the classic novel about French Foreign Legion desert exploits, the Douglas Heyes–helmed Universal offering featured enough Hollywood b.s. written in to keep technical expert D.R.O. Hatswell at the hotel bar for the bulk of his off-time.

Many of the movie's 20-plus players covering the stunt work were legends by career's end: Freddy Waugh (who wore orange cowboy boots), Ronnie Rondell, Jr., Chuck Hayward, Bob Herron, Everett Creach and Gary McLarty all labored as Arabs and Legionnaires, sometimes in the same scene. They were costumed in white robes and headdress or heavy wool French uniforms featuring dark tunics with double rows of metallic buttons, so the 125-degree temperatures around the Yuma, Arizona, dunes location made even simple tasks difficult. Doug McClure, Guy Stockwell, Leslie Nielsen and Telly Savalas starred but stuntmen handled 95 percent of the equine load. While actors and stunt players remained thirsty in Buttercup Valley, Gilbert recalled a water truck constantly cooling down the horses during desert shooting.

Performing second story high falls back-first from fort walls, Mick also executed perfect "flop overs" (falling forward to his death below). Long before airbags were invented to soften landings, stunt-tech in '65 was lots of cardboard boxes lashed together on the ground, to minimize landing impact. Considering the 25-foot height required for a full forward somersault in vertical, slow fall, the guys were tough as nails to walk away from the daily grind. Gilbert revealed, "We had a saying: They shoot until it hurts. And *we* [stuntmen] shoot despite it hurting."

There were also wild stirrup drags and horse falls. Mick used the softer sand landings to embellish the stunts. He was shot out of the saddle, sword-slashed, bumped, bombed or tripped; Gilbert's time with his father-in law's falling horses paid off in spades. The conditioned animals did rearing-and-kicking pull-overs (horse and rider toppling in closeup for dramatic effect); Universal's accountants could see that Mickey was in almost every payroll report.

Decked out as Arabian warriors one afternoon (complete with long curved swords, beards, tribal headdresses and flowing robes), Mickey, the Couch brothers (Bill and Chuck) and Freddy Waugh spotted some lost extras circling the dunes about half a mile away. They made a sword-waving charge at the trio with shrieks of cold-blooded murder promised; the extras disappeared in haste over the valley's distant hills. "We were kids in costumes," Gilbert freely admits. "It wasn't a political act, just misbehaving in wardrobe!"

Paramount's 1966 production *Africa: Texas Style* was Gilbert's next slice of fun. Produced by Ivan Tors following his vast commercial successes with *Sea Hunt* and *Flipper*, it leaned more toward roping impalas than brahma bulls. The concept was based on an American cowboy hired to work on an African ranch by an ex-military Britisher capturing wild animals for zoo sales via horseback, instead of the usual Land Rover.

Having hung a sign advertising boarding along his property's fences, Mick was curious the morning a black limousine rolled majestically through the open front entrance of his ranch. Stopping gently by the main barn producing a swirl of dust, the big Lincoln settled without disturbing nearby grazing horses. A dour chauffeur in suit (complete with patent leather brimmed cap) lurched from the driver's side to crisply open the back door. A fifty-ish, well-coiffed woman emerged, followed by a cigar-chomping older man, bush jacket cinched at the waist. They avoided piles of horse dung when approaching Gilbert's roping ring. Mickey watched the couple from the corner of his eye.

They were his neighbors Tori and Ralph Helfer, owners of Africa U.S.A., a spread featuring "exotic game" including lions, tigers, wildebeest, zebras and ostriches. Gilbert was soon listening to the story of two show horses that were not rideable. Would he give them a try? Feeling sorry for the horses' situation, he agreed. He appraised the stallions the next morning in their corral. When he approached, the larger of the two aggressively charged Mickey with snapping teeth and flattened ears. Returning with a leather halter from his nearby roping horse, Gilbert ducked into the pen. Stepping toward the massive blue roan, he gently slapped the animal's snout as it reared menacingly, front hooves clawing the air. "What are you doing with *that* thing?" Ralph demanded in a frightened tone. "Teaching him," Gilbert answered with a swipe against the roan's exposed flank. The stallion turned to deliver a powerful kick, but trotted off to a feeding stall instead. Approaching the horse again, Mickey spoke in a gentle tone as it nervously turned to reverse direction. Intercepting the stallion in mid-step, Gilbert closed the gap between him and the horse, petting him on the neck while instilling trust, then miraculously walking easily next to him. Slowly calming the roan enough to slip the halter on (after gently rubbing its face with it), the champion rodeo rider led the horse from the corral, presenting it to the owner without incident. Following days of concentrated re-training at Mickey's ranch, both stallions were rideable for their owners. The Helfers were shocked when given instructions to enjoy the horses and no bill for services.

In a fateful twist, Mick's payment materialized through Helfer's partnership with Ivan Tors on *Africa: Texas Style,* shooting in Kenya with *real* wild animals including elands, lions, cape buffalo, tigers, zebra and wildebeest, all to be roped from horseback. Gilbert signed to double the lead, Hugh O'Brian, and to stunt-coordinate.

Director Andrew Marton was known for risky, cutting-edge action styles (like those exhibited in his second unit direction of the *Ben-Hur* chariot race and his massive Normandy invasion sequences in *The Longest Day*. He and Tors were a perfect match for East Africa, combining dangerous critters in far-off exotic locals with "the known" entity of American cowboys giving chase on horseback. Their "animal know-how" from past productions like *Clarence the Cross-Eyed Lion* (1965) nurtured a synergy of creative problem-solving mirroring John Wayne's 1962 blockbuster *Hatari!* Lensed from fast-moving Land Rovers, the rugged action flick filled theaters throughout the summer.

18. A Career Begins

Doubling *Africa: Texas Style* star Hugh O'Brian, Gilbert (right) ropes a 600-pound wildebeest while his father-in-law Joe Yrigoyen (left, doubling for Tom Nardini) prepares to toss his lariat at the same target. The California cowboys had to avoid being gored off their horses in the process.

Starring Hugh O'Brian, Nigel Green, John Mills and Tom Nardini, the movie was shot by the U.K.'s Paul Beeson. Gilbert hired his father-in law Joe Yrigoyen to oversee all equine issues. First, Joe was to supply four of his best trained roping horses for the production. Shipped Air France as special cargo (following weeks of acclimation to chimpanzees, lions, tigers, etc., housed at the Africa U.S.A. ranch), Yrigoyen's well-muscled roans were employed for their brave temperament as well as "quarter horse" agility and speed around the fast cats and horned cattle they would be pursuing. The picture proved a "one-way ticket" for the horses. Returning stateside from Kenya with such creatures was nearly impossible due to U.S. quarantine rules and expense.

The action included dodging rhinos, roping lions, bulldogging cape buffalo and riding zebras. Each day's call sheet presented its own difficulty and danger. They were working with natural herds of 2000 buffalo along the Kenya-Uganda border, and the slightest mistake could produce a deadly stampede. Sniffing human scent, hearing a backfiring Jeep, or just seeing an airplane would set them off. Weighing five to six hundred pounds on average with razor-sharp horns, the usually docile grazers turn deadly when startled or confronted. They were capable of goring predators like tigers, lions and hyena, so men on horseback posed little threat to the nearly fearless buffalo. In the jungle, survival depends on group awareness, speed and ferocity when attacked. While filming sequences with O'Brian on horseback (doubled by Gilbert for the dicey stuff), the director nearly caused a tragedy. He was told to remain in place while Mickey and company approached the herd downwind—but he disregarded the instruction and ordered camera vehicles moved. According to Mickey, "We were approaching along a higher plateau when we saw a dust plume rise and the camera car suddenly moving, pushing the herd away." Warnings to stop by radio did no good. Vibrations from the ground felt like an earthquake. "I think they stampeded the buffalo," Joe said, as their horses' ears perked forward and nervous whinnies emanated from their throats. A rolling plume of dust engulfed them. The guys aligned their horses *with* the sea of frenzied cape buffalo and were suddenly enveloped from all directions. The two faced the danger of being trampled should their horses fall. But they survived, and the close call led to better clarity with the director. Marton's attitude improved: He began to *ask* for Gilbert's feedback on everything. Sixteen different species of African wildlife were captured for the series: elands, ostriches, zebras, giraffes, lions, tigers, warthogs and more. Gilbert recalled bulldogging a 600-pound steer to the ground by its horns.

Explaining how to ride a wildebeest, Gilbert said that "staying low as possible" when landing upon the steer was imperative. Avoiding the animal's three-foot-long horns is also important! Gilbert courageously straddled the beast's neck and chest with his thighs. His boots plowed through loose soil (heels first, carried violently forward), but failed to slow the massive hulk. Gaining full control of the critter's head by gripping the razor sharp horns from behind and forcing the neck down (like a full Nelson), Mickey executed what he called a Hulu handle. Exerting incredible strength and split-second timing, Mick flipped the wildebeest onto its back in a snarling heap. Rolling over the dazed animal, then pinning it momentarily against the turf, the cowboy bound rear and front hooves in a single roping motion, leaving the 600-pound steer hogtied until the scene was cut.

One challenge presented by Marton proved trickier than bargained for: Roping a rhino. On foot!

The situation was too unpredictable to risk a horse. Mickey moved with a dancer's precision (football cleats for traction), avoiding his two-ton horned tango partner. Applying rodeo experience gleaned from dodging Brahma bulls, he manifested a combination of quick feet, timing and a boxer's symmetry to jink the charging beast with each pass. Advantaged by lighter body weight, agility and nerve, he coaxed the giant animal ever closer with each grunting, horn-first lunge, using an African method of teasing the rhino (a high-pitched baby voice) to get it to attack. Mickey played "catch me if you can" with the 5000-pound animal, using a tree to hide behind and waving his arms to spur on his massive playmate. Running around the base of a stout Cordia tree like a child circling a Maypole (with the snorting rhino in tow, a foot behind), Gilbert grew more daring each turn as the director screamed for action. Quick to learn that humans are too fast to catch when darting behind trees (and tiring with each attempt), the rhino soon refused to even budge. Once the animal was exhausted enough to tether against the tree, principal Hugh O'Brian could then safely slip between the lens and rhino without danger of being gored. "I smacked him in the face with my rope, trying for one last charge," Mick revealed. "He didn't care about his closeup. The rhino just wanted to be left alone."

Teasing rhinos presented problems, but capturing wild lions and tigers proved a cinch for Gilbert. Relating the intricacies of roping large cats from horseback, Mickey explained the method of such insanity. Having utilized Yrigoyen's most fearless and fleet-hooved quarter horses to "face down" some hungry male lions in Kenya one afternoon, Gilbert revealed that large felines are no different than housecats when it comes to an offered bit of string. "When you toss the lariat, they see *it*, instead of the thrower. And we used trained lions for closeup shots near our horses." Standing off camera, two African sharpshooters with scoped rifles waited, just in case "friendly cats" forgot their place, or wild ones posed a threat. But not a single shot was fired during the series.

Animal trainer Tony Harthorn learned that movie work can have its price, when a large male eland eviscerated his midsection. The animal had black ebony corkscrew shafts three feet long with wicked sharp points. Within scent range of a breeding male, an "in heat" female moved for closeup coverage, triggering the lovestruck bull to charge Tony from behind.

This was the first time such an attack had occurred. Harthorn was put aboard a decrepit bush plane (with no lights) to take off from a short field at night for a hospital in far-off Nairobi. Gilbert's quick thinking saved the day, and Tony's life: He rounded up 20 automobiles to line the runway at the tiny Nanyuki Air Field with headlights guiding the plane. Harthorn pulled through (despite kidney damage and a punctured lung) following a month of recuperation.

Wrapping principal photography in November '66, Joe Yrigoyen and Mickey made a gift of the four roping horses to a local government big shot, Minister of Defense Dr. Njoroge Mungai (the sole Western aficionado in Kenya; he adored Roy Rogers films and bent every rule that production required). Reduced to tears by the gift, he gleefully rode the horses. The 6'6", 300-pound African was costumed in full cowboy regalia specially made in huge sizes: red floral neckerchief, ten-gallon hat, cartridge belt with six-shooters, chaps, boots, spurs and vest that resembled half a pup tent. According to witnesses, the Mungai looked like Deacon Jones in the Lone Ranger's costume. It was too expensive to fly the roans back home, so the gesture became producer Ivan Tors' good will investment in his future of filming in Africa. Which he had plans to do, remembering the success of his past animal series.

Following viewer approval of *Africa: Texas Style,* Tors and right-hand man Harry Redmond, Jr., jumped at the chance to use miles of wildlife footage shot for the previous show. They started a new series called *Cowboy in Africa* and incorporated d.p. Paul Beeson's fantastic stuff from Kenya with Ted Voigtlander's stateside grabs at Helfer Africa U.S.A. Ranch in Acton, California. Gilbert was hired by producer Helfer as action coordinator and Chuck Connors' stunt double on the knock-off. Tom Nardini was covered by Mick's mentor, Joe Yrigoyen. Mickey stood 5'11" and lanky ex-ballplayer Connors 6'4". "Fighting stunt guys smaller than me, made them easier to toss around!" Gilbert laughed, remembering something more vital. "But learning to rope left-handed made it really possible to fool people." Complementing the illusion, Connors mastered *his* right-handed lasso toss, matching Mickey in wider shots. Connors played an American roping champ and Ronald Howard an expatriated British colonel running an African game preserve. The existing footage from Uganda and Kenya was interspersed with new stuff shot stateside, using Helfer's critters: zebras, impalas, wildebeests, cape buffalos, ostriches and giraffes.

Producers persuaded Mickey to double Connors in a daring helicopter-to-truck transfer. Pursuing rhino poachers fleeing on horseback, he descended by rope ladder from a chopper 30 feet above, flying 70 MPH. Next he was supposed to swing into a bad guy and kick him off his horse. Things went considerably awry during filming. He missed the kick owing to the pilot's failure to fly close enough, and Gilbert was left clinging for life. The chopper pilot banked and turned while accelerating, unaware that Mickey was *still* clutching the ladder; and Mickey thought the pilot would realize his predicament and land him safely. Soon G-forces threatened to rip him from the ladder. His facial skin rippled with eyes strained to focus as violent inertia forced blood from his brain; Mick nearly blacked out. The chopper reached 90 MPH in straight-away (including three Gs of accelerated maneuvers with a full-throttle 180 degree turn at the end. But Mick's time as a gymnast saved his life. Transitioning from full arm extension (body hanging below) into a trapeze sitting position on the ladder's bottom rung (legs forward and arms entwined around the vertical lines), he held fast, and jumped clear as the helicopter eased down. He angrily confronted the pilot; the chopper jockey's expression of horror was enough to explain all. Unable to see the hanging stunt player and lacking ground radio communication, he had no idea Mickey *remained* on the ladder. Subsequent takes went more smoothly. Able to descend the ladder and swing into the baddie at the precise moment, Mick kicked him off his horse as planned.

Richard Widmark still refused to do horse work without Gilbert, his hero from *Alvarez Kelly*, and the actor brought him aboard his newest picture, the dark western *Death of a Gunfighter,* shot in early '69. Directed by Don Siegel, *Gunfighter* was a Universal movie shot around Newhall's Golden Oaks and the Janss Conejo Ranch. Arizona's Old Tucson "played" the town. In addition to handling Widmark's equestrian duties, Mickey's prowess with high falls was put to use. Blasted from a tower roof by Widmark, Gilbert fell eight feet onto a slanted overhang, *then* down another dozen feet to the street, without a cut. Gilbert softened his landing by preparing a two-foot-deep trench filled with sand, then covering all traces with a canvas tarp and dirt. Audiences groaned as he landed in a facedown heap, unaware that a safe landing had been achieved via equal impact with toes, knees, elbows, forearms and palms, all used simultaneously. "Done properly," Gilbert says, "the ground-hit is little more than diving into a pool."

19

Cleopatra to *Return of a Man Called Horse*

Mickey Gilbert had his fair share of stunt-loving directors. Names like George Roy Hill, Andrew McLaglen and Arthur Penn aside, one helmer who truly adored action players was Sam Peckinpah. Gilbert was hired by Joe Yrigoyen for Peckinpah's *The Wild Bunch* (1969), lensed by Lucien Ballard and starring William Holden, Ernest Borgnine and Robert Ryan (with world class supporting performances from Ben Johnson, Warren Oates, Strother Martin, Bo Hopkins, L.Q. Jones and Dub Taylor). The Warner Brothers film was was a breakthrough for director and studio alike. Ballard employed long lenses resulting in deep depth-of-field coverage, holding background and foreground images in razor sharp focus. This gave master shots (amid rural backdrops in Durango and La Goma, Mexico) a painter's effect of life passing around one's subjects. Peckinpah and Ballard experimented with varying film rates from 24 to 120 frames per second to decelerate gunplay into a ballet of violence.

The Wild Bunch consisted of 79 shooting days in Mexico, 1200 camera set-ups, 333,000 feet of film, and *everyone* catching dysentery except Holden and Peckinpah owing to booze consumption rather than water. The movie company had a shared vision of its master's call: realism regardless of pain. It was far darker than standard studio westerns by virtue of flawed characters being the picture's "heroes": ex-professional soldiers who evolve after service to rob trains, banks and payrolls. The counterculture switch was not missed by critics.

Thirty hand-picked cowboys were brought to Mexico by Yrigoyen, a veritable Who's Who of the equine craft including Louie Elias, Bob Herron, Whitey Hughes, Tony Epper, Roy Snickner (a writer and quasi-producer of the movie), Gary Combs and the Canutt brothers, Tap and Joe. Mickey was surrounded by industry pros of top standing. The picture's premise (and promise of extraordinary gags) fit his agenda perfectly. He was able to strut his stuff alongside the film world's cowboy-booted best, exhibiting both athletic form and proprietary planning in the execution of his stunt work.

Not all was smooth on location. With a reputation for running his set like Captain Bligh, Peckinpah was notorious for firing crew members on the spot if they failed at their given duties. For the first three weeks of production, Gilbert watched as caterers, grips, prop guys, wardrobe gals, drivers, assistant directors, soundmen and dialogue coaches were dismissed by the hot-tempered helmer for one perceived neglect after another. If a sombrero blew off the head of a Mexican extra during a take, the costume assistant handing out hats would get a ticket home. Dialogue changes not current? Say goodbye to the script supervisor. And so forth. Peckinpah wanted only perfection from his craft-mates, and Mickey wished to serve the "madman" well, so he took a chance and approached with an idea. He said that he was Joe Yrigoyen's son-in law, and a staring bout ensued. Breaking his silence upon seeing a curious glint in Peckinpah's beady eyes, Gilbert outlined his concept for a twist on the already ambitious express office shootout. At one point, a dropped bag of gold coins was to be scooped up by a man leaning down from his saddle in a galloping run; Mickey played his surprise card: "Shoot the horse out from under *me*." And so Mick was blasted backwards from his saddle, transitioning into a stirrup drag, holding the loot as he's pulled along. When Robert Ryan orders, "Shoot that horse!" the animal tumbled by remote control rig (as if actually hit), allowing Gilbert several seconds of drag time right through frame

Instantly hooked on the new idea, Peckinpah asked the young stunt player if he could deliver as promised. Mick assured him he could. The sequence was rapidly scheduled. Warned by Lucien Ballard that those who fail to impress were fired, Gilbert forged ahead.

"The first part went perfect," Mick said. "Louie Elias was shot off his horse, and I sped forward a second later, to scoop up the bag of coins. Blown from my saddle via Peckinpah's cue, I laid back into my drag, towed by one foot with a cable through my boot—connected by quick release around the stirrup." They utilized Yrigoyen's old-school trick of upending a horse by control wires rigged beneath the saddle and connected to the animal's bridle and bit; a jerk on the cable rotates its head to an extreme angle, inducing a

Gilbert is stirrup-dragged by a horse during *The Wild Bunch*'s express office robbery scene. Note the carefully cocked-forward position of his head.

fall. Short lengths of plastic tubing were employed so that the horse would not be cut. Wire guides threaded the mount's far side, trailing 70 feet off set to Joe's hands. Gilbert released himself from the stirrup as the horse was "shot" and felled in the second set-up. Rising with coin bag in hand, Mick is blasted several times with high-powered rifle hits.

With the falling cable removed in post and Joe beyond frame, the edited sequence was breathtaking in seamless physical complexity and action; it garnered whoops of appreciation from crews viewing the dailies. Peckinpah was suddenly enamored with Gilbert and told him so. A few days later on set, the director told Mick it was the best stunt he had *ever* seen.

Instantly becoming the helmer's go-to guy, Gilbert donned wigs, false teeth, eye patches, beards, mustaches and costumes of all types to work in every scene. If the moment required a Federale cut down by machine-gun fire, then off to effects Gilbert went for enough squibs rigged beneath his costume to "kill him six ways from Sunday," as Peckinpah was fond of saying. Cast as a Mexican soldier in Mapache's army for the train bridge explosion, Gilbert was first to try his brother-in law's newest stunt tool, the air ram. Inventing the pressurized-air device to replicate explosion hits and airborne launches, Joe Finnegan introduced the rig on the picture. "It could throw you six to 12 feet," Mickey recalled. "So if you leaned slightly forward, you could *really* fly." Rookie effects man Bud Hubbard used nearly 60 sticks of dynamite to blow the bridge (putting five stuntmen in harm's way at $2000 each). The resulting bang drowned one horse after knocking it cold, and tossed Gilbert twice as high as bargained. "Luckily, the ground was soft by the Nazas River. My 15-foot fall was painless."

Enjoying the costumed play-acting, Gilbert added accents, fake limps and character names, practicing dialogue over lunch to the joy of Peckinpah who would playfully ask his new find, "Who are you today, Lon Chaney?" He was everything from a Mexican soldier shotgunned off a horse by Bo Hopkins, to a wounded deputy plummeting 15 feet from a rooftop to the ground. Mickey had the director and Yrigoyen feeding him assignments several times a day.

Mickey eventually performed so many gags that producer Phil Feldman repeatedly recognized him in dailies; he played a total of 32 parts. But not before witnessing movie history, so far as the gunshot effects were concerned. Immersed in total historical firearm accuracy, Peckinpah ordered separate recordings done for each weapon. He didn't want the one-size-fits-all carbine sound used for the past 30 years. He had the sound folks sample such gear as Colt's M1911 semi-auto pistol, Winchester's M1897 pump and Browning's M1917 heavy machine gun. Their efforts excited paying audiences and led them to expect nothing less in the future.

Having a goodbye drink at the hotel bar, Peckinpah and Gilbert discussed one of the helmer's favorite subjects, rodeo. In the planning stages of *Junior Bonner* (released in '72), Sam offered Mickey the stunt coordinator job on the spot. He liked Mick's wild ideas of shooting cowboys riding bucking bulls—live action, documentary style. More on that later.

First came a turning point in Gilbert's career that would catapult him to the level of Hollywood's top coordinators. The 1969 western *Butch Cassidy and the Sundance Kid* starred Robert Redford and Paul Newman, with direction provided by George Roy Hill. The 20th Century–Fox picture was a sexy, hip sort of "Robin Hood Meets the West," except that two American bank robbers play the charming leads. *Butch Cassidy and the Sundance Kid* became more than just fiction on the screen. It reflected the changing values of the times in which it was made, including ideas of what a hero can be on screen.

Gilbert's participation was not of standard form. He was phoned after midnight by production manager Lloyd Anderson, who asked, "Do you do high work?" (extreme high falls). Mickey verbally signed on to double Robert Redford, agreeing to grab the four a.m. "red-eye" flight from Burbank to Colorado that same morning. He was informed that he was slated for the picture's famous "buddy leap," where Butch (Redford) and Sundance (Newman) are trapped high on a cliff ledge by a posse. With rapids beneath, the duo—fully expecting death—join hands, then plunge 200 feet to the water. When Mickey heard the first part at 11 minutes past one in the morning, all sounded fine. It was the story's second part (playing itself over in Gilbert's brain) that kept him from sleeping during the two-hour flight.

A previous stunt coordinator (and Redford double) had disappeared following five salaried weeks of location hunting in Mexico for a "death-defying" cliff. The poor fellow was ultimately scared into quitting after returning stateside via scouting Colorado's Animas River Gorge with its 200-foot sheer drops. He later wired production he was too busy for the show's schedule, having taken work elsewhere. Mickey's turn came next. This was a huge opportunity, and he knew it. Redford's career was in overdrive. Doubling the actor in a major film could launch *him* (Mickey) into the stratosphere—especially amid Hollywood's re-birth of "western cool."

Arriving at Boulder's La Plata County Airport, Mick was no sooner settled into his motel room than the phone rang: Production manager Lloyd Anderson wanted to take him to see the location as soon as possible. The following morning was set for a go-see. Hanging up the call, Gilbert was excited. He unpacked his essentials for scout work: a Polaroid camera and spare film, binoculars, broken-in cowboy boots and 100 feet of 10mm climbing rope.

Mick, production manager Anderson and director George Roy Hill spent the afternoon getting to know each other. In the pre-dawn black of the next morning, Gilbert felt confident as he shouldered his kick-bag and rope for the walk to the waiting scout vehicle. Hill, Anderson, Mick and a Teamster drove for an hour in silence. They snaked along Durango's mountainous roads at questionable speed.

Arriving at the location, Mick confidently strode to the cliff's edge and peered down. Two hundred feet below, on the surface of the rapids, he saw indications of shallow water and submerged boulders. He sought to show Hill and Anderson their great mistake in location selection. Fearing for his safety, Hill and Anderson balked as Gilbert walked along the edge. He secured his climbing rope to a stump, then tied the other end around Hill's waist. Then the stuntman tossed a grapefruit-sized rock off the cliff as he stood (untethered) by the director. Both watched its descent; it landed in two inches of water over sandy soil. Mick emphasized to all that the jump *was* possible—but not *there*.

Gilbert gave the pair a detailed description of how to get the shot. The river could be deepened via back shovels and floating dredges with specialized crews, or it could be dynamited to deepen it. But all of that would be expensive. Patience running out, Hill blurted out the line Mickey awaited: "How the hell do we do it, then?"

He said, "Go back to L.A." Now an explanation was in order. The only dredging required was that of Paramount's back lot pond to 18 feet, adding rapids and fake rocks to duplicate the spot along the Animas. Employing a 24-foot-wide matte-glass painting of sky and clouds from the actual location (converted by scenic master L.B. Abbott), the "mocked-up" river below formed a seamless blend from top to bottom of frame when viewed through the camera's linear plane. Insuring audience belief that Redford and Newman *could* have done it, a 120-foot construction crane was utilized to mimic the height and length of the vertical fall during the pair's descent. Gilbert and Howard Curtis (a parachute expert and famous cliff diver) leapt from an earthen platform rigged on wooden planks, secured to the top railing of the Condor crane's basket. Reaching 90 MPH after five seconds of free fall, they sliced through the artificial river's surface boots first. They instantly dropped through 18 feet of water to the floor of the pond (full of underwater blower motors duplicating rapids and real boulder formations). Placement of their actual landing became dangerous owing to obstructions in the "white water." Every detail was considered, including the use of a soft suede holstered gunbelts for both to simultaneously grab when leaping (keeping each level throughout the fall). No rehearsal or second takes were possible for the 125-foot drop. Gilbert revealed, "I picked Howard 'cause I knew as a professional skydiver, when we said *go*, he would jump with me … no bullshit. Having a fella hesitate or wait too long in the process is a sure indication that things will go badly, or you'll get separated in the fall and maybe hit one another underwater."

Starting "the big jump" with Durango "plate" footage, the sequence cuts to the actors' jump from a boulder-backed perch behind them, leaping hand in hand into the void. This was accomplished via Redford and Newman jumping from a fully dressed eight-foot platform on a sound stage (with furniture blankets softening the landing below and the aforementioned matte painting incorporated with matching lighting above.) The brilliantly edited sequence then switched to a long overhead shot of Gilbert and Curtis at the Paramount pond.

Gilbert and Curtis took three quick strides to exit the 12-story-high Condor. They descended rapidly from frame toward the water beneath, arms flailing in medium closeup. They looked just like Redford and Newman with makeup and mustache and identical wardrobe; more tricks than met the eye were utilized to pull off the illusion. Torrents of bubbling water were created via high-compression pumps and hidden blowers. A near-exact duplicate of the swift-moving Animas was achieved in Paramount's pond.

A brilliant camera pan followed through Abbott's matte sky, then pulling focus down the cliff as the guys drop; it was a masterpiece of smooth operation. Cutting as the heroes break the water's surface with tremendous force, it was the literal translation of Hill's vision.

They jumped in tandem from a moving platform 12 stories up, the fully extended "basket" swaying in the wind and loaded with a dirt-filled platform, two stuntmen and a camera operator with 300 pounds of gear. The listed weight limit of 500 pounds was exceeded and *then* some. A narrow "sweet spot" had been dredged to give the stunters the 18-foot minimum depth required for water landing. Missing the mark by more than 24 inches in any direction would have meant striking boulders or submerged motors.

Convinced of Gilbert's superhuman capabilities owing to that first stunt gone well, George Roy Hill became a fan of the stuntman's for the picture's remainder. He bowed to the stuntman's knowledge of all things "iffy." Mickey's reward came by way of bit parts whenever Hill could slip him in. Mickey said with a glint of satisfaction, "I told George on the scout that I liked doing stunts that allowed me to deposit the check the following day, without use of a wheelchair, or lawyer in case of terminal deadness."

Gilbert put his personal stamp on every stunt for the rest of filming. He and "the

Mickey Gilbert (doubling Robert Redford) does a leapfrog from his saddle to double-ride on the horse of Jim Arnett (Paul Newman's double) in *Butch Cassidy and the Sundance Kid*. Note the extreme height of Gilbert's launch, his boots above the horse's neck.

boys" routinely expanded bits of action. Blown off a horse? Add a spinning back-fall on the way down. Shot from a rooftop? A forward somersault before landing was the norm. They constantly made the simplest of storyboarded gags better. The posse chase became a study in cleverness. Doubling up on *one* horse as their pursuers close in—Mickey as Redford and Jim, Newman—the duo drive their rider-less horse in the opposite direction, hoping to loose Joe Lefors' white "skimmer" hat, along with Lord Baltimore and the rest of the posse. While seemingly simple, the sequence possessed a difficulty few could grasp just watching.

Requiring Arnett to keep his gelding at a constant speed as Gilbert trotted along parallel; Mick would then vertically blast himself from the mount—landing on "Cassidy's" horse, just behind the saddle. Performed with a dexterity born from years of gymnastics (including jumping exercises with weights for pole-vault), Mickey's three-foot launch from the stirrups was accomplished via abdominal and thigh strength, combined with his horse's forward gait to provide momentum. Landing while the animal's back is arched rather than bowed being critical to avoiding equine injury, the subsequent "sticky landing" was accomplished by precise timing while locking one's thighs upon impact, riding normally throughout the transfer as the horse adjusts for two men. And *not* falling off the churning hind quarter.

One stunt that almost "blew up in everyone's face" was the second train robbery. Filmed along a remote stretch of Silverton's narrow-gauge track in Durango's foothills, the classic mail car stick-up was a "big deal" to the director. He envisioned a billboard with Newman and Redford, a mushrooming fireball and the train car blown to smithereens. The final result was close to his expectations. First there's a comedic attempt by Cassidy to talk Woodcock the mail guard (George Furth) into opening the door rather than have it blown up with him inside. The actual blast was more than anyone could have foreseen. Mickey watched as the effects man liberally planted primacord explosive, gasoline and two-foot mortars and knew that if he stood where the director wanted him to stand, the result would be deadly. He refused to do the stunt as planned, despite the effects fellow's guarantee that everything would work out well. Gilbert told Hill that injuries could include blown eardrums and concussions, plus burns should the gasoline ignite too rapidly.

He finally talked the helmer into letting him stand 20 feet from the blast. Cheating perspective by camera angle and lens choice, d.p. Conrad Hall's five operators (Jordan Cronenweth, Earl Clark, Thomas Del Ruth, Dave Friedman, Ed Hutton) still required plexiglass or plywood fortification as a safety precaution. When cameras rolled, Gilbert and Arnett were propelled violently through space as the hot airless vacuum of deafening explosion impacted their bodies. Boards from the mail car flew six stories skyward as the shock wave expanded, lifting the two men six feet off the ground and a dozen yards backwards. Their eyebrows, necks and ears were singed. Both were close enough to the blast

In *Butch Cassidy and the Sundance Kid*, stunt players Mickey Gilbert (left) and Jim Arnett react to a big bang as an explosive effect turns out to be more powerful than anyone figured.

that their headaches and tinnitus lasted for days. "Had we been on the original marks," Gilbert said, "Jim and I would have been blown to bits."

A supposed "expert bike rider" was brought in for the montage sequence of Butch doing trick headstands to impress Etta Place (Katharine Ross). Gilbert, watching him rehearse, knew his director had been duped. "Bill" stalled for six weeks while on salary and supposedly practicing (although *no one* had seen him touch the bike). He was revealed to be a fraud following several failed attempts at headstands at Mickey's request.

Newman became interested in the bike gag after he was playfully pelted with apples at the orchard location by Gilbert and Arnett. The actor got off the bike and returned fire. Mickey dashed past the hail of fruit and scooped up the bike, intending to ride away. Reversing the normal seated position, he straddled the seat backwards and rapidly pedaled the bike in the opposite direction. Taunting Redford and Newman in a childish voice with each subsequent pass, he rode "no hands," arms folded over his face. The actors were amazed by the stuntman's skill. Newman sold the alternative gag to Hill and Mickey doubled him for the backwards ride.

Mickey signed on for another 20th Century–Fox "horse picture," director Andrew McLaglen's *The Undefeated*. The Hal Needham–coordinated stuntfest starred John Wayne and Rock Hudson, with supporting roles filled by Jan-Michael Vincent, Ben Johnson, Merlin Olsen and Roman Gabriel. It was the story of a Confederate colonel (Hudson)

During *Butch Cassidy and the Sundance Kid*'s Bolivia bank robbery montage, Robert Redford spins after dispatching a heavy (Gilbert), seen falling in the background of the shot.

leading his bedraggled boys through Mexico in search of a better life while Yankee counterpart John Wayne seeks to sell horses to the unpopular government; the two disparate groups must team to defeat revolutionaries and bandits while defending their own lives. Gilbert was hired to ramrod a stampede sequence utilizing 300 head of longhorn steers and horses. Owing to Mickey's professional rodeo chops, he was singled out to wear 16mm helmet cams for coverage of everything from stirrup drags to ground level footage of cowboys roping longhorns from horseback while standing amid the massive wave of hoofed animals. This footage was blown up to 35mm and the action edited into the rest of the picture, giving a realistic, frenetic pace to the coverage.

Gilbert continued on the film via high falls (shot off roofs as both Mexican soldier and revolutionary). He also showed his proficiency with exploding horse tumbles, stirrup-drags through a mangrove swamp, and air ram–launched explosions duplicating cannon hits. "The rams would be buried in shallow pits, then covered with burlap and loose dirt. Then, as effects guys trigger the pyrotechnic charges, we time *our* launch to coincide with the explosion. You can get six to ten feet vertically, but care must be used on landing to avoid busting an ankle."

Sam Peckinpah made good on his promise to hire Mickey for his next picture. *The Ballad of Cable Hogue* was shot in late 1969 at the Eaves movie ranch in Santa Fe, New Mexico. Mickey doubled Jason Robards, who led a small cast including greats Slim Pickens, L.Q. Jones, Stella Stevens and Strother Martin. The stunter was called upon to do a comedic variation on the Pony Express mount: hitting the dirt instead of saddle leather. Taught the nuances of the gag by master John Brady (son of Big Buffalo Brady, a famous rodeo trouper), Mickey paid homage to his teacher with an over-the-top version that got real laughs in theaters. He vaulted over the horse 11 times before Peckinpah was happy; by then, Gilbert was slightly more than sore.

Hal Needham soon summoned Mickey to join him on *Little Big Man*. An ideal vehicle for Gilbert's horse talents (stirrup drags, falls, etc.), the Arthur Penn picture was a graphic look at the 1870s military's debauchery as applied to the Native population of Montana's Little Big Horn area. It was an up-close look at the historic battle: Lakota Sioux, Northern Cheyenne and Arapaho tribes vs. the U.S. Army (culminating with General George Custer's 7th Cavalry over-commitment at a Crow Indian encampment, known as the Battle for Little Big Horn). A few of the indigenous extras working the show were descendants of the actual natives involved. Returning to the set after an all-night party, a group of Native American extras were killed in a car wreck involving alcohol.

Hardly for the faint of heart, *Little Big Man* was a masterpiece of western action and history put on film, albeit slightly painful to all parties concerned. Its multitude of stunt gags included gun battles, horse falls, knife fights, mounted saber attacks, stirrup drags and "shoot-offs" from front, rear, side and back by arrow, bullet and lance. There were many opportunities for the stunt players to show their stuff. And show they did. Gilbert did front somersaults as horses were shot from beneath him. The day's work left marks.

Mickey and the rest of Needham's crew delivered an artistry of western violence seldom witnessed on film: back-flips off running horses, gunfights and knife brawls, etc. A continuous adrenal pulse kept the picture physically believable. Yet the sensitive Calder Willingham script allowed for the tale's humanity.

The stagecoach hijacking was a work of art. Attacked by a band of renegade braves while leading a stagecoach containing all his worldly goods—including his new wife Holga (Kelly Jean Peters)—the hero jumped from horse to horse in a deadly game of

Gilbert, dressed in buckskin as an Indian brave, stands nearly straight up in the saddle as he prepares to club a Union cavalry officer fighting on foot in *Little Big Man*. The stuntman selected one of the tallest horses for this scene. The disparity between standing equine and actor is impressive.

follow the leader, after the Indians dispatching the teamster driver and coach's occupants. Performing the dangerous sequence, Gibbs doubled Hoffman for master shots of the sprinting six-horse team. However, the comparatively safer closeups were done with Hoffman already in place on each horse's back; quick-cuts of the leapfrog move were accomplished by good editing (amid shots of the diminutive double from behind), rather than risking the actor's hide.

Employed time and again, the trope of teams of horses pulling loved ones has served as the hero's vehicle of gallant rescue since matinee audiences first tasted popcorn. The "horse over horse move" calls for finesse, requiring a pommel-horse forward vault to launch onself over the rear haunches of the galloping animal before you (then "sticking" the landing by way of clinching thighs as your butt hits the hide); bouncing off or falling could prove fatal by way of crushing wheels or trampling. Hidden planks were placed between the rows of horses (rigged to the harness gear as foot holds); Hoffman and Gibbs alike benefited from their presence.

One bit in the picture tougher than it looked was Little Big Man's passage through the 7th Cavalry's snow bound attack, where he and "Old Lodge Skins" (Chief Dan George) witness the village's massacre to the tune of the "Gary Owen" battle hymn. Wading into the frozen waters of Calgary's CL Ranch in Alberta shooting the "invisible escape from the soldiers" sequence, Hoffman and the elderly Chief were nearly incapacitated by the river's early spring temperatures. But stuntman Freddy Waugh fared worse. Landing skull-first from a horse fall onto the frozen Canadian tundra proved too much, even for a man known to wear orange cowboy boots. Knocked unconscious, he needed several slaps across the face from Gilbert before he came around.

Trading cowboy costumes for ape suits in early 1970, Mickey answered a 4 a.m. call from second unit director Chuck Roberson to work on 20th Century–Fox's *Beneath the Planet of the Apes*. The picture was a comparatively low-budget attempt to replicate *Planet of the Apes*' box office magic, without benefit of a brilliant Rod Serling script holding it together. Even the ape prosthetics of makeup genius Dan Striepeke were less believable than those in the original. However, stunt-wise, the picture was first-rate. Action it *did* have—especially horses.

Humans were scooped up in nets, shackled, imprisoned in crude wagon jails, and generally beaten down at every turn. Gilbert played both pursuing ape and loincloth-wearing, fleeing victim. Both were brutal beneath the unforgiving sun of Red Rock Canyon State Park. One particular gag took some flesh from Mickey's legs each time he did it: getting caught in nets stretched between one ape on horseback and another. Gilbert was forced to do multiple takes by cinematographer Milton Krasner's need for coverage. According to Gilbert, "The net would clip you at the ankles. The idea was to lift your feet slightly as you ran, so you could fall back into the webbing, without getting fouled up as the rig swept forward. Once you were in the net, the danger of striking the ground with your head were pretty real, so you had to keep your chin up." The possibility of being rubbed raw on one's bum was real. Without substantial costumes, the stuntfolk felt every pebble when dragged.

By 1970, Mickey Gilbert was a well-known pro who could double anyone, fall a horse, leap from a cliff, and do things in automobiles that made insurance men weak. He was seldom out of work. At the invitation of pal Jim Arnett, Gilbert got a few weeks work on Paul Newman's pet project, a logging picture titled *Sometimes a Great Notion*. The Universal film was shot on rugged locations in the Columbia River gorge; Newman wanted the dangerous realism of the craft saga brought to the screen, going so far as learning to wield massive chainsaws like a pro. He practiced his newfound skills in old friend George Roy Hill's office while the helmer was out; the actor dissected the director's favorite antique desk in one clean swipe. He left the building as if nothing had occurred—but he later had a replacement delivered.

Taking chances with more than chainsaws, Newman wanted Mickey to help him pull off a gag so dangerous that Fox's insurance company balked. To get a shot of a runaway log rolling down a steep hill and nearly decapitating Hank Stamper (Newman), Gilbert devised a bounce pit rig that sent an 80-foot-long, four-foot-diameter tree right over his head.

There was no way to test the log rig before filming. The breathtaking results were testimony to the skills of both stuntmen and second unit d.p. Rexford Metz. In another scene, Newman and Richard Jaeckel (playing his brother) get rid of a "union man" by tossing sticks of dynamite at his boat. The effects folk wired underwater charges to detonate on cue for large explosions and big geysers of water. They were marked by two-foot-round pieces of cork, a visual alert to each charge's location. Gilbert was in a boat when he gave the signal to blow the charge, unaware that the boat was directly over the charge. The skiff was lifted five feet out of the water and Gilbert launched ten feet through the air and into the drink. There was a 24-inch hole in the boat's floor. Gilbert was dazed, but surfaced immediately, continuing the scene in character and swimming away. Suddenly ad libbing, he flipped off his enemies while dogpaddling slowly out of frame. Newman liked it so much, it was used as is.

In the fall of '71, even before his *Sometimes a Great Notion* checks cleared, Mickey was signed for another Newman vehicle, *Pocket Money*. Gilbert doubled Newman, who played Jim Kane, an aged cowboy duped into doing a crooked rancher's bidding. Handling the equestrian duties including some spectacular quarter horse roping sequences, Gilbert was the darling of the set. Between d.p. Laszlo Kovacs' camera set-ups, the stunter entertained director Stuart Rosenberg with comedic rope tricks like lassoing passing wardrobe girls or lariat-dancing with extras.

Mickey did not want to choose sides in the personality clash between stars Newman and Lee Marvin (the story has it that Lee was drinking heavily during the picture, and Newman resented the unprofessional behavior). Marvin conned a prop man into loaning him a large pistol. Demanding to be allowed to fire it despite warnings that 11 a.m. was too early to shoot a .357 Magnum, Lee took target practice off the hotel's second floor balcony. He emptied the gun into trash cans 30 feet away, the sixth round echoing for several seconds. Crew members' doors opened as they peered through half open eyes. Production kept a lid on it without police reports.

Pocket Money fared poorly at theaters. While critics were not privy to the real issues interfering with the picture, they did smell a rat when it came to the two stars' chemistry. "None whatsoever" was the *Philadelphia Enquirer* film reviewer's opinion.

In November '71, Mickey spoke to stunt coordinator Buddy Van Horn about some horse chases that director John Sturges wanted for the non-conventional western *Joe Kidd*. It starred Clint Eastwood and featured good character bits from Robert Duvall, Don Stroud, Paul Koslo and Chuck Hayward. Lensed by Bruce Surtees, the action flick had a scrubbed look fairly uncommon to films of the genre.

Joe Kidd was filmed amid Lone Pine's Alabama Hills, Inyo National Forrest and Old Tucson. The locations ranged from brutal cold to desert heat. Gilbert with his talent for spectacular horse spills and envelope-pushing equestrian chases stayed busy as part of the "heavy" gang (along with Chuck Hayward), until killed off when blasted from horseback. (He did a crisp reverse somersault in midair before landing in a dead heap.) Mick's style was thick icing on the stunt cake.

True to his word, Peckinpah hired Gilbert for his ode to rodeo, *Junior Bonner,* in January '72. Gilbert was drafted to stunt-coordinate and double Steve McQueen in the picture's many bull-riding and rodeo sequences, while Loren Janes handled quarter-horse work and all other McQueen stuff. Gilbert was the real deal, from his "hooey" (finishing knot to tie a calf's legs) to his bronc-riding form.

Driving all night from Los Angeles to arrive at the company's Prescott motel by noon the following day, Mick was met with curious looks when telling the front desk he was there to see the director. The blanching clerk coughed and spat out a response akin to gibberish, her only clear sentence being, "Is he expecting you?" She waved him past, a horrified look on her face. He strolled through the lobby and out a double set of glass doors. Passing a pair of dusty SUVs with Los Angeles tags, Gilbert noticed a gaggle of men in suits ten feet from the director's door. Wearing rumpled suits, they stood in a cloud of cigar smoke backlit by the white Arizona morning sun. The balding studio types were hotly debating with each other. They turned in unison as Mickey strode past them toward the door.

"Where ya going there, Cowboy?" someone asked. Informed of Gilbert's appointment with Peckinpah, producer Joe Wizan warned him to avoid the room, mumbling something about girls and waiting since 10 a.m. as he nervously mopped his brow with a handkerchief. When Mickey knocked on the door, an angry growl was heard: "*Who is it?*"

Mickey announced himself: "The Kid."

There was a barely audible "Sorry. Hang on a second." A metallic thud signaled the door's opening, Gilbert looked up to see Peckinpah standing naked, a nude girl on each arm. He was back-slapped into the room as the director waved towards the sweating Hollywood boys outside, inviting them to "cool their heels" a while longer. This was following by 16 rambling minutes of the director talking about his vision for the picture (Gilbert averted his eyes the whole time).

Peckinpah's love letter to a vanishing west, the picture was a dirt- and sweat-rimmed look at a violent way of life, and what "sport" folks could find in it. It featured McQueen as Junior Bonner, Robert Preston as his father "Ace" and Ida Lupino as his mom. Supporting roles were played by Joe Don Baker, Ben Johnson and Dub Taylor.

A myriad of Casey Tibbs rodeo sequences covered everything from bronc riding to which "rough stock" to use. One big gag took more than a livestock coordinator to pull off: the Palace Bar fight scene. It required 20 stunt players; Gilbert sought to import Hollywood brawlers to Arizona, but was instantly denied on the basis of cost. Agreeing with Peckinpah to hire and train amateurs in the Prescott area, Gilbert headed out to find talent. He scoured local spots like the Santa Fe train station, courthouse and Whiskey Row. While strolling between booze joints, he hit the mother lode. Standing 6'8" and weighing 300 pounds, Sioux Indian James Shreeve was rolling down the pre-dawn road driving a tractor when Gilbert spotted him: "He was so huge, he dwarfed the John Deere!" Approached with an invitation to earn cash beating up cowboys, the giant responded with a smile: "Who do I have to kill?" Gilbert paraded each new find by Peckinpah as he held court at the motel bar. One look at Shreeve sent the helmer into a little jig.

Mickey trained the locals at the YMCA. He ran his 20-some novices through the carefully choreographed fight scene, but he saw "camera nerves" on the first take: rushed, disjointed movement, rendering the footage unusable. Realizing that time was short, Gilbert informed the d.p. and director that he was going to roll cameras without cueing the players. He told them to continue "rehearsing" at half speed (winking at Peckinpah to roll film as he did); the resulting calm produced terrific action. No longer burdened with fear of the camera, the rookies beat the crap out of one another for two days, staining the famous bar's fancy redwood floors with their sweat and blood. Perfect cuts by editors Frank Santillo and Robert Wolfe made it all work. *Junior Bonner* made a dismal box office showing; it wasn't the "Steve McQueen" folks wanted to see.

Still Hollywood's go-to coordinator for equine action, Mickey lent his faculty with horses to 20th Century–Fox's *When Legends Die,* starring pal Richard Widmark. He was tasked with teaching supporting actor Frederick Forrest roping skills and advanced horse work. Skipping off to Almería, Spain, after New Year's 1973, Gilbert reunited with John Sturges for *Chino,* starring Charles Bronson. He was contracted to purchase horses for the company (requiring nearly 200); Mickey found the herd, and also a crooked unit production manager. Cowboy contractor for the large stables being built to house the horses before delivery, Mickey was constantly at odds with the UPM—and getting thrown under the bus for refusing to play along. Questioning Gilbert's competence when meeting in Rome, producer Dino De Laurentiis was swayed after the stuntman addressed him formally, assuring Mr. Dino that he had nothing to fear with a good friend like Sturges referring him.

Securing the 200-head herd for the movie required three weeks' assistance from

Tony Tarruella, a Spanish assistant director who knew every rancher in Almería), and Augustino Medina (a gypsy wrangler). "Trainable" animals were needed for a crucial breaking sequence culminating in Bronson being bitten. Different horses were brought into play for various sections of the gag.

Traveling through Almería's fabled, Texas-like horse country, Gilbert was fortunate to find two identical three-year-olds that suited his needs to perfection. Acquired from two separate ranchers, the unbroken horses were given "cold shoulder" treatment pre-training; Mickey wanted the "wild" left in the animals, keeping the transformation as realistic as possible. The horse is cut from the herd via Bronson's rope work (actually Gilbert's), then transported to the ranch proceeding introduction to the corral in the wild state. Chino produces a seemingly tame horse, but then the filly attacks him from behind, biting him on the shoulder. Getting it all on film for d.p. Armando Nannuzzi was no small trick. Gilbert continued to segregate the two horses from human contact as much as possible (feeding being the exception); he wanted their raw essence preserved for the corral work with reared-up kicking and pawing action. At the same time, Gilbert was overseeing a second trainer employed to prep the shoulder-bite shot.

Wrangler Rudy Ugland staged a wardrobe-clad "double dummy" on a movable base with a vertical shaft holding it erect. It bore a likeness to Bronson. Two other black horse-doubles were trained for rear-ups and forelock strikes. With two cameras rolling nonstop, Nannuzzi and Giuseppe Bernardini obtained their images like wildlife photographers; no dolly movement or focal zoom. Thousands of feet of film were required. A beautiful dance of mutual adoration and submission between animal and man, the sequences were some of the film's finest.

Gilbert, doubling Bronson, began approaching a true unbroken horse in the corral. Moving ten soft steps toward the wild filly, lariat in hand, he tossed a neck shot; his arm was too quick for the horse to avoid the rope. He pulled the sliding lasso taut against the three-year-old's neck with his left hand, then took several paces to a snubbing post on his right. Three quick wraps around it secured his line, and the horse, in one fluid motion. The horse circled the post as it fought its restriction; this forced it closer to Gilbert as he reduced the distance between them with quick, sideward steps, hands moving along the lariat. Soon exhausted, the filly resorted to nervous reflex via urinating and pawing the ground. Mick calmed it with soothing words and gave it several minutes before proceeding. Rudy Ugland led in one of the tamer "double horses," helping Gilbert swap it out for the actual wild one, still tied to the snubbing post.

With cameras rolling, Rudy queued the horse's head left then right with stomping feet signals, standing just out of frame. "Reaching in" and snapping the bridle halter over the horse's head, Mick (doubling Bronson) tied him to the post. Cameras cut during resultant pulling and kicking; Mickey slipped off his lasso, then covered the animal's eyes with a dark bandanna, using the halter rigging to hold all fast while he verbally calmed the horse. A quick transition to saddling coverage was achieved, bringing the horse closer to tame with each cut. Once the actor could sit atop the horse safely, multiple takes were done before switching *back* to the second unbroken filly, saddled and blindfolded like the first. Wranglers muscled it into its predecessor's position, whereupon Mickey (again doubling Bronson) continued to break the horse, step by step, on camera. Matching wardrobe, mustache and hat made Mickey a convincing Chino to the camera's eye.

20

All in a Day's Work

Returning stateside in spring of '73, Gilbert hit the ground running to re-establish himself with stunt work outside of the equestrian world. James Starrett's action vehicle *Cleopatra Jones* was as far from cowboy boots as one could imagine. Tamara Dobson played the title role and Shelley Winters the heavy. The Warner Brothers picture also featured Brenda Sykes, Esther Rolle and Bernie Casey. Newcomer Antonio Vargas' "Doodlebug" character is *not* to be missed.

The tale of a heroin manufacturer and her notorious dope gang taken down by a special agent, the flick had as many violent stunt gags crammed into it as the producers could afford. Taking the call from coordinator Paul Knuckles, Mickey performed a high fall complete with machine-gun blasts, squibs and airbag landing. He was contracted along with friend Howard Curtis at half-rate for the 35-foot fall over the upper balcony railing; subsequent squib placement from chest to knees left the guys bruised and scorched by wrap. Plummeting head down, the duo relied on gymnastic chops and aerobatic dexterity to assume a diving position for the fall. At the last moment they transitioned to forward backflip for a safe airbag landing. Gilbert recalled, "It's a short swan dive with a tuck-flip onto your back as you hit. Only you're also setting off squibs as you fall."

It was done "down and dirty," without rehearsal or hesitation. Subsequent takes were flawless, and the high fall experts were sent on their way at sequence's completion. Jumping studios but staying on the same side of town, Mickey picked up another exploitation picture by way of the mob, Universal's *The Don Is Dead*, later that same month. Helmed by action pro Richard Fleischer (*The Boston Strangler, Tora! Tora! Tora!*) and shot by Richard Kline, the "mob-sploitation" flick starred Anthony Quinn as an aging Mafia chief betrayed by his own. Gangster regulars Al Lettieri, Abe Vigoda, Barry Russo and Joe Santos rounded out the vendetta crew, bent on serving their don's wish for justice after the beating of his mistress.

Mickey was contracted to do a special fall connected to a garrote while being yanked down a flight of stairs. The gag was complicated by the backwards orientation of his feet. Lacking the ability to "bridge" his arches to reduce injury (reducing the strain of the rope by raising his body), he instead had to rely upon balancing on his toes, each backward step he hit while being choked. The bruising on Mick's throat lasted longer than memory of its infliction.

Having grown bored with machine-gunning and garroting, Mickey did a quick featured horse fall in Michael Crichton's *Westworld* in the summer of 1973. Coordinator Dick Ziker drafted him to be blasted off a galloping horse as a robot cowboy fleeing the town sheriff. It was an "in and out" job, says Mick. "It took longer to get through wardrobe and breakfast than to nail the gag itself."

Mickey worked again for old friend George Roy Hill, but this time there were no 200-foot cliffs to jump or rivers to dredge. Only a hop onto a moving street sweeper and simple staircase hurdle. The picture was *The Sting*. As Robert Redford continued to request Gilbert's talent as a double, his "stunt stock" continued to grow. Hiring producers assumed they had to pay top dollar for such talent. And pay they did, as Gilbert earned more than a quarter million dollars in '73 alone. In *The Sting*'s boarding house sequence, Johnny Hooker (Redford) jumps over an elevated bannister and down a stairwell one flight. Performing the ten-foot plunge six times, Gilbert barely warmed his hamstrings upon landing. Ensuing assignments were equally simple. He played an angry pursuer who hitches a ride on a passing street sweeper. A hidden handle was added to the truck, for Gilbert to grab, and he barely broke a sweat for his efforts. "*The Sting* was really George's way of saying 'Thanks for *Butch Cassidy and the Sundance Kid*,'" Mickey recalled. "He coulda had *anyone* do the gags I did, Redford wanting me or not."

Coordinator Steven Burnett drafted Gilbert for six weeks doing all things equestrian on Lucille Ball's soft-focus comeback *Mame*, which began filming in January '73. Tasked with staging the fox hunt sequence, the stuntman hired trainer Al Yanks (the fellow responsible for Lee Marvin's drunken horse in *Cat Ballou*) and real-deal horse whisperer Glenn Randall, Jr., to draft "dressage folks" in Los Angeles. They rounded up 50-plus members of various dressage, show and event jumpers to make up the bawdy fox hunter's ensemble. A comedic slapstick approach to the gags was director Gene Saks' thing.

Coordinating the jumping was Gilbert's thing, and he took the reins on second unit work with Michael Moore. Hardly capable in the saddle, Lucille Ball was doubled by Stephanie Epper. Donning a red "Lucy" wig and padded frock coat, Mick committed himself to the cheat shots. Performing several leaps over wooden gates, stone walls, hedges and water, the stuntman did his best to mimic an inexperienced, frightened rider. Slipping saddle left and then right, losing foot placement from stirrups and dropping reins while grasping mane, Mickey did it all to appear comically out of control. This footage was intercut with Phil Lathrop's "rocking horse" coverage of Ball on a soundstage with pastoral background projected behind. The entertaining sequence was the picture's most ambitious.

January of '74 saw Warner Bros launch the biggest western spoof in cinema history, Mel Brooks' *Blazing Saddles*. Outpacing *Towering Inferno*'s $100,000,000 box office, *Saddles*' $120 mil payday gave Brooks the last laugh—all the way to the bank. Al Wyatt Sr.'s collection of pros (more than 80 cowboys, trick riders and stuntmen) was impressive.

Doubling Gene Wilder for riding gags, Mick took pains to imitate the actor's every physical nuance, in and out of the saddle. Horse work was not Wilder's favorite thing, so Gilbert handled anything more than a slow trot. Executing his saddle falls, jumps and drags for the outlaw sequences or "in town" pranks, Gilbert recalled that keeping a straight face was more difficult than the gags. "Mel Brooks was always on," he remembered. "Between Cleavon Little, Harvey Korman and Slim Pickens ad libs, you had to bite the inside of your cheek to keep from busting up and ruining the takes." Mick proudly spoke of horse-fall mechanic Dave Sharpe executing a picture-perfect stirrup drag, decked out in a '70s business suit. In the picture's "big fight" climax, Gilbert demonstrated his gymnastic acumen, reacting to punches with back-flips and sailing over the bar. He was only on *Blazing Saddles* for a few days, but considers it one of his favorites. Having bonded with Wilder, he would be called upon twice more to double the comedic star, in *The Frisco Kid* and *Silver Streak*.

20. All in a Day's Work

Beginning in March 1974, Phil Kaufman's Eskimo epic *The White Dawn* was filmed during Nunavut, Canada's, spring thaw around Baffin Island. The story, set in the late 19th century, focused on three stranded whalers saved by an Eskimo tribe. Unexpected events lead to violence, and there's death on the ice floes. Warren Oates led a first-rate cast including Timothy Bottoms and Lou Gossett, Jr. The Atlantic Ocean in March was still frozen solid 30 feet down. By helicopter they located a stable section of real estate large enough to make base camp. They shot footage of the ice-breaker boat's foray into the Arctic. Glacial ice walls collapsing into the sea sent huge plumes of frigid sea water 60 feet skyward.

Perhaps the picture's most compelling action was its coverage of the whaler's long boat harpooning a whale. It was adeptly shot by cinematographer Michael Chapman. Mickey and the effects crew made it all happen without loss of human life—but at times, it was close.

The sequence begins with footage of a harpooned whale dashing beneath the ice to dislodge the shaft. In cut-aways, we see the longboat pulled across the ice like a kid's toy. It was rigged by effects man Henry Millar, Jr., and construction coordinator Bill Maldonado with ropes and pulleys leading to a flip-ramp; when it capsized, its occupants fell into the sea. There was a camera below the ice; camera operator Ken Post could barely position it before his arms would go totally numb from the cold water. As Oates' double, Gilbert had much the same problem, concerned that frigid water would overcome him while he was immersed in the heavy costume (fur coat, britches, hat and gloves).

Positioning himself at floe's edge near a four-foot-deep slush stream, Gilbert inserted his wetsuit-clad arm up to the shoulder in the soup. By the count of ten, his elbow and wrist joints began to throb and burn as though on fire. Within 12 seconds it was unbearable and he yanked his arm from the drink. Mickey decided a safety cable was a must, so that he could be fished out if knocked unconscious. With a line attached around his waist beneath the heavy fur jacket, Mick bravely performed the stunt. The rig worked as designed, submersing the stuntman for 14 seconds, nine of which were cut into the picture. He came to by two propane heaters in an 8 × 8 Army tent, surrounded by Eskimo women who were stripping away his wet clothes. Each layer removed fell like a hundred pounds thumping soaked to the floor. The ladies had Gilbert down to skivvies before they stopped. After he thawed, he wanted no more water work on the picture.

Mickey and a hundred other stuntmen were drafted by coordinator John Daheim for Universal's *Earthquake*, made in direct competition with *The Towering Inferno* which shot at the same time. He was challenged with 60-foot-high falls into airbags (replicating folks plummeting out of tall buildings), and dodging three-ton blocks of concrete released from construction cranes. The $500 "bump" for each fall, combined with extreme hazard pay, made Mick and the boys lots of dough.

Working the film's dam-breaking sequence, Mickey was at Universal's dump tanks, preparing to be hit by walls of water and swept away. Topping 5,000 gallons each, the three tanks provided a "flood" ten feet high and 30 yards across. The flood was created to sweep into town, washing away everything including 20 guys on foot. Familiarizing himself with the area he was to be swept into, Gilbert saw the possibility of being struck by moving debris. Deciding that floating *with* the powerful surge of water was prudent for survival, Mick mapped a route through the water's path that would be safest to follow. Stunter Bennie Dobbins thought he had a better idea. Attached to a wooden street sign via hidden steel cable beneath his wardrobe, he clung to the post when the wave hit, arms and legs flailing.

As the water subsided, Mickey surveyed the wreckage for signs of Dobbins. Dobbins was 15 yards from the street sign, lying prostrate and unconscious in a puddle, entangled by fence slats and wire. Rolling his friend over, Gilbert saw a bleeding gash over one eye. Responding to revival techniques (face-slapping and smelling salts), the groggy stunt player was taken to the emergency room by Mickey (Dobbins just wanted to "go home and rest up"). Shards of park bench were surgically removed from his forehead, 11 stitches applied and a broken cheekbone set. "And you fellas do *this* for a living, every day?" the doctor asked.

"Not on weekends, Doc," Mick responded, "We have to draw the line somewhere."

It was Dobbins' bad luck to miss out on the remainder of the *Earthquake* pickings. Then Mickey (and 100 other stuntmen) took work on *The Towering Inferno*. Directed by John Guillermin, ably shot by Fred Koenekamp, and produced by disaster master Irwin Allen, the 20th Century–Fox picture was stunt-coordinated by Paul Stader. It boasted a bevy of stars, both A-list and slightly past their prime. Steve McQueen, William Holden, Paul Newman, Robert Wagner, Faye Dunaway and Fred Astaire did their best to make the film watchable; the stunt crew made it believable. The movie showcased world-class high-fallers, burn specialists, window gag artists and "firemen"—the names were the best in the business. From Steven Burnett to Howard Curtis, Loren Janes to Dar Robinson, there was a level of talent second to none. And Mickey was every bit their equal. A back-stairs mock-up was constructed for the water and fire effects. The studio hydrant pressure was so great that Mick was blown off his feet when first hit with water. *Towering Inferno* was a one-dimensional disaster platform, without much story. Nevertheless, the stunt crew earned more than ever.

Constantly moving up Cinema City's stunt chain, Gilbert was again paired with George Roy Hill to double Robert Redford in *The Great Waldo Pepper*. The director who tested him on *Butch Cassidy* had another challenge. A 15-foot balcony fall, without pads. Beautifully photographed by Robert Surtees, Frank Tallman's aerials were equally extraordinary. Tiger Moth biplanes were employed for the barnstorming, flying circus and other flight sequences. The picture utilized professional wing-walkers for the real airborne stuff, resorting to studio inserts with static planes on gimbals for the actor close-ups. Redford played Waldo, Bo Swenson his arch-rival Axel Olsson.

Mickey jumped at the chance for a good sock on the jaw and fall. Surveying the set height while planning to land back-first on the card tables below, he figured that cardboard boxes were adequate to break the fall. He planned to hide them beneath the table (pre-sawing the legs halfway to assist the snap); his idea was squashed when Hill informed him the entire set was "in frame." While he was strategizing the trajectory and impact of his fall, the helmer hollered "*Ready*" before Gilbert could object. "Action" began with Bo Svenson delivering a round-house to Mick's jaw, whereupon he hurled himself over the balcony. He plummeted 15 feet back-first, then hitting a real oak table. He landed in a heap. The stunt was perfectly executed yet damaging to the point of momentary paralysis. As the pain subsided, Mick remained still for a bit, until able to slowly rise and walk outside the stage. The walls of the studio reverberated with Mick's vocal vetting, screaming *ouch* while crouching by the elephant doors. Outside, Redford approached with concern. He cautiously checking Gilbert's neck, back and pupils for damage. He found none, and a gentle hug ensued.

Moments later, both returned inside arm in arm, to crew applause. Bowing from the waist in mock appreciation, Mickey was confronted by the director, who had a foul look on his face. He called the stunt "wild," but added that the table sitter's response was non-existent (he was dumbfounded by the athleticism of the gag), and Hill asked for another take. Knowing his first effort to be a true exercise in gymnastic skill to make the midair turn after the punch just right, Mickey's brain raced to figure a second, survivable take. Another table was quickly prepped. Mickey did the gag again, landing flat on his back. This smash-through was even more dynamic (and painful) than the first. Hill was the first to thank Gilbert for his sacrifice. He left the picture once he caught his breath and could walk again. A cash bonus was in hand as he departed and promised himself to never perform such a non-padded fall again.

Mickey flew off to join Terry Leonard in Spain for *The Wind and the Lion*. Directed by John Milius in early '75, this story of a Berber's kidnapping of a wealthy American woman in 1904 Morocco was A-list from start to finish. Featuring Sean Connery, John Huston, Geoffrey Lewis, Candice Bergen and Brian Keith, the MGM offering was entertaining by sheer force of talent, and contained larger-than-life battle sequences. Leonard and a couple of Tinseltown toughies (augmented with a company of Spanish National Guardsmen costumed in period) employed every horse and sand gag they could muster. Mickey procured falling and drag horses from his last film in Almería (*Chino*). He was shocked to learn Leonard's secret for riding through plate glass on horses. Requiring a rider to take a horse through a large garden window (doubling Connery in robes and headdress), Leonard preferred to "blind" the horse via attached ping pong balls painted like eyes. Spurred through the real glass, the animal would suffer any consequences. The horse stumbled on landing, nearly throwing the coordinator, but the gag played okay. Gilbert and Larry Randall worked the movie as two stunt professionals, conscious of the safety of all, vs. "doing what you gotta do" (the Leonard type).

The picture featured a Preakness of horse falls with dramatic explosions in its final battle sequences between American and German forces. Real dynamite was used for some gags. Between complex mounted sword fights, dozens shot off horses, and explosions hurling stunt player and volunteer Spanish Marines through the air, the picture was close to "David Lean scope." It strove for turn-of-the-century accuracy of action. The story was based on Barbara Tuchman's essays that appeared in *American Heritage* magazine in August 1959 (titled "Perdicaris Alive or Raisuli Dead"); the "kidnapped" American was actually a Tangiers expatriate.

While howitzers and Maxim machine-guns lit up the action, it was a small troupe of American horse stunters who made the battle personal. Gilbert enlisted previously trained bays and roans used on *Chino* for the picture's rough stuff. For forced tripping of horses, a rig known as a Toe-Tapper works like this: A series of aircraft cables are attached to the inside-rear of the horses' two forelegs (snugly taped in place), from leg-joint to hooves, terminating beneath the Frog. A washer locks all in place—through small holes drilled in the keratin edge of the hoof. The exterior of the hoof is comprised of dense, dead tissue, like human fingernails, and the rig is painless to install. Inter-connected to a single center retractor under the horse's stomach (run through the saddle with its wire terminating into a hidden handle the rider pulls to activate the fall), the ensuing mechanics drew the animals' legs under, with frontal trippage rapid and safe. Enabling stunt players to add flourishes from near explosions, like front rolls, somersaults and back flips from the falling horses, Mickey and the guys went from soldiers to Berbers and back, often in the same sequence.

Pulling off the picture's frenetic battle scenes via multiple costume changes, makeups and horse switches, the Hollywood group of eight (augmented by Spanish special forces) looked more like 80, after editor Robert Wolfe cut the sequences. One set-up where Gilbert's warnings to his rambunctious boss went unheeded was during the large, mounted charge incorporating scores of mounted Berbers, utilizing dozens of buried "cork bomb" mortars laid two feet beneath the sand. Dramatic images of riders thrown skyward were unparalleled for their time. Launching Mick ten feet or more with each explosion, Terry Leonard thought to best his pal by way of a flagbearer trick—that went totally wrong. With Toe-Tappers at every turn, Leonard's "heroic" soldier rides forward during the battle, flagpole tucked gallantly in his boot, allowing one hand on the reins, the other to trigger the falling rig. Simulating being blown off the galloping steed (planning a back flip in the process), the coordinator beckoned to Gilbert to watch a pro do his thing.

There was danger in having a flagpole down one's boot while working a Toe-Tapper. Mickey warned Leonard of his mistake and suggested cutting down the shaft to avoid possible impalement, as he and the rest of the flagbearers had done. Refusing, Terry did the sequence as he planned. The horse cartwheeled owing to a misstep, and the long pole struck Leonard and broke his collarbone. He was now unable to double Sean Connery for the picture's duration; Mickey gladly filled in, doubling his day rate for his trouble.

Still on horseback, Mick had a speaking part in John Wayne's *Rooster Cogburn* in late '74. Shot amid the studio's sprawling Six Points of Texas sets, the "done before" saga paired pro Katharine Hepburn (can you say John Huston's *African Queen*?) with the Duke subbing for Bogart, complete with the impassable rapids scene "borrowed" from the previously mentioned Huston picture. Even the preacher's angle was played; Hepburn's Eula Goodnight was the daughter of a murdered clergyman. "Bumped-up" by old friend Michael Moore, the assistant director helming the action sequences, Gilbert was given a speaking role in addition to the normal bang-bang stuff. Playing Hambone, a heavy, he not only had time to learn his four lines, but to play tricks on "fellow thespians" as well. During pre-production, he met co-star Richard Jordan, a New York stage actor cast as outlaw leader Hawk, at Western Costume. Mick was less than taken with the fellow's "trained actor" ego. Knowing that Jordan had no experience on westerns, Gilbert encouraged the newbie to select an all-black wardrobe with felt hat, heavy vest, chaps and fancy matching guns, knowing that they would be shooting in the torrid summer temperatures of Rogue River, Oregon. He conned Jordan into every weight-adding accessory in sight.

The first week of filming amid Grant's Pass heat, the method actor refused to wear his guns to rehearsal. Between the large silver Conchos on batwing chaps and the solid black shirt, just moving was an effort in that getup, once outside. While mounting a horse without assistance proved difficult, one piece of costume after another became the butt of inside jokes around the set. Those "in the know" laughed each time he wobbled from his mount, perspiration running down his face, black britches tugging at his lanky frame as he attempted to walk. Swearing about sodden underwear beneath his leaden chaps, high-heeled boots (suggested by Gilbert to make him taller) and headaches from the black hat, Jordan understandably *never* did another western. *Rooster Cogburn* was the nation's 25th top grossing picture of '75, but its lack of originality doomed it with critics, and put an end to plans for more films in the series.

When not laughing hysterically, Mickey earned his keep on the production with a stand-alone saddle-shoot off and stirrup drag that was picture perfect. Hambone was dispatched by Marshal Cogburn's lever action Winchester: He was hit multiple times with squibs blowing, before executing the 100-foot stream drag.

Mickey returned to Charles Bronson's camp in March 1975 for *Breakheart Pass*, hired by Terry Leonard to be the heavy in a mounted swordfight scene between them. It was shot in Lewiston, Idaho, around the Camas Prairie railroad circuit. The picture was rife with action for the seven players hired by coordinator Yakima Canutt. Lensed by studio pro Lucien Ballard (with special train sequences by d.p. Robert McBride), the United Artists production netted Mick a cool $2500 a day for two weeks' shooting. He played Indians and cavalrymen within the same sequences with gags from horse falls (requiring galloping rear flip-offs when shot with bullet or arrows), blasted from behind or launched from the saddle via tossed spear.

Mickey and Terry had left Los Angeles with little more than toothbrushes for the one-day sword work promised. But upon their arrival on the set, Canutt immediately began discussing complex horse falls. They half-heartedly objected to the added work, and were both assured they were on the show for its duration. The duo were suddenly the biggest moochers on the picture, borrowing everything from back supports to knee pads. Enjoying each day, the duo counted "fly-ups" and "kick-backs" in $1000 increments, laughing as they hit the ground at their good fortune.

Mickey was drafted to play a cavalry officer shot by renegades during a firefight through a train's caboose. He was expected to spin upon impact and *fall* between moving train cars. The plan nearly cost the pro his life. Spying a lower stairwell, Mickey offered to roll down the steps in order to spice up the somewhat generic stunt. Warned the action occurred on a trestle over a 500-foot gorge, Mick assured all that it was well within his capabilities. The gag was to be shot with no additional preparation (like a safety handle rigged to the edge). Gilbert heard Canutt shout *action*, then violently turned with the squib's explosion. Falling faster and farther than anticipated, Mickey found himself clinging for life to the train's undercarriage, one arm supporting the entire weight of his body. Applying a gymnast's leverage and strength, he rotated his trunk atop the bottom stair, saving himself. Clutching the tread at 40 MPH inches above the elevated trestle, and realizing that he had nearly" bought the farm," he chastised himself for failing to use backup. Admiring looks from the director and crew (believing it all part of the show) failed to cheer him. "I learned a lesson that day: Beware of overconfidence." The stuntman refuses to watch the footage, stating, "I have no desire seeing *myself* almost killed … the nightmares were close enough."

On the heels of *Breakheart Pass*' near-disaster came Mickey's most prized work: *The Return of a Man Called Horse*. Hooked by producer Sandy Howard with a script messengered to his house, Gilbert was tapped as coordinator. It was all horse and buffalo gags. Meeting with director Irvin Kershner about the hunting sequences, Mick sold the room with descriptions of real buffalo chased amid mounted hunters shooting rifles, arrows and throwing spears. All should be covered in sharp focus from the hunters' p.o.v., without over-editing or cheap effects. Equestrian action expert Michael Moore was hired to direct second unit. The movie benefitted from talent like Richard Harris starring as British expatriate John Morgan and d.p. Owen Roizman capturing the vital energy of the Sioux. And Gilbert's extraordinary mechanical buffalo rigs and genius for externalizing carnal wounds on camera made "the hunt" a neo-classic.

Gilbert knew that buffalo required control harnesses like any other "falling" animal, and designed and built his own. His oversized Running W's consisted of one-inch leather straps and hardware, camouflaged with buffalo hide. All terminated in a wire and ring bracket, attached from foreleg to knee, instantly "hobbling" the bull when pulled by remote cable. It ran the length of the buffalo's belly (tight against the body and ending just behind the front legs). A cable rig trailed behind the animal. Mickey (on horseback, near-naked in Sioux costume) would activate the trip wire, tripping the animal without obvious contact.

For arrow and spear hits, Mick welded a two-inch-diameter threaded pipe, 90 degrees to a curved steel plate the same size. They were fur-covered and secured to the bison. Spear shafts and arrows were mated to receiving brackets. Once "screwed" to the animal and protruding, the look was perfect, with blood added. The old rodeo hand devised a funnel line by which bison would appear in frame one after another. Intercut with shots of the entire herd in stampede, the illusion was compelling. The entire sequence rumbled through theaters for six minutes with thundering animals filling the frame as bison were felled, one after the other, without a single animal actually hurt.

Gilbert was also asked to get the herd to stampede on cue without losing control, and once again his knowledge and imagination made the impossible, possible. He conditioned the buffalo to break into a controlled trot (rather than all-out panic), and also set up a catch-pen at one end of the meadow familiar to them. He "ran them" from horseback, then fed and rested them, before finally returning them home at coaching's end; the pampered animals became used to the course of action. Within weeks, the "herd" was somewhat controllable.

Mickey knew enough to gently separate calves and their mothers from the 1500-bison herd, penning them in plain view of their fathers. He picked ten trainable bulls from the group for closeup spear and arrow rigs. Then he fitted those ten with the previously mentioned flying W harnesses and wound brackets. Becoming totally used to the routine, the bulls performed without objection. Gilbert and Gary McLarty integrated themselves on horses as a new part of the workout.

Cowboys firing pistols started the herd stampeding. After 100 bison had filled the frame, Mickey signaled to open the holding pens; the rigged buffalos rushed out and joined the herd. Arrows and spears protruding from the pre-fall animals, Gilbert and Leonard (mounted on horseback) trailed close behind the bison with W's and tripped them in the middle of the actual stampede. Dozens of takes were required.

The bison were then driven through a narrowing canyon to compress the herd; the rest was accomplished via a cattle sluice provided at Gilbert's request. Funneling 1500 head through a 20-foot gateway, the result was a fire hose effect of buffalo. With snorting nostrils and wild eyes, they churned the dry ground until ten-foot dirt devils rose into the air. Rigged bison were kept in the foreground, the untrained behind; the spear and arrow receivers were carefully hidden in closeup shots. As Terry Leonard doubled Harris on horseback, Mickey would time it so that when Leonard fired, he (Mickey) would simultaneously yank the trip line and bring down a bison. Harris was sometimes in the frame, Sharps .50 caliber rifle in hand, bagging one bull after another. Yet he was no closer to the herd than fate, insurance or producer Sandy Howard would allow.

Mickey also wanted to capture the most difficult of gags: a thrown spear's full trajectory and impact on its target. It seemed a shot that would be impossible to get without tossing an actual spear into a real animal, but he used sleight of hand to make it work. He chose Bob Orrison, a stunt player often cast as renegades owing to bareback riding skills. First, we see a brave (Orrison) on horseback in pursuit of a massive bull. He throws a spear; a rapid cut picks up the buffalo running with a shaft *already* imbedded via hidden mount. Interspersed shots of Orrison heaving the spear were transitioned by Gilbert tripping the wounded bull as the weapon impacts. Using camera pan with the Sioux's arm in motion, follow through of the spear in flight captured the buffalo collapsing to the turf, the shaft protruding from its flank as it fell dead. Though the spear was thrown just shy of the animal, choice framing of Orrison and clever cutting made audiences believe its impact nonetheless.

Adding a touch of realism to the film's depiction of tribal violence, Gilbert suggested having Yellow Hand women defending their camps by use of bolas. Two billiard ball–size stones were tethered together via a 12-inch cord and thrown in such a way as to encircle a victim's legs. They were historically implemented to capture deer, rabbits and coyote; in Mick's vision, they hobbled enemy horses. But they had to be thrown by a strong and practiced arm; missing a horse's forelegs and striking its thigh or torso would likely injure. So Gilbert himself did the work. He wore a squaw's buckskins and was made up with wig, rouge, eyelashes and breasts, as no local extras were good with the rig. (And he survived tasteless gibes from cast and director alike.) It was another example of Gilbert's dedication to the art form. And if "art" is in the details, then he was painting masterpieces.

A dozen years later, *Dances with Wolves*' producers wanted Mickey to coordinate their buffalo hunt sequence. He deferred and suggested the use of animatronics instead. The new technology spared Kevin Costner the attention of the Humane Society, which would *not* have allowed Gilbert's previous methods to be implemented in 1990.

Mickey Gilbert switched from saddles to horsepower in '75 on the high-octane Warner Bros. comedy *Gumball Rally*. A "pop" movie based on a car race from New York City to Los Angeles, it was helmed by action director Chuck Bail (who started as a stuntman on *Bonanza* and *Gunsmoke*) and featured Michael Sarrazin and Gary Busey. It was written amid America's gas shortage and people's desire to drive fast despite it. Mickey and a company of 40 handled everything from Ferraris to motorcycles, blowing every speed trap imaginable with law enforcement around every bend.

Hired by stunt coordinator Eddie Donno for a 70 MPH car-to-car transfer, Gilbert got carried away. He tried 100 MPH takes, leaping from one Corvette convertible to another, driving in parallel lanes. Aiming for the panel behind the seats, he was sucked over instead, the victim of buffeting and wind shear between cars. He could have smashed into the convertible's rear panel (and off the trunk at 95 MPH); only Gilbert's focus and hand strength kept him from dire injury.

"Car-to-car transfers require a continuous move," he explained. Owing to centrifugal force, inertia and forward momentum, he equated the move as "energy flow" from the first object *transferring* to the second, with an invisible geometric bubble holding all in gravitational pull.

Filled with Jaguars, Porsches, Ferraris, Rolls-Royces, hopped-up Dodges, an A.C. Cobra and a muscle car Camaro, the picture ran out of ideas long before money during production. It was reduced to an everlasting succession of high speed "overtakes," steer-arounds and underpass antics. But *Gumball* made money and spawned sequels.

21

Sydney Pollack, Redford and Belushi

Blazing Saddles had paired Mickey with a longtime personal favorite, Gene Wilder. Mickey was invited in March '76 to work on Wilder's next picture, the comedic action flick *Silver Streak*. He would not only double Gene, but serve as stunt coordinator as well. The story of a mystery writer who sees a murder on a cross-country train ride, then becomes the target of the killers, the film was a perfect canvas for rail-borne antics. From old cowboy roof-walking sequences to near-misses between trains, the picture was believable from the stunt end. But a simple misstep early in shooting nearly cost Gilbert his life.

The photography was first-rate, with coverage from multiple helicopters, fast picture cars and train mounts engineered by key grip Dicky Moran.

Setting-up a treacherous uncoupling scene with Wilder (Gilbert) inches from the track, having slipped between cars, Richard Pryor's double, Alan Oliney, was to clutch him back to safety from the brink of death. Noticing nothing solid to grab in an emergency, Mick had a hidden bar welded to the train's staircase—a last minute thought which probably saved him. Running the first take at full speed, Gilbert was bent over in position to "fall" (with Oliney holding him to his mark), when things went badly. When he struck a four-foot-high metal signal sign at 50 MPH with his butt, the impact ripped him from his partner's grasp instantly. Legs flying as as he was pulled away from the train, only by his hold on the safety bar was he able to keep from tumbling down the track. Thrown back onto the iron coupling knees first, once again Mickey's gymnastic faculty surfaced as he reversed grip on the pipe and held on. Body smashing into the rear of the train car (out of frame and not visible to crew), it seemed he had fallen. Hanging from the bar straddling the coupling (toes inches above the track), he rode out the take while waiting for the emergency signal to stop the engine.

Composure regained by the time Max Kleven ran up to the train, he greeted the second unit director calm and collected, standing on the coupling lock, arms tucked nonchalantly behind his head. Grips frozen by the track as the engine lurched to a final stop were slack-jawed having thought Mick bought the farm; yet there he stood ready for another take. "Alan thought I had fallen beneath the train," Mickey said. "When he saw me leaning there like I was waiting for a bus, his look of horror turned to Christmas morning, and I was the gift under his tree."

Taking Wilder's lumps, Gilbert was thrown from the Silver Streak three times in the picture. He described the preparation necessary for the job: At 35 MPH, his first train fall was similar to leaping from a moving car. He scoured the route for big rocks and trash while laying down a 20-foot sand landing strip along the track; three days of subsequent takes were painless for all.

In *Silver Streak*'s exciting conclusion, the train smashes through Union Station. Gilbert was afraid that extras might be crushed and wanted cardboard cutouts instead of people; then he opted for 30 highly tutored stunt players. They performed a ballet of movement *around* the carnage without so much as a scratch. The train gag was an audience favorite.

A wrap party thrown at the hotel became the setting for adolescent pranks. Mickey tossed a clothed "stunt dummy" from his eighth floor Vancouver room that night, then made a hasty getaway before investigating police officers could get to the bottom of the "Hollywood Jumper." (The rumor at the front desk was that a producer had leapt to avoid excessive bar bills.) The Mounties drove away with the souvenir.

Mickey did more train work on Hal Ashby's *Bound for Glory* in April '76. A biopic of Woody Guthrie, the David Carradine vehicle was a rough-and-tumble look at Depression era life along the tracks. Stunt coordinated by Buddy Joe Hooker and lensed by Haskell Wexler (he earned a Best Cinematography Oscar), the picture was shot in Stockton and Altamont, California, as well as parts of Pittsburg and Iseltion, Oregon. Gilbert recalled being part of the picture's opening sequence, among 900 extras (and 30 actors) following Woody (Carradine) as he walks through camp. "[The Depression] was before my time," Mick said. "But between the ragged extras (me included), and staging of the hobo camp … it felt real." Gilbert was employed in the big fight, and also tasked with rail-riding beneath actual train cars. He was required to do several high-speed passes with cameras mounted around him; he was "riding" the train car's superstructure at 60 MPH, just inches from the tracks. He wrapped a pad around the metal bars, and credited the strap and his narrow butt for saving his skin.

Gilbert reunited with Gene Wilder in early '77 for the actor's second directorial outing, *The World's Greatest Lover,* a spoof of Tinseltown's silent era. In the movie-within-the-movie, Gilbert did the sheik's horse work. The picture co-starred Carol Kane as a Zasu Pitts type, Dom DeLuise as the studio head, Danny DeVito as an all-knowing A.D. and James Hong as a yes-man.

Gilbert mimicked the Valentino prototype with galloping chase sequences, horse-to-horse transfers and falls. His biggest challenge was training a stunt gal for Carol Kane's work. She would have to leap from a moving train onto the sheik's horse and land face to face with him for a kiss. Timing that stunt would be difficult for a pro, much less a rookie who happened to be production executive Frank Baur's youngest daughter Chris. Mickey gave her the gymnastic conditioning needed to effect a midair torso turn and pull off the gag. Experienced in riding motorcycle and horses, she shined in the sequence, and went on to a successful stunt career.

Working with Hal Needham for his next paycheck, Gilbert landed on the Warners lot for Burt Reynolds' *Hooper*. Greenlit after Needham's $100,000,000 success with *Smokey and the Bandit, Hooper* was in the works before *Smokey* was out of theaters. The picture incorporated every stunt vehicle known to man, plus record-breaking high falls, fistfights and more. The 70-plus stunt crew were really the stars of the film. Performing a perilous 232-foot plummet doubling Reynolds, airbag expert A.J. Bakunas set an industry high mark for non-parachute falls. Gilbert says that when doing a 20-story drop, the airbag looks as small as a postage stamp from above: "Wind shear and forward inertia can carry you off, and landing dead center is imperative. Every foot off mark decreases the bladder's ability to absorb the impact." Landing poorly can result in serious bodily damage.

Mickey, playing a motorcycle cop, did a stunt while chasing Hooper's speeding car. He wore a waist belt beneath his wardrobe with one end of a steel aircraft wire attached, the other end attached to something stationary. He gunned the bike, traveling 20 feet at 35 MPH before being yanked rearward off the seat.

After working on *Who'll Stop the Rain* in the jungles of Mexico, Gilbert was tapped by coordinator Buddy Van Horn to return to Warner Bros. and Clint Eastwood for *Every Which Way But Loose*. He did biker gang stunts (along with Gene LeBell, Gary Davis, Orin Harvey, Chuck Waters and Jerry Wills). The James Fargo–helmed farce was barely a few days' work for him, but still a challenge. "Coming into a family like Clint's Malpaso for a few days was fun but difficult. With Eastwood in nearly every set-up, we *all* had to be on our A game." He returned to his Santa Barbara ranch, where the phone rang as he walked through the front door. It was coordinator Al Wyatt, Sr.: Laboring on the low-budget Quinn Martin pilot *Colorado C.I.*, he offered Gilbert lots of vehicle work, fights, skiing gags and the lure of doing a high speed car chase in a Jaguar along the Continental Divide.

Mick landed at Denver International Airport amid morning snow flurries and arrived at Grand Junction's ski area location by noon to acclimate himself to altitude. Checking the Jaguar XJ6 intended for the high-speed driving sequences, he was steering the refined sports sedan around white packed ribbons of curvy road like a skier. The rear wheel drive Jag performed with an athletic prowess that gave Mickey an idea.

Skiing the next morning, he saw dynamic but empty trails. His mind envisioned the swift Jaguar transitioning from paved road to snow. His desire was to add a "James Bond" level of excitement to what was essentially a movie-of-the-week–level production. He hooked Wyatt with the idea, then sold it to the producers by way of a sightseeing tour.

Gilbert had the effects crew enclose the Jaguar's underbelly. This smooth bottom would slide over frozen drifts. They also fitted the vehicle with studded tires. Now the Jaguar was snow-worthy as he put it through its paces. A hidden ramp made Gilbert's street-to-trail transition as dramatic as possible; forward momentum and suspension bounce lifted it ten feet into the air on launch. Trajectory flat as the Jaguar soared 30 yards down the hillside, it impacted the snowdrifts with the force of a two-ton bobsled. It disappeared from view beneath hills of white powder (tunneling through 20-foot banks), but Mick's foot-to-the-floor acceleration got it to surface like a breaching whale. The sedan drifted and slid across 100 yards of glistening snow to finish the shot. Decades ahead of the *Fast and Furious* films showcasing "drifting" and the Jaguar commercials with vehicles dynamically traversing snow fields, Gilbert's stunt pointed the way.

Continuing with automotive gigs, Mick was hired by director Joseph Ruben for his film *Our Winning Season*. He read the "coming of age" drama (revolving around high school jocks during their senior year amid fast cars, girls, drugs and first loves) and found that the pages called for little action.

Enter the genius of Mickey Gilbert. To enliven a chicken race between Dennis Quaid and a rival, Mickey turned for inspiration to the car jousts of his youth. Knowing the point of excitement to be the last-second swerve, and subsequent victory owing to one's guts vs. desire to avoid impact (brains), he sought to visually bring that split-second of terror to the screen.

Beginning with high-speed passes of two cars facing one another at 400 yards (closing at 80 MPH), a two-lane blacktop was created with a drive-in movie theater set built off to one side. Two head-on runs were filmed with cars barely missing one another (then a third with increasing speed and last second turn of the wheel before impact); the first vehicle ran into high weeds while the second was launched airborne, crashing into the front entrance of the drive-in, straight through the movie screen. Persuading Ruben to construct the set at Atlanta's Raceway Track with breakaway wall sections and soaring plate-glass windows, Gilbert included a marquee sign, ticket booth, concession stands, and lot full of cars to mirror the real thing. Filled with details down to kiddy swings, men's rooms, trash cans, and plush landscaping, the mock-up required two weeks to build. A hidden ramp 75 feet from the drive-in entrance below road surface with an 8-degree upward pitch, "blob-launched" cars at 80 MPH, 25 feet into the air. To do it, elements of controlled flight had to be incorporated. Like a jet catapulted from an aircraft carrier, "straight line of ascent" was imperative to success. Ensuring the cars' straight approach with the ramp, Mickey straddled a bold white line leading 100 feet to the jump. Driving dead center, his "practice" runs put the vehicle exactly in place for optimal launch. Building a "ditch-turn" to abort the jump BEFORE hitting the ramp (should anything go wrong), Mick used traffic signals to cue the sequences throughout. Rigging green, yellow, and amber lights along the route, there was no mistaking stop from go.

Calling in longtime pal Freddie Waugh to act as right-seat ballast (doubling Scott Jacoby), Mick played Dennis Quaid's Paul Morelli behind the wheel. "I told Freddie *nothing* about the ride, when hiring him on the phone," Gilbert laughed. "Just that it would be wild." The theater facade was constructed with a breakaway section of sheetrock wall 12 feet square (rather than 2" × 6" studs and plywood) as the target point for the car to break through.

When the night shot began, cinematographer Stephen M. Katz deployed eight cameras: five "inside" the structure, three out. Shooting high speed (to slow action down), four operators including George Bouillet waited patiently for the sequence to begin. Watching the Mustang 300 yards away, the guys flicked their cameras on as blinked headlights became a green go, and the vehicle took off, tires spinning.

With the guys having buckled their stunt harnesses down tight and given the crew their flashing headlamp ready cue, the red signal before them flicked yellow, then green. Sharing a perfunctory "Geronimo scream," Gilbert got down to business. Ramming the accelerator pedal down to the floor, Mickey's 400 horsepower Mustang reared forward with a screaming lurch of tires and tremendous acceleration—reaching 60 MPH in under five seconds. As they closed on the "last ditch" junction rapidly, a blanket of cloud suddenly enveloped the raceway. Nearly Biblical, it cut visibility to nil for Gilbert. Hitting the brakes the instant the track's signals turned red (camera had killed the shot), Gilbert and Waugh pulled over to catch their breath, just 70 feet shy of the go ramp.

Starting 15 minutes later after weather cleared, the duo was again poised at the starting point, waiting for the go cue. Wasting no time when the second light clicked from yellow to green, Mickey took off, barreling towards the takeoff point. Two hundred yards from the ramp, the Mustang cleared 65 MPH as the occupants readied themselves for the jump. Shoulders back, neck straight, breathing controlled, arms clutching the wheel slightly flexed, Mick was increasing speed when the lights went out—instantly followed by the walkie talkie blurting "Cut! Cut! Cut!" Veering into the ditch lane at the last moment, he brought the car under control by instinct and camp lighting, still burning by small generators. Stopping along the track's grassy edge in near blackness, Mickey began to think the gag trickier than envisioned. Breaking for dinner while electricians fixed the power issues, Gilbert was approached by director Joe Ruben. Spooked by the delays both mechanical and spiritual—he had suffered a car gag gone wrong while shooting *Joyride* the previous year—he wanted to cancel the jump. Convincing him otherwise, Gilbert and Waugh strapped into the Mustang once again, as the juicers got the lights going—to cheers of crew and drivers alike.

Lights turning red, yellow, green, Mick floored the Ford for all it was worth. Tires smoking on launch, the rear end waggled and gripped as traction bars dug the wheels into the track. Tachometer racing past 4000 RPM, the vehicle reached 70 MPH in a blink. Straddling the all-important white line dead center of the car's hood, the ramp entrance loomed closer as the duo roared past the point of no return. Flying 80 MPH past the ditch turn, the final 200 yards to the jump happened in a split second. Meeting the ramp with surgical accuracy, the Mustang took flight like it was blasted from a Howitzer. Clearing the ticket booth while continuing on an upward trajectory, the Ford blasted through the neon marque without losing altitude. Propelled forward despite the one-foot drop for each two traveled through space, the vehicle struck the theater wall 28 feet up, spanning 200 feet in the process. Striking the breakaway section mid-mark, the Mustang blew out the drywall like paper as it crashed through. Sailing over rows of drive-in parked cars, the Ford continued with flat trajectory, eviscerating the movie screen like a cartoon busting the third plane and flying sixty feet past the screen to land on all four wheels with a violent thud. The sequence's success was owed to Gilbert's driving acumen, as well as counter-weighting the car's rear end to offset the forward weight imbalance. Hobbled on impact, the Mustang's four wheels were splayed out like a child's toy. "If it was a real horse we would have shot it!" Gilbert joked.

Considering Samuel Arkoff's American International Pictures paid the way, the bust through the theater gag was the movie's most memorable moment, and worth every well-spent cent.

Producer Walter Mirisch's Australian-made *The Prisoner of Zenda* (1979) had great locations and texture. Mickey was tasked with a series of "period" stunts including a swordfight atop an open coach, drawbridge leap and high fall from a castle turret into a moving wagon. Re-establishing connections made on *The Wind and the Lion*, he contacted wranglers and shopped for horses. He needed one capable of jumping from a drawbridge while it was being raised. After testing five horses in a pasture with six-foot cliff jumps (riding each to the edge to see if it would get spooked), Mick picked two that jumped fearlessly. A week of leaping six-foot obstacles prepped the large geldings until full jumps were made without hesitation. Ready to perform the drawbridge gag the first night of filming, Mickey informed cinematographer Arthur Ibbetson that rehearsal was not an option. Mick cantered his steed in tight circles behind the heavy door waiting his cue. "Action!" was called and the spirited horse bolted forward. With Gilbert in the saddle, the animal leapt in a rising arc off the ascending platform's edge and landed perfectly. Mick: "The secret to making it work was conditioning the horse." He added that he and the horse had practiced for a week with heavy planks bolted together (doubling the drawbridge door). "Approaching the obstacle at the same speed, then galloping off the fixed platform, the horse gains confidence in the move. By shoot day, the six-foot jump was no big deal, despite the drawbridge effect."

Mick also lent good old Hollywood horse sense to an Englishman's idea of an open coach swordfight, when British stunt player Joe Dunne wanted to spice up his otherwise lackluster demise. The original plan was for Gilbert (doubling Peter Sellers) to run through Dunne, who would then fall from the coach. Dunne wanted to flip off onto the horses' flanks, tumbling dramatically to the ground. The victim's fall was worked ass first, avoiding trampling, while still giving "more."

While hardly testing Gilbert's horse talents, the picture did allow for a tricky high fall that *could* have meant curtains. He was slated to drop 40 feet off a castle turret into a moving donkey cart; the smallest distraction of Teamster or beast might make him miss the mark. Six feet wide by 12 long, the wagon was padded dead center to absorb impact, but its sides and back presented dangerous targets if accidentally struck. If the wagon was not moved precisely on cue, or at the right speed, a falling person could miss altogether. Mickey cast a Spanish stuntman named Timoteas (a veteran of *The Wind and the Lion*) as cart wrangler to ensure his own safety.

Mickey plummeted the distance with hands clawing and feet kicking before landing back first in the wagon with a dropped boulder's impact. The wagon's reinforced wheels and axles kept it from imploding.

22

Stunt Heaven and Helicopters

Roger Creed was drafted by director Sydney Pollack to ramrod *The Electric Horseman*'s action, both two- and four-legged. The stunt coordinator hoped to subcontract Gilbert to handle the movie's "high-priced talent": an ex-racehorse formerly called Lets Merge.

Mick drove all night, arriving at the movie's base camp by dawn. He found the thoroughbred's trailer and approached a paddock marked "Rising Star." Met with hostile, bared teeth and wild eyes, he thought he had the wrong horse until nearby wranglers confirmed it was indeed the correct animal. Mick was disturbed with production's plan to shoot with the horse prior to his coaching. He was slated to double Robert Redford aboard Shining Star in the picture's climax: Sonny Steel (electric horseman) riding, in a lighted suit, down the Las Vegas Strip into the night desert beyond. Seeing the racehorse brutally steadied by an ear-hold just before rolling that first evening, Mick questioned the wrangler (Joe Lomax), as to the rough treatment's necessity. Assured it was a "spoiled horse," he was soon witness to the Rising Star's personality, firsthand.

Gilbert had just sat in the saddle when the horse viciously chomped him on the hip, tearing him from the saddle. Informing the shocked wranglers that the stallion had *not* been worked as instructed, he invited all to watch the racehorse's first lesson in etiquette. He returned moments later with spurs over his boots, the rodeo hand reverting to his past profession of bronc rider. Gathering the bridle firmly in hand while quietly ordering the wranglers to release the horse's ears, Mickey climbed resolutely into the saddle again, quickly spurring the horse into an easy trot on the Strip's cement surface. Attempting to throw Mick, Rising Star broke into a bucking bronco, complete with hind legs wildly kicking. It swung left to right in a whirring motion, with a rocking leap each time, landing on all four hooves with a thud. Mick withstood the animal's most energetic attempts to unsaddle him. Thirty seconds of fight transitioned into an uncoordinated trot, with neck arched and back legs slowly committing to forward motion. When it was finally smoothed to a gentle gait, Gilbert rode the ex–race horse well into the surrounding desert. The horse had a controlled, easy gait and gentle bobbing head 20 minutes later, as Mick informed camera that all was ready.

The take started calmly as Pollack whispered *action*, the horse proceeding gently forward along the loose soil. The moment its hooves contacted the roadway, Rising Star started bucking more violently than before. Mick had to employ every ounce of rodeo savvy he possessed to bring the horse around. Gilbert allowed the thoroughbred to "run itself out" and calm down.

Mick located a stretch of soft riverbed to conduct a mini-training session. He and Rising Star progressed from slow canter to full sprints in less than 15 minutes. After a spirited backstretch run, Mick figured out the horse's problem: It had a serious pre-existing injury. But the company was ready to shoot.

With Mick aboard, the relaxed horse sauntered 600 feet back to camera. "Let's try another one," Gilbert told Pollack, who was slumped head in hands, a defeated look in his eyes. Returning to his mark 30 feet away, Mickey passed the wranglers who had failed to pre-train the horse as requested. He gave them a look of scorn, the silent gesture indicating that they would *never* work for Gilbert again.

His electric suit re-lit, Mickey shifted forward in the saddle as Pollack conferred with cinematographer Owen Roizman. Soon the director was ready, the camera rolled and Rising Star stepped before it as if on rails, Mick's "toe prod" signal enough. Crossing dirt to highway, the racehorse was perfect. When it ambled back into the desert sands, all held their breath as Gilbert's twinkling suit lights diminished, and the mag ran out at 400 feet with a *tic-tic-tic* sound.

Mick later took Pollack aside and told him the horse was disabled, with heavy calcium deposits from left foreleg to knee. This meant the end of its movie career. He told Pollack that all-out galloping sequences would finish the horse. Utilizing old-school makeup tricks like shoe polish to replicate the horse's markings, another horse was made to look like Rising Star for full sprints. Meanwhile, Mick retrained Rising Star to jump four-foot hurdles for the police chase scenes where he (Mick) would double Redford. At Pollack's insistence, Mick pushed the horse for the final helicopter pursuit; the horse came up limping after full gallops. A suitable photo double for the once great runner was obtained; a white brushing of forelegs rendered the stand-in passable.

From time to time, stunt players get a negative rap with animal safety, but it was always Mickey Gilbert's policy to harm nothing in the process of making movies. Folks like Gilbert protected those horses, impalas, chickens, lions, dogs and tigers. He always cared.

Returning to cowboy fare, Mickey began work on *The Frisco Kid* in the spring of '79. His job was to double star Gene Wilder for horse and wagon work throughout the comedic western helmed by action pro Robert Aldrich (*The Dirty Dozen*). Wilder played Avram, a Polish expatriate rabbi making his way to head a San Francisco synagogue; Harrison Ford played a repentant ex-gunfighter who befriends him, and William Smith the heavy. The picture was full of rough equestrian work including breakneck pursuits down steep embankments and a 40-foot horse and rider high fall into water; in other words, it was made to order for Gilbert. The coordinator who employed Mick, Chuck Hayward, was more intent on playing cards with the wranglers than helping Aldrich, so Mickey was soon the director's go-to guy.

Mick stepped up after Hayward failed to furnish ideas for the 40-foot jump. "At first Aldrich shut me out," Mickey revealed. "He told me if he needed help making movies, he'd let me know."

Then came the game changer. Aldrich *et al.* struggled to find camera placement spots for the picture's climactic shoot-out along the beach. The director got no help from Hayward. After an hour without rolling cameras, Gilbert suggested how to shoot a variety of horse drags, shoot-offs and chases along the Santa Barbara coast line. This resulted in the movie's most fluid action sequence. After viewing dailies, Aldrich assigned Mick the second coordinator slot, giving him sole responsibility for the film's remaining stunt work.

Free to plan the movie's most memorable action gag (doubling Wilder for a rider-and-horse high fall into water), Gilbert pulled out all the stops to make it world-class. He engineered a massive drop chute complete with a set of stairs able to support the horse's bulk. Soon this structure towered 50 feet above Columbia's Burbank Ranch. A greased platform up top was at a 45 degree angle to slide horse and rider into the drink. Early attempts saw the gelding loose-footed and plummeting tail first into the water (with Mickey scrambling to avoid getting knocked cold on impact beneath it); subsequent takes went as planned with small variations in the ramp's pitch. Aldrich was so happy with the stunt that he offered Gilbert the chance to be his stunt coordinator on all projects forward. But the director unexpectedly died soon afterwards.

At an aeronautics testing stage in Alta, Utah, Gilbert and about 30 other stunt players were tossed around the mock-up interior of a Concorde cabin for 1979's *The Concorde...Airport '79*. They were $6,000 richer following six days performing forward somersaults, back flips and twisted half-gainers, and crashing into padded bulkheads. At the end of it, Gilbert said goodbye to second unit helmer Newt Arnold and coordinator George Sawaya, check in hand. "We had that sequence choreographed down to the last tumble," he said. "Using our gymnastic strengths, [we] made it a floating dance of jumps and collisions. *Except*, when you smack into the ceiling. That hurts no matter *how* much padding you use."

Another well-paid gig came his way in July '79: Gilbert and 80 of his pals wrecked 103 cars for Universal's stunt fest *The Blues Brothers*. Employed by coordinator Gary McLarty for the John Landis bang-'em-up, his first task was a rear-end gag and subsequent motorhome jump into a pond. In the scene, he is doubling Charles Napier as Bob's Country Bunker proprietor Tucker McElroy, who gets his foot glued to the accelerator during the Good Ole Boys Winnebago chase scene; he also drove the cop car chasing Tucker. Slammed into by Napier's pickup truck (trailing the Winnebago at high speed), Gilbert doubled the officer driving the patrol car while McLarty filled in for the angry redneck. "Roll cannons" blasted the vehicles into violent horizontal flips. A dynamite-powered blasting piston was welded to the vehicle's underside by steel plate and fired via hotwire by battery through a driver's switch. Roll cannons are inverted mortars capable of flipping an automobile like a child's toy.

Mickey calls McLarty "the whiz kid" and described how he managed a bit requiring 40 cars horizontally sliding down a muddy embankment. The sequence required 40 drivers, eight camera operators and two cranes to cover, in three takes.

The logistics of big-time car stunts necessitated employment of many folks, from tow truck operators to tire guys to motor cops. Part of the machine, Mickey earned a grand a day for his efforts. He was not only old-school capable but New Age–articulate by 1980. Brought in to enhance the director's vision of action, he read scripts even before actors were cast.

At Robert Redford's insistence, Mick was engaged by producer Ron Silverman for the 20th Century–Fox prison picture *Brubaker*. He doubled the star and coordinated the horse-heavy feature. Co-starring Yaphet Kotto, Jane Alexander, David Keith and Morgan Freeman, it was based on the real-life work of Arkansas jail reformist Thomas O'Murtin at the Tucker Farms system in the early '60s. *Brubaker* was filmed during the rainy spring of 1980 at Ohio's defunct Junction City prison farm. Prior to shooting the picture's polo match, which entailed multiple saddle falls, Mick ordered the soil softened by wetting and removal of rocks. Elimination of those hazards allowed the stunt company to perform the sequence with ribald horse bumps, riding falls and spirited rough play with no harm to horses or humans.

But a hanging nearly went wrong. In the movie, an elderly black inmate is lynched. Actor Richard Ward, cast by Redford and helmer Stuart Rosenberg for his authentic looks and gravelly voice, reported to Mickey the morning of the shot to be fitted with the hanging hardware: a leather and fabric harness running around the legs, up the back and across the shoulders. It would all be hidden under Ward's wardrobe. Ward was born in 1915 and by nine he was in vaudeville with his sisters (they called the act "Dot, Flo and Dick"). The skinny youngster transformed into a tough-as-nails prizefighter at 20, then retired from the ring and worked as a homicide detective with the Manhattan District Attorney's office for ten years. Post–World War II service he took his life's experience "on the road" with Baltimore's Black Theatre. His acting career began when he starred as Willy in *Death of a Salesman* and received rave reviews.

Gilbert was preparing the harness when the 65-year-old asked, "Will this affect my pacemaker?" Realizing the stunt too much for the ailing man, Mick called a time-out. He explained to Rosenberg that the work could kill Ward (pacemaker or not). A simpler version depicted the noose being placed around Ward's neck, and then a stand-in of remarkable likeness did the rest.

Beginning in March of '80, Mickey was doubling Gene Wilder on Columbia's *Stir Crazy*. The job involved handling Brahma bulls and bucking horses inside Arizona State Prison, cheered on by 350 inmate extras. It was directed by Sidney Poitier and starred Richard Pryor in the sidekick role, Barry Corbin as crooked warden Walter Beatty, George Stanford Brown as the mother killer inmate and Craig T. Nelson as the warden's henchman. Mickey coordinated everything from a bank robbery in the opening reel to actual rodeo jobs like clowning, calf roping and bull and bronc riding. Doubling Wilder in the film's mechanical-bull test sadistically conducted by Warden Beatty, Mickey stayed planted despite the prop man's best attempts to throw him. Mick recalled the atmosphere at the Arizona State Prison as bizarre; only Wilder seemed focused and relaxed: "We were in 'the yard' with murderers, gang guys and guards on towers with automatic rifles. Making a movie was just an added challenge. Keeping a straight face around Pryor was nearly impossible."

In the last months of 1980, Mickey worked forgettable titles such as *Hard Country, Circle of Power, Honky Tonk Freeway* (doing truck roll-overs), *...All the Marbles, When I Was King* and *S.O.B.*, the latter being the only film worth watching. In it, he portrayed a stuntman in the movie-within-the-movie. Mick was earning a fine living but hardly content in the "here today, gone tomorrow," suitcase world of stunt guys. He longed for a gig in town that would fulfill his earning requirements while feeding his performance appetite.

The answer to his prayers: *The Fall Guy*, a TV series imagined, produced and written for stunts—and with Mick in charge of the works.

23

Old Gringo Rides

The Fall Guy was inspired by the success of the 1980 movie *The Stuntman* and Hal Needham's ode to stunt players, *Hooper*. It came to the small screen courtesy of creator-producer Glen Larson, with star Lee Majors portraying Colt Seavers, a bounty hunter and stuntman. The weekly series was chock-full of car pursuits, high falls, fight gags, horse work and more.

All did not go smoothly during the shooting of the pilot. Two weeks of shooting with Rick Sawaya doubling Majors had not turned out to everyone's satisfaction, and thoughts turned to Mickey.

Bill Catching thought of Mick as "just a cowboy" so he was intrigued when told of Mick's Jaguar jump in the snow and leaps from moving helicopters. Invited to the Fox lot for a meeting with Catching, Mick was given a back lot tour of the set for a complicated car jump and subsequent landing in a farm wagon. Behind the studio commissary, he was shown a large carnival location constructed with fascia fronted buildings including glass-windowed ticket booths, refreshment stands, vendors, toss games and rows of flagpoles dotting a long circular drive. A large hay wagon sat in the middle. Catching said that Colt Seavers would double Farrah Fawcett in a movie-within-the-show sequence involving a car landing in the wagon. Mick was suddenly distracted when a short fellow strode by shaking his head and muttering a loud doubtful grunt.

"Who was *that*?" Mickey asked Catching. He was told that it was Glen Larson, and that the producer imagined him to be no better than their current stunt coordinator, Paul Baxley. A new GMC Jimmy was accidentally demolished the previous week.

Mick told Catching that the error was in the engineering of the gag, not the execution, and he guaranteed that he could give the producer what he wanted. "I know I can jump a car and land on a dime," Gilbert promised, "much less the back of a hay wagon." Shifting into teaching mode, Mick pointed to a nearby Cadillac and explained the equation of ramp height, takeoff speed, forward momentum, timing and pitch of launch. The car had to hit the wagon with a perfectly flat inclination to "stick the landing."

Mick approached from 65 yards back, hitting a seven-foot ramp with a 58 MPH takeoff. The two-ton Ford Mustang was airborne like a mortar. A 70-foot span was crossed to make the vertical drop onto target. Mick had counterweighted the trunk (controlling forward plunge from the heavy engine). Mathematical equations had come into play when figuring the flat landing. Fighting gravitational pull by 2:1 (every two feet traveled laterally, drops you one foot down), the car's forward imbalance threatened to crush the wagon.

To counter the effects of these principles, Gilbert had to reinforce the wagon while somehow reducing the impact, without detracting from Larson's storyboarded intent. His fix was simple enough. He gave the wagon reinforced axles, heavy struts and truck-size shock absorbers; steel rings were welded around the wheels and secured with rods driven four feet into the ground. Wheel displacement solved, there was now the problem of making sure the wagon was not crushed beneath the Mustang's weight. The wagon, made of wood, would break point without reduction of landing impact. Gilbert's brilliant solution: 1000 watermelons in the back of the wagon to absorb the automobile's landing. His choice of "organic padding" was genius. The melons' crush reduction via water content and rinds made for a soft landing.

While jump logistics were solved by a mixture of metal and produce, Mick's methods for building the ramp road (figuring the speed of the Mustang without rehearsal, and controlling the distance traveled) came from innate knowledge and experience. Sketching the location on paper, Gilbert outlined the carnival set with wagon in the semi-circular square, his ramp leading to the jump and dotted path of the car through its course of travel. He constructed the ramp with a steep takeoff; then the base height of the structure had to be figured, as well as the length and height of the landing zone. Those three things dictated distance, speed and flat lift of the Mustang (and its straight-down fall into the wagon). To lay out the ramp *before* actually building it, Gilbert stood at the estimated point at which the car was to launch. Cueing his son Tim to drive by at 60 MPH, he traced the vehicle's imaginary trajectory from start to finish through the sky

Mickey's first *Fall Guy* stunt: getting a Mustang airborne and landing in a wagon-full of watermelons.

with a sweeping arm and hand. Watching multiple drive-bys, Mick would shift his feet in small increments each time the Mustang sailed past. Tracing the car's path to the point of flight, a series of numbers called to an assistant, and foot gouges on the ground translated to placement of pilings to build the raised ramp.

"First shot" the following day, Gilbert awaited his cue behind the wheel. He was doubling Farrah Fawcett so his blond wig was taped snugly in place and he wore makeup and woman's wardrobe complete with inflatable breasts beneath. He mashed down the accelerator on the '68 Ford as cameras rolled; the wind vacuumed through its open windows. Gilbert gripped the steering wheel with flexed arms as the car raced along. His stomach bottomed with the Mustang's shocks as the vehicle shot up the ramp. Speed and momentum combined at launch; the result was six seconds of flight upon clearing a parked Cadillac convertible and sailing past building frontages. The Mustang seemed to defy gravity before falling as planned, plopping squarely into the wagon like a two-ton kiddie car. It impacted the fruit mound with a hollow thud. Holding firm, the Mustang vapored and seized as melon juice swamped its engine compartment. A final stillness of the landed hulk was suddenly replaced by a loud "*Cut!*" megaphoned through the air. Gilbert took his hand from the steering wheel, and waved "All okay!" to camera and crew standing by.

Led by Majors and Bill Catching, the stunt players applauded wildly. "You're *my man!*" exclaimed the actor. Mickey was surrounded by cheering cast and crew members. Leading the pack was the grumpy little guy from the week before, slowly clapping. The smile on Larson's face told Mick he had the job. Hired on the spot by Catching to handle car gags, Gilbert ultimately made the show his own throughout five years as its stunt coordinator. Testifying to to his stellar performance, the watermelon wagon footage was used in the series' opening montage.

Larson wagered on Majors because of his popularity from his *Big Valley* days to *The Six Million Dollar Man*. The actor's self-deprecating sense of humor and "aw shucks" good nature on *Fall Guy* was a hit with viewers. According to Gilbert, Majors was generous in sharing laurels when the series became a success. The idea was to hire the world's best stunt players each week, then design a plausible story line *around* their specialty. Whether motorcycle jumps, speedboat near-misses, helicopter play or basic car chases, the producers brought in "the *best guy*" to showcase *that* gag. Larson was giving television viewers what was usually reserved for features like *Smokey and the Bandit*. Actual crew members were given bit parts in keeping with the show's "behind the scenes" Hollywood action.

It was a gold mine idea to give Colt Seavers two professions, stuntman and bounty hunter. Many a stunt player got rich from the series via credits for story ideas and action sequences. Mickey wrote and second unit–helmed four years of *Fall Guy* stunts, and came up with ideas others could never have dreamed. Bringing in nearly $20,000 a week, he was also paid $3000 a week as Majors' double, as well as routinely bagging $10,000 in additional writing fees. Eventually crying foul, producers limited Gilbert to lesser amounts, but this did not dampen his enthusiasm. He cooked up hundreds of stunt sequences, then backtracked and devised stories that could lead up to them.

The Fall Guy was a bonanza for stunt men. One episode featured a chopper snatch from a Lincoln limo racing along the Pacific Coast Highway (the driver dead and foot crushed to the accelerator). The woman was to be lifted through the stretch's sky roof; steady flying and precision driving were required to make the shot possible.

23. Old Gringo Rides 175

The show also employed the finest *gal* stunters in the biz, like May Boss. One imaginative car-under-an-18-wheeler slide was given new life with Gilbert's comedic touch of the roof being sheared off and the motorist driving away.

Mick takes pride in a chase scene involving a Porsche and Colt Seavers' pickup truck, a 1980 (4 × 4) GMC. Mickey mapped out the scene's Topanga Canyon route. "I would see a section of road, or an overpass, and my mind would imagine *what* could be done with it to make it a good chase." Such was the case of the Porsche vs. pickup joust. After Fox inked a deal with GMC to for *The Fall Guy*'s official truck, Gilbert put his mind to work. He presented Larson and Catching with the concept that Colt's truck become a character in itself, like Bond's Aston Martin and *The Dukes of Hazzard*'s General Lee. His idea for the Topanga Canyon scene: Pursued

Fall Guy stunt genius Gilbert takes the direct route in the truck, soaring over the guardrail to get ahead of a bad guy's Porsche. A large number of GMC vehicles were used over the years on *Fall Guy*—and often crashed, firebombed, cliff-tossed or rolled to total destruction.

through a small town, the "bad guy" Porsche accelerates ahead, then rips a violent U-turn with the "good guy" truck following suit. Colt is unable to keep up with the car, so he *jumps* his truck over a tight switch-back to intercept it. This was done via a compression ramp tech. The producers and GMC were so enamored of the action that they decided to have writers "fly" the pickup in *every* episode.

The "Superman gags" didn't come without hours of preparation. The section of targeted "leap road" was reinforced with a substratum of compacted asphalt, topped with sandy soil. The Teamsters and their back-graders weren't the only ones with extra work. Transportation boss Howard Bachrach had second unit wrench Jim Nordberg upgrade everything from control and sway arms to shocks and coil springs. The addition of 35-inch Cepek tires with a half-foot lift-kit enabled the pickup to handle the toughest of roads—at least until landing. Then, numerous back-up trucks would be repainted and prepped to use. Further customizing, Gilbert added 12 shot-bags to the truck's rear end, as counterbalance to GMC's six-cylinder motor. Mickey said, "The truck would have nose-dived into the ground, or even somersaulted on some of those jumps. Without the slightly canted back stance when landing, the motor might have dropped through the front end every time."

Second-season additions to the truck included skid plates, and its engine was shifted to the back of the cabin; as a result, pick-ups could be re-jumped, so that they were no longer wrecking a truck per gag. The modifications worked well enough to sail the Jimmy even higher. When the truck was spotted at filling stations, customers cheered, and begged to know where the show was shooting next. The producers feared that mobs of fans would follow the truck to nearby locations.

Pressed to come up with bigger and better stunts each week by the network and GMC, Gilbert dangled from more helicopters than all the other stunt players in Hollywood combined. He and the revolving stunt stable of 70 labored six- and seven-day weeks to pull it all off.

Mick sold Fox executives on an 1100-foot cliff gag with Majors fighting a bad guy as their convertible heads for the precipice. A hidden driver lying on the floor controlled steering and acceleration as Majors and the meanie traded punches. Doubling Majors, Gilbert was knocked into the back seat of the moving car; the bad guy was replaced with a dummy; and then Gilbert grabbed a rope ladder lowered from a helicopter that has been following the car. Mick is pulled out of the car seconds before it goes over the edge. "That was wild," Gilbert remembered. "The chopper literally pulled me from the back seat just as the convertible was dropping away. At that point, all I had do was stand on the bottom rung of the ladder and hold on for dear life." A small parachute stashed under the rear seat was Mickey's insurance policy against death or dismemberment.

Gilbert next doubled as Colt and was chased up a tree by an enraged 500-pound lion. Actually, there were two: Trainer Monty Cox employed the old switch routine with two identical African males. Simba (declawed and defanged) was docile; Jumbo was not. The latter was the "menacing" lion as attacks start, while Simba performed the soft-mouthed kills on camera. Mickey addressed Simba with a playful sing-song voice before his cage, then signaled cinematographer Ben Coleman to ready cameras. Mick dug a final "dig-in" with cleated foot, then visually scanned the distance between his present location and the safety of the tree. The camera rolled.

Gilbert blasted forward as the cage door's release was sprung. Racing the 15 feet just two strides ahead of the lion, Mick could feel the big cat closing on him as he vaulted up the tree. With the first half of the sequence "in the can," Simba was returned to his cage; the scene was reset with Jumbo in place. Provoked via raspy-toned teasing, it clawed the air in Gilbert's direction. Mick again scanned the ground between himself and the tree. Cameras rolled and he bolted, the lion shockingly close behind. Surging after Gilbert, Jumbo closed the 15 feet in three strides. Its front claws just reached his left heel when the safety cable (keeping Jumbo from reaching the tree) "clotheslined" the cat by the neck, flipping it heels over head in a backward snarling tumble. Mick had barely made it. Jumbo was returned to his holding pen near Simba's, and both were left to calm down after the anxiety of playing chase. But the cat pursuit was not finished. The pair escaped to a nearby dry streambed, and Jumbo was itching for a full-out brawl with Simba, who was frightened and backing away. Trainer Cox and Gilbert to the rescue, nudging the aggressive lion with a truck's bumper to keep it from attacking the weaker cat.

Mick recalled filming a complicated Jeep and truck chase and the rookie stunt driver (and friend of Lee Majors) who insisted he "knew what he was doing"—but Mick was worried by the newbie's lack of preparation. Sure enough, instead of driving the Jeep as instructed, he hit a ramp dead center and went airborne, a two-ton missile with tires. Mick had agreed to record the stunt with the fellow's VHS camera, and had the viewfinder to his eye as the action unfolded. When the frame filled with truck grill and bumper, he knew he was in trouble. He stood transfixed for a millisecond, then reflexively attempted to get clear. He was already dropping when struck by the Jeep. With only forearms raised in front of his face for protection from the 20 MPH blow, a flashbulb-like explosion of light (and pain) exploded in his skull, rendering him unconscious. He came to with Gary McLarty and half the crew circled around. His eyes were not fully focusing, there was a loud buzzing in his ears and the pain was intense. Standing with help, Gilbert, shirtless and bleeding, asked, "What happened?" The Wrangler's control arms and body bolts had raked him over from front axle to rear; it was amazing he was alive, much less vocal. Mick was airlifted to Santa Clarita Hospital for emergency trauma evaluation including CAT scans of skull and vital organs. Numerous sutures closed the gashes. After a 24-hour stay to clear up dizziness and double vision, he was released in good shape. When this writer asked him how he survived, Mick simply gestured upward (indicating a higher power).

Continuing to thrive, as well as survive, Mick embarked on a litany of stunt-driven pictures to earn his living. He worked four weeks of nights on the low-budget teen flick *Fast Times at Ridgemont High*. Starring Nicolas Cage, Anthony Edwards, Forest Whitaker and Sean Penn as the stoner character, the Amy Heckerling–helmed "coming of age" story provided skateboard play and car stuff for the stunt players. It was filmed all over the San Fernando Valley including schools in Canoga Park and Van Nuys. "I loved those Vans," Gilbert said of the checkerboard slip-ons that Penn wore on his feet (and which later became must-have footwear nationwide). Under the pretext of doubling Penn, from car wreck to fistfight, most of the stunt players had conned wardrobe for a pair by picture's end.

Mick worked constantly throughout the 1980s. *Swamp Thing, The Being, Eye of the Tiger, The Golden Child, Blue Thunder, Harry and the Hendersons, Big Shots, The Milagro Beanfield War, Little Nikita, We're No Angels*—he was everywhere at once. The checks rolled in and his bank account swelled. He even got the occasional speaking roles, which are a cherished opportunity for stunt players/actors hoping that some small amount of exposure will catapult them to stardom (as it did for Burt Reynolds).

Gilbert's three lines in *Blue Thunder* (playing a policeman driving a patrol car) made him the envy of all.

Blue Thunder featured state-of-the-art helicopters. Aerospatiale Gazelle's three main rotor blades and 13 rear fenestrons made the movie's flying chases a piece of cake. Multiple choppers were used as shooting platforms to capture the fast-moving French machines' amazing flight capabilities. They were ably lensed by John Alonzo utilizing downtown Los Angeles' Figueroa and South Main as backdrops; the picture's "training exercises" were recorded over Lancaster, across the Mojave Desert at speeds nearing 200 MPH.

24

Return of the Westerns

Gilbert was assigned to double Jeff Bridges in Sidney Lumet's *The Morning After*. The 1986 suspense thriller had a "follow the leader" sequence at full gallop between Glenn Close and Bridges that pushed both horse and rider to their limits. Gilbert looked so much like the star that Lumet felt compelled to push the gags' boundaries. Mickey succeeded in exciting director and viewer with a mounted slalom through trail and trees.

Cable and film markets continued to expand, ushering in an era of ever more content on multiple networks. It was a time when anything with an action theme could get made. And it usually did.

Case in point: Screen newcomer Steven Seagal's fight-fest *Above the Law* (1987), its second unit directed by Mickey. Written and directed by Andrew (*The Fugitive*) Davis, the picture was Seagal's first major starring platform and Warner Brothers employed top-shelf talent including seasoned actors to help him along. Gilbert was brought in to spice up the film's action workings lying flat and bland in Davis' script. But even he couldn't perform miracles.

Gilbert says that Seagal was soft-spoken and well-mannered during pre-production meetings, but when shooting began, he was a different fellow—and this one was insecure. The movie's fast-moving, *Miami Vice*–like opening sequence (filmed in Chicago's warehouse district) required the actor to run, duck and dive during a big shoot-out. When his prop pistol jammed, Seagal was enraged. Showering the prop man and second assistant director with a torrent of curse words, he stalked off like a child until the gun was back in working order. Gilbert advised the newbie to relax, rather than chomp at the bit like a straining bear. Gilbert also offered to have his friend Gene LeBell (a hero of Seagal's) help the actor with grappling gags in upcoming scenes.

Shooting continued with the star still acting like a child with a short fuse. Second unit helmer Mick had other issues to solve, like creating an original high fall that audiences would remember. Trapped by bad guys atop a 12-story parking structure, Seagal's character Nico Toscani slams his car into reverse, pinning one unfortunate to the rear bumper and driving through a retaining wall, sending the baddie plummeting to his death. Here's how it was really done.

A balsa wood recreation of the wall was made and a dummy double slammed through it. Then an actual stunt player fell backwards from 12 stories. A stunt player with full faith in Gilbert's rigging was needed to execute a blind backwards fall from 120 feet into an airbag, so special preparations had to be implemented. Foremost was the man: Mick chose Peter Horack, a steely-nerved pro known for his high-fall acumen. Next came the rig. A platform jutted eight feet out from the crashed-through opening 12 stories up. Horack was to launch himself backwards into space, without direct vision of the target bag below. Unnerving, to say the least! A blind fall like that would put off probably 95 percent of stunt players.

If all went according to plan, Horack would land flat on his back on the airbag; the slightest variation could cause him to miss landing on its dead-center sweet spot (which meant serious injury) or miss it altogether.

As prep work continued, Peter verbalized doubts about the jump. "Mickey," he sighed, "I can't see the bag." Gilbert assured him that all was fine and explained that the fall required an inverse action to arc him rearward into the pad. Demonstrating the rearward trajectory, Mickey dropped a 25-pound shot bag to insure the airbag's position. It impacted dead-center and Peter seemed to be reassured.

When cinematographer Robert Steadman's cameras rolled, Horack didn't. After again saying that he couldn't see the bag, he was reminded that cameras were rolling. Thirty seconds of film passing through six cameras amid total silence but the whirring sound of the high speed Panaflex. Peter was again informed by Gilbert that all was ready. His eyes locked on Mick and, blowing out air like a trumpet player, he launched him rearward. "Bye-bye, Mickey" were his final words when pushing off. Imagining himself diving into a pool, with no thought of height on release, Horack waved his arms and kicked his legs so that viewers would know that it was not a dummy. He impacted the bag with a resounding thud after following Mick's advice. The slightest twisting of torso could have carried Peter into a tumble, or worse, a soaring inverse tangent overshooting the landing zone.

Mickey eventually tweaked or re-wrote nearly every fight scene in the script. In the marketplace tussle, Seagal's stunt double Matt McColm had to break through a glass window carrying a man on his shoulders. McColm required special training to pull it off in one continuous take. (Mickey said, "It's difficult penetrating the glass, not to mention adding 200 pounds to a guy's shoulders.") Borrowing from his father's track and field coaching, Mickey conditioned McColm with weighted broad-jump drills and leaping exercises that quickly developed the vertical strength required to pass through the window while remaining upright in the leap.

But Seagal had problems with the set-up and ultimately refused to do his bit. In actuality, he was embarrassed by his inability to execute some of his own physical work (despite his tough-guy persona). The newcomer was nervous, and everyone could smell it. Atop a slow-moving train, the idea of making six-foot jump from one car rooftop to another filled the actor with such fear that he insisted on McColm doing all of his stunts. Via cheating angles and using inserts of Seagal, that problem was solved.

Finishing the film in June '87, Mick distanced himself from the Seagal franchise. After *Kinjite: Forbidden Subjects* (the worst-titled and -branded Charles Bronson flick, ever), he returned to his western roots with horse work on 1989's *Old Gringo*. Based on Carlos Fuente's novel *Gringo Viejo*, it featured Gregory Peck and Jimmy Smits. Jane Fonda's chemistry with these men, unfortunately, was hardly *Cat Ballou* level.

With Gilbert stunt-coordinating, the quality of the action sequences far out-distanced that of the movie itself. In Mexico City, location fun began when the Gilberts checked into the hotel. There was discussion of Mick's wife Yvonne doubling Jane Fonda; Yvonne was Jane's spitting image, wardrobe, makeup and hotel maids all agreed. But her protective hubby refused to allow it and she did not work the picture.

Seeking the perfect area for the picture's opening battle sequences between federal troops and revolutionaries, Gilbert scouted Hidalgo Santa Maria Regla's Canyon of the

Prisms. There he found tall columns of basalt rock with sheer, towering 70-foot cliffs; canyon walls reached 80 feet and sandwiched a dry creek bed below. The spot would be photographically perfect once a few improvements were made. The rocky surface was softened for horse falls; truckloads of sand were brought in, then graded by backhoe to create safe "landing zones" for dispatched riders and their mounts. Fifty eight-ton loads were required to create the soft-fall areas.

An ecosystem was engineered: Dunes and brush areas were created in contrast to the natural flat bottom with varying heights and levels as a perfect setting for mortar explosions, horse shoot-offs, cannon play (including air ram devices sending stunters skyward) and cavalry charges. The sand-wash was the set (surrounded by canyon walls and stone balconies above), and there was a 200-foot-wide river base for staging the battle. And stage it Mickey did. But not without a fight.

Attending a production meeting, Gilbert reported that 15 stunt pros were en route from Los Angeles to handle the key horse gags, supported by dozens of local Mexicans in secondary roles. Mick was told no stunt folks could come. There wasn't enough money to pay them. To get his way, Mick threatened to quit. He asked for a plane ticket home (polite language for "*I'm off the picture*"), and producer Wisnievitz begged him to reconsider. He said the money would be found. Mickey was given his 15 players from L.A. and stayed to make the picture, his way.

The main battle sequence Gilbert envisioned was of David Lean proportions: monumental, with dozens of cannon explosions, horseback combat including saber fights, train loads of rifle-bearing revolutionaries, and Federales on foot, scampering to hold their lines. The 300-extra melee had fights within the fight, and multiple master shots of the entire fort and railyard. Gilbert implemented buried dry-ice and water pots that created a mist of battle haze that hung over the location. The remotely triggered devices spewed volumes of smoke from each "cannonball hit" as flying dirt combined with springboard-launched stunt players filled the frame. Sturdy plywood camera blinds were constructed within the dunes to capture galloping horse gags. The coverage was highly dramatic.

Rows of revolutionaries descended upon the fort over the man-made dunes, creating an undulating foreground motion as their horses galloped past. Cannon fire from the fort exploded amidst waves of mounted riders with dozens of horse falls, blow-offs and stirrup drags filling the frame. Hand-to-hand combat was staged in the periphery to enhance the realism. Sombrero-wearing revolutionaries battled uniformed Federales with reckless abandon. The 15 Hollywood Yankees and 60 Mexican locals formed a cohesive unit under Gilbert's leadership that produced first-rate work.

Mick's greatest creation: a high fall from a 70-foot cliff representing a dream sequence by Gregory Peck's character to start the whole battle. Its preparation and execution was nothing short of amazing. Gilbert's son Lance was in the saddle. It would be his first high fall.

Doubling a cavalry soldier riding along a high ledge, Lance was to be shot off the horse, then free-fall, rifle in hand, to the ground below (actually into an airbag below; it was a 70-foot plunge). Lance was required to fall forward from the saddle, then over the cliff edge into a somersault; from such a height, a back-first landing was a must. He nailed the high fall with Dad, mother Yvonne and brother Tim rooting him on; young Lance was part of the working family from that leap forward. For the same dream sequence, Mick's other son Troy was to rear a horse, then gallop to the cliff's edge where horse

(Troy still aboard) would jump off. Mickey employed two separate horses. The first was conditioned by trainer Rudy Ugland to stand up on back legs and paw the air with its hooves. The second was coached to approach cliffs without hesitation. An aircraft cable was attached to the horse (a special hidden rig beneath its saddle). As it reached the edge of the cliff, the arm of a 120-foot construction crane lifted the animal past the lip and over the precipice in one fluid motion.

Lowering the package of 1200-pound horse and rider by decelerator rig before high-speed cameras capturing slow motion footage, a special "Britchen" harness was fitted to the animal. Constructed of heavy canvas, nylon webbing and leather straps, it utilized a belly and chest halter integrated into the saddle with cut-outs for legs, neck, and tail allowing free range of motion. Engineered with a steel cable running up through the saddle pommel and attached to the crane's down line, the combined devices could transport rider and horse gently through space while "erasing" telltale wires via a tricky printing process in post. The entire sequence went something like this.

The first trained horse galloping toward the cliff's edge, the camera cuts while the Britchen rigged mount is brought in. Riding the second horse, Troy fired his rifle, causing the trained colt to rear up on hind legs. Resuming its charge toward the cliff, camera is again cut while the harnessed animal is fixed to a construction crane, extended 80 feet to allow free movement of the running horse below while booming and swinging the camera crane arm to shadow it. The animal's natural leap into space appeared fluid. With the take-up spool action of the decelerator compensating forward momentum, horse and mounted rider lowered smoothly from space as though on a ray beam. Producing nearly invisible harness pieces by way of brown nylon strapping and horsehide covered hardware, a combination of operator excellence and brilliant engineering kept the four-legged "package" stable and level throughout the descent in addition to the rider's bulk. Picture perfect in execution, focus, originality, and timing, the unit was wrapped with Gilbert sure he had created a masterpiece.

As often happens in Hollywood, scenes wind up on the cutting room floor. *Old Gringo* director Luis Puenzo dropped the massive sequence owing to "running time" issues. What Mick called "his best battle *ever*" landed in a million-dollar garbage bin.

While a professional letdown, the picture was a good experience for Gilbert based on time spent with Gregory Peck. Peck, on horseback, would watch Mickey and the boys utilize Toe-Tappers and execute stirrup drags. Mick has fond recollections of Peck astride his white horse through many hours of equine play: "He was well over 70 and it was hot. He would occasionally nod off in the saddle." Mick put his horse's wrangler in charge of the mounted, sleeping star.

In talking with the present author, Mickey was reluctant to go much further than three or four interviews. At that point, his answer was often "No recollection." The normally vocal stuntman now had a look of bored indifference. It was as if a curtain had dropped. He was willing to discuss the last third of his career in only the most general of terms. Only when really big films came up was the conversation two-sided, but even then, the volume of facts was greatly reduced. Tired of me personally? Quite possible. Facts blurred by 40 years passed and 1000 movies done; you bet, partner. Pictures like *Coupe De Ville* hardly registered. I wondered if Gilbert had run out of descriptive verbs in recounting his extraordinary career.

Pursuing his tales to the end, I made one final round trip to Santa Barbara. I rose at dawn in Sherman Oaks. Rolling through his ranch gates at 9 a.m., I was greeted by the tallish cowboy with Tony Lama boots and buff-white Stetson hat worn straight; piercing blue eyes beneath the brim, a warm smile creasing his lips. "Park that kitty-cat and come up to the house," he said.

Sitting down with hot mugs of coffee in hand, Mickey and I began the dance we had done five times before. Legal pad ready and tape recorder on, I would name a picture, ask questions about stunts and actors. Gilbert would respond.

However, unlike previous sessions covering the old-school stuff (1955 to 1985), these movies were from the '90s on—a far busier time. Working so many projects on multiple sets, Mick's memories were usually blurred.

We talked about the 1989 remake of *We're No Angels*, a 1955 film featuring Humphrey Bogart, Aldo Ray and Peter Ustinov. The new version starred Robert De Niro, Sean Penn and Demi Moore. Writer David Mamet and director Neil Jordan could not save this turkey, but the stunts were wonderful. Gilbert arrived in Vancouver and was whisked north to the location even before dropping luggage. Cleveland Dam and its spillways were nearly a football field long and 20 feet wide, the six successive chambers of the waterway sloping gradually to a collective base. The De Niro character was to dive off the dam side of the waterway bridge and then be drawn beneath it; he was to drop into an inlet, then be swept into the spillway channel, ultimately falling to the bottom. Mickey described the workings of a decelerator to provide a controlled plummet for De Niro's double (Mick's son Troy), combined with cheating camera between two active spillway ducts and one dormant. The stuntman between would look fully immersed, yet actually be clear of the water's tremendous weight. Thrilled to get the shot as envisioned, Art Linson and Fred Caruso bought-in totally. Explaining the precision of the hydraulic descender's ability to lower a stuntman *down* the spillway as quickly as the water moves (while being able to stop him at any point), Mickey insured the "look" would be that of uncontrolled falling without the risk. Placing his son in the gag gave evidence of his sureness it would work.

Inspecting the voluminous collector below the spillways to ensure unimpeded entry into the basin at stunt's climax, Mick and Troy donned "dry-suits" to survive the wintry 40 degree dive. No such luxury would be possible for the stunt; only costume would do. Performing decelerator tests with a 180 pound double-dummy while submersed to check safety clearances, control of depth was obtained while fall-speed was matched to the spillways' flow. Engineering a five-foot mark beneath the water via the operator's take-up spool, Gilbert used a precise stop point to avoid accidental impact with the collective's bottom. Yet, there was still a problem.

Spying large chucks of cement and rebar construction material submerged at one end of the basin, not visible from the dam bridge or on the ground, Gilbert moved the termination point of the fall twelve feet to avoid the hazard. Only cautious preparation of his "look-see" dive avoided possible catastrophe.

Marking camera positions from full frame below (looking up), and atop the spillway filming transversely for dramatic overhead coverage, Gilbert warned second unit cinematographer James Devis that no water could be in the center channel while filming. Cheating the angle was paramount to capturing the action without seeing the empty passage, and keeping Troy safe in the process.

The morning of the shot, the center spillway was shut down. All was made ready. Camera operators nervously fingered already checked magazines and lenses. Grips stood by with safety lines, interested looks and cigarettes dangling from their mouths. De Niro's double wardrobed, hair dyed, and harnessed in place to the decelerator-rig atop the dam awaiting his cue, Mickey scanned the location for anything out of place. Spotting a small boat with an operator hurriedly mounting an Arriflex camera to short "sticks" (tripod), he was sitting at the base of the empty spillway, totally exposed to the other camera positions. The radio crackled with a request to flood Troy's spillway as a police order to vacate saw the uninvited camera boat move away. Following three levels of NO (stunt-coordinators, director and finally producers), with unkind utterances aside, the shot was done Gilbert's way. "It was beautiful," Mick remembered. "Troy pulled it off without a hitch!"

Mick did a quick stint in May '89 on *Coupe De Ville*, stunt-coordinating open convertible gags along backroads of Coral Gables, Florida, and numerous North Carolina counties. He took the job to help out producer pal Joe Roth. He was hired by producer–unit production manager James D. Brubaker for *Problem Child* six weeks later. He was stunt coordinator and second unit director, injecting physical action wherever possible. Intended to transition talented television star John Ritter to motion pictures, the comedy was a top-grossing film of 1990 but just another payday for Mickey.

On the western reboot *Young Guns II,* Gilbert was saddled with second unit chores and stunt coordination. It was directed by Geoff Murphy and retained original cast members Lou Diamond Phillips, Kiefer Sutherland, Christian Slater and Emilio Estevez as Billy the Kid (and had a great cameo by James Coburn portraying John Chisum). The picture's fast-paced action was perfect for Gilbert.

The script provided infinite possibilities for horse chases, shoot-offs, stirrup drags, falls, leaps and gunfights. For Mickey, it was 11 weeks of paradise, with a paycheck. Sons Lance and Troy were integral members of Gilbert's troupe of horse players. (They doubled Estevez and Sutherland, respectively.) There was an unspoken communication between father and sons that transcended the coordinator-stuntman roles. This was blood, and as equestrian works goes, you'll see none sharper than the boys' work in *Young Guns II*.

It was filmed by A-lister Dean Semler in Cochiti Pueblo's "tent rocks," White Sands National Park in Galisteo, New Mexico, Sonora deserts (both Arizona and Mexico), the Eaves Movie Ranch outside Albuquerque and Old Tucson. Therefore, it mirrored the vibe of mid-'60s westerns. Surrounded by such impressive locales, Gilbert was inspired to use their beauty as well as danger to stage stunts.

Mick incorporated the tent rocks into a posse chase with the Young Guns driving their horses down an impossibly steep ravine with Pat Garrett and others in pursuit. Only the riders' ability to keep the animals' necks up kept them from tumbling head over heels down the hill. Mick: "You have to center your weight back in the saddle, while holding the horse's head almost straight-back." To simulate the shooting of a horse, Mick employed a hide-covered squib attached to a pony's neck; a remote triggering device made it go off before the animal rolled three times. Lance Gilbert's fall looked agonizing to audiences, but it was harmless to stuntman and steed alike.

In one scene, Lou Diamond Phillips, mounted on a horse, has his hands bound behind him and a noose attached to his neck, seconds away from hanging. In an ensuing action scene, someone's revolver fired too near Phillips' horse during the take. Lurching forward in panic, the suddenly riderless colt bolted down the road, yanking Phillips behind, the rope caught around his throat. Recounted by the actor as a near death experience on various talk shows thereafter, its result was an unavoidable incident owing to an over-zealous extra's lack of experience.

Young Guns II featured all the western action Mickey ever knew, including Pony

Express mounts, saddle transfers, stirrup drags, fistfights, knife-throwing and more. And yet there was humor. Just after production wrapped, Gilbert received a call from Sutherland and Phillips. They, and their co-stars, were pulling practical jokes on each other throughout production, and now they wanted to "celebrate" Estevez's birthday by delivering a cow to the set of his current picture. Mickey paid a rancher pal to bring a milk cow to the set of *Men at Work* in Indian Dunes. "They brought the heifer up to Emilio's table at lunch, then handed him the rope and walked away." The actor was distracted by the laughter heard every time the cow mooed to be taken home.

Continuing in the cowboy vein, Mickey's next interesting challenge came via Irby Smith, producer of *Young Guns II*. His next, *City Slickers*, had Billy Crystal portraying a middle-aged big-towner on a getaway "cowboy" vacation, and Smith wanted Mick's know-how for all the horse work and cattle drive sequences.

Mickey began by planning the picture's climactic cattle drive through a rainstorm. Raw steers were purchased and transported to the Ghost Ranch's holding pens in New Mexico for conditioning. Mick hired a dozen cowhands to teach the herd of 500 steers to "turn as one." The cows were working as a cohesive group even before production began. Through repetitive tutorials, they grew accustomed to the cowboys' control. This allowed them to shoot herd drives over the desert terrain, then down steep grades into the moving water. "Without the training, we would have been chasing steers all over the desert. This way, you had a manageable herd, allowing make-believe to seem possible (and safe), working 500 head with actors in the middle."

Finding a good location for the river-crossing scene was vital. Gilbert led Ron Underwood on a scout through Durango, Colorado's, alpine country. It was comprised of boulder-strewn slopes, dense woods and plunging valleys. Adding to the excitement of the sequence, Gilbert ordered the construction of rain towers soaring 60 feet skyward (pump-fed with river water), to provide a torrential downpour. Gilbert also took advantage of a 100-yard downward grade leading down into a three-foot-deep channel. The steep banks were a natural sluice to control the steers. The animals plunged into the river, the forced flow of 500 heifers looking highly dramatic on camera. Throughout this footage, editors inserted shots of actors and stuntmen twirling ropes with exaggerated arm movements, Stetsons half-covering their faces.

Gilbert used Crystal's double Brian Burrows and his own sons Troy, Tim and Lance for the tricky mounted stuff—everything from the pursuit of a calf swept away by the current to swimming horses with riders swamped by the elements. A special tripping pit was dug to make Crystal's horse fall end over end in the scene where he tosses his lariat at the young heifer. Burrows did the stunts; insert shots of Crystal (wearing a wetsuit under his costume) were done in small rapids. Ritter fans churned up the water's surface, making everything look believable. The sequence ended with multiple set-ups of Crystal holding the calf in waist-deep water, one of the picture's most memorable moments.

Crystal complained of being cold after the first take, and Mick instructed him to urinate in his wetsuit to keep himself warm. Crystal took the suggestion, and said it did make him feel better. Pranking the actor, Mick feigned disgust and said he would have to pay for the wetsuit.

The Last of the Mohicans was helmed by Michael Mann, who met with Mick in his (Mann's) Beverly Hills offices. As Mick arrived, Mann and special effects supervisor Tommy Fisher were having an awkward exchange over foam cannon mock-ups; Mick was soon in a stare-down with the infamously macho director over the picture's stunt work. Mann attempted to impress Gilbert with scores of stunt wannabes and action "extras" undergoing martial-arts fight training (out-of-period hand-to-hand jiu-jitsu and kung fu). Watching a video tape of the workouts left Mick snickering. The fighting was full of aerobatic moves, fancy punches, sweeps and downright silly brawling action; he saw everything from British soldiers performing crescent kicks to Iroquois warriors proficient at Drunken Monkey and judo throws. Mick told Mann how ridiculous the idea was, and said he would not work on the film if the director insisted on approaching it from that angle. He then carefully described Colonial fighting tactics of the 1750s with descriptions of swords, flintlocks, clubs, knives and long rifles pitted against Huron and Mohawk braves wielding bow and arrows, stone hatchets, lances and other implements of destruction. The famously unchangeable mind of the director was changed, and with a quick cowboy smile Mick offered to do the picture. Mann agreed to give Mick full control and the men shook hands.

Mick second-unit–directed all the film's action. His ability to always see "the bigger picture" gave the movie an authenticity it would have otherwise lacked. In the fight scenes, the participants were pre-conditioned by Gilbert, who had the knack of handling large groups of men well. The main battle sequences would bring into play hundreds of action folks playing both British and Huron. Mick's fight training program was Colonial hand to hand. Some also needed to be proficient in sword fighting (click-clack in stunt industry terms), including slashing and run-throughs without poking anyone around you. Everything was practiced, from stabbing and scalping to bludgeoning and bullet hits. Dale Dye was assigned the chore of teaching proper British drilling, the manual of arms, bayonet use, period calisthenics, marching and overall battle tactics. For the stunters playing Hurons, Mick focused on *their* brand of mayhem including scalping, knife-fighting, tomahawk-slashing and equestrian tricks. For the length of the filming, they all needed to have the same haircut: a Mohawk, leaving only a short tuft of inch-wide hair from the base of the neck to forehead. The "look" is fierce. Daily buzz-cuts and razor-shaving were required to maintain the look. Everyone playing Hurons had to submit—except Gilbert's son Troy. Because of his equestrian talent, it was necessary that he play both a Huron and a British, so a special "Huron hairpiece" was made for him.

It was necessary for wounds to appear on the bare skin of some of the Hurons. Gilbert came up with sheer body suits (worn beneath the minimal native wardrobe) that would hide the effects wires and detonators required. Combined with the prosthetic makeups of Vincent Guastini, the "body suit solution" allowed for full range of movement for stunts while supplying a most realistic effect for Dante Spinotti's camera. Squib hit "flesh panels" were applied to body parts of the braves, so that gruesome bullet impacts (complete with flying "blood") from the Pennsylvania long rifles could be simulated.

Despite the massive scope of Gilbert's *Mohicans* duties, the smaller details of Mann's vision for up-close violence were also on the stunt coordinator's mind. He implemented springboard and mini-mortar blasts hurling cannon fire victims ten feet skyward, not to mention prosthetic forehead pieces utilized for scalping gags. Mickey had a hand in all.

In one scene, there is a gruesome assassination attempt on British Colonel Munro. Serving as guide to the Brit troops, the Huron scout Magua (Wes Studi) had their trust. Calmly strolling from the column's front to its rear, Magua pulled out his tomahawk and planted it squarely in the skull of an unsuspecting soldier. The actor playing the soldier wore a prosthetic head piece and neck section with a tomahawk *already* imbedded in it; the pre-positioned weapon was seen as he turned and revealed it. The bleeding, gaping wound drew gasps from audiences every time. The soldier's murder is one of the picture's most graphic moments. And it was very much Gilbert's.

The picture's epic battle finale pitted the trained British and Huron stunt players against each other. Word had filtered to Gilbert of *both* units' savage disposition. Conditioned as though *real* combat were to occur (and foolishly told as much by instructors), each side was nervous and excited to face the other. Gilbert knew that such an atmosphere would create chaotic, non-flowing fight sequences, and came up with a plan to change their attitudes. He ordered a full-dress rehearsal including costumes, weapons and makeup. The men gathered at sunrise after being housed in frigid tent towns the sleepless night before; their gathered ranks were a magnificent mixture: uniforms and buckskins, feathered headdresses and tri-corner hats, beads and brass buttons, white wigs and long black braids, tomahawks and muskets. Addressing them by loudspeaker, Gilbert ordered the ranks to attention. Tensions were visible in braves and troops alike as they fingered rubber knives and checked mock rifles. "I saw fear," Mickey recalled. "And I knew I had to use the moment to turn the situation around."

Gilbert sternly ordered both sides to ready position. They he relayed a second command to the combatants; this time speaking with a drawl: "On the count of three, walk across to the nearest opponent and shake their hands. *Then hug each other!*"

Hard looks turned to smiles, the moment becoming pure camaraderie as "opposites" surged forward, smiles and names offered rather than punches. A feeling of kinship descended over the herd. Brotherhood cemented, the stunt players were ready to make the picture as real as they could make it, without *really* harming one another.

Trainers thought the move lessened the ferocity they had drummed into the players, but Gilbert recalled that many stuntmen thanked him for removing the fear factor. They rehearsed for over a week before filming the grand battle, and the results were unparalleled. A chaotic sea of fighting men amid horses and explosions. Mickey provided carnage as far as the camera's eye could see. With military precision, the two dozen platoons (containing 30 action players each) were led by numerous sub-bosses (Gilbert's sons Tim, Lance and Troy and other experienced fellows). The footage was visceral and violent. Many "micro-skirmishes" were visible throughout the battlefield, filmed in a way that called to mind Freddie Young's deep focus methods in *Lawrence of Arabia*: action in the background, "personal" killings like scalping, stabbing, and close-quarters gunfire in foreground.

In the climax, Uncas (Eric Schweig) fights to save Alice (Jodhi May), and Lance Gilbert was chosen to double Schweig as he is thrown off a cliff. Lance was slated to plummet 80 feet, rifle in hand, and land in a catcher rig bolted to the rock face; if he missed it, he would drop three football fields to his death. In North Carolina's Chimney Rock Park, rigging stunts was difficult. Their efforts an exercise in bravery, a team of skilled rock climbers installed a queen-size platform containing an airbag to break his fall. It extended six feet beyond the curvature of the cliff at eight stories down. Lance needed to drop straight down to hit the mark. Mick felt that his son was not entirely focused, so he positioned himself at the edge of the bag with climbing harness and ropes, and hopes of improving Lance's chances should anything go wrong.

Lance pushed off with his feet and the arc of his descent was instantly bad. Zapped by thoughts of losing a child, Mick felt adrenal panic race through his body, hurling him to the airbag's end like a diving third baseman after a hot line drive. Striking the rig on the outside of proper practice (but arresting the fall nonetheless), Lance's impact at Dad's feet was frightening. Containing a higher, thicker retaining lip than other airbags, the model used for that gag probably saved his son's life. And Mickey knew it. A lesson had been taught between master and student, and the look on Lance's face confirmed the paternal schooling found its mark.

Mick worked the picture's water-bound finale with doubles for Cora, Hawkeye and Chingachgook. Strong current from Hickory Nut Falls pulled the heavy boats toward a lower inlet during the canoe chase. Shooting the boats rowing towards lens with the falls in the background, Mann and Spinotti failed to realize the danger of the boats being drawn too close to the edge of the upper inlet as undercurrent pulled the heavy mock-ups downstream. Instructing talent to beach their canoes for camera with the huge falls just 50 feet down river, the shooting perch atop a 12-foot boulder gave a wonderful cinematic view but little safety. Mickey's was better. Concerned for the doubles' wellbeing should anything go wrong during the breaching, he tasked sons Tim, Troy, and Lance with last-chance lines at the inlet's far end to catch the canoes, while stationing himself at frame's edge. Accidentally creeping into the shot numerous times in as many takes, the helmer cursed Gilbert, refusing to move his camera or alter the frame in any way.

Fighting to hold one of the bulky canoes after a sudden current nearly ripped it from his grasp, Mick's attention was on the dug-out when he heard Mann's voice booming above the roar of the falls. The director was cursing him for blowing the take. Mick waited until he finished, then questioned his sanity. Weeks of frustration (battling climate, insects, production problems and Mann's Napoleonic style) boiled over. Grabbing a heavy five-foot oar, he flung it 20 feet end over end straight at the director. It missed Mann's ducking head with inches to spare as it whooshed past. There were frozen stares, soon shattered by assistant director Michael Waxman hollering, "That's a wrap!" Left with boats and gear to gather, Mick and the boys lingered at the location as Mann and the crew began hiking back to the base camp. Assuming he would be fired, Gilbert instructed his sons to stay with the show upon his dismissal. By the time the Gilberts arrived at the base camp, all vans back to the motel had departed. Only a stretch limousine was parked in the lot. Mickey gulped when the sizable director stepped from the open back door and begin walking toward him. Mann strode forward until they were face to face. Smiling in apology, each agreed to allow the incident to pass, and they hugged at the helmer's bequest. They had a working friendship for the picture's remaining weeks. *Last of the Mohicans* became one of Mickey Gilbert's crowning achievements.

Mick was hired by Hunt Lowry in late '92 for the Bruce Willis stuntfest *Striking Distance*. It was directed by action pro Rowdy Herrington (*Road House*), a Pittsburgh native who did extensive location shooting in that area: the Allegheny River's Point Park locks, the Monongahela River and Mount Washington. Gilbert made good use of Pittsburgh's hilly streets while scouting initial chase ideas.

That's when he got a look at a future that chilled him to his stunt bones: an early Sony computer-animated video-proximity of the stunts to be performed. Computer-animated live-action gags *without* actual stuntmen. Despite vehicles appearing in block form, their movement and exact camera angle replication were a clear advancement over anything Mick had ever seen. Fearing loss of employment to total extinction, he met with other coordinators about it. Regardless of his warnings, digital effects quickly became the industry norm for many filmed stunts. The profession has changed since the cardboard box high fall and saddle-drag days. But not completely. A punch was still a punch. And folks still like a good chase. Even if it *is* 60 percent CGI.

Striking Distance was the story of a former homicide cop who stumbles upon a serial killer, and risks life and pension to catch him. The film featured boat chases instead of car gags, and the Allegheny water locks offered Gilbert a playground for stunt action.

Coordinating the picture's first big stunt sequences, Mick brought in sons Troy and Lance to drive the boats, doubling Bruce Willis and Robert Pastorelli, respectively. Launched 100 feet with each take, the boat sank before reaching dock at day's end, despite the crew's best efforts to keep it afloat.

Mickey gaffed a car-boat sequence that was hard to top. With son Tim driving along the Allegheny River frontage, the resulting chase by Willis' boat included an improvised flare gun barrage. Traveling along dirt service roads at 60 MPH for practical exteriors, the parallel attack was complicated by the flares' trajectory (streaking across the night sky in drooping arcs) before striking the vehicle. Crashing through the back window via special effects—insert shot, the signal flare ignites, issuing volumes of sparks and fire to help sell the shot.

Lifted by explosion, the flaming automobile flips end over end. (This was done via a hidden ramp to catapult the car, and a small effects cannon welded to the rear frame and triggered by the driver.) Safety considerations for the gag included Lexan sheeting encapsulating Tim's driver's compartment to protect him from heat and billowing flames; an ambulance and fire truck stood by, just in case. The car landed with a terrific impact. The forward inertia and G-force required incredible strength and focus from the driver, just to remain in control.

It was a familiar challenge for Gilbert to come up with fresh stuff for *Striking Distance*. He admits that the "Tom and Jerry" concept of chase is very much in his heart. Logistics-wise for stunts, it can be a major undertaking to secure the proper locations that can also accommodate the small army which is a film unit. *Striking Distance* was no different. Its "edge of your seat" automotive sequence (Willis after Robert Pastorelli) utilized sons Troy and Lance in respective double work. Even youngest boy Tim was in on the family fun as the driver behind the wheel of a police cruiser. Six cars in all were put through their paces. Steep streets upped the danger and excitement level,

Days spent scouting Pittsburgh's neighborhoods with location managers Charlie Miller and Steve Parys turned up usable long hills and byroads with an antiquated four-lane stretch of paved street, perfect for filming. With a crossroad every 100 feet, the service road allowed for ramps to be constructed, and ten-degrees-pitched lifts were built at each junction. Speeding Fords were launched in a crazy Joie Chitwood type of aerial display. Impact of the cruisers loosened siren lights and sprang hoods. Second unit shooter Tom Priestley, Jr.'s, coverage was spot-on in combination with cameras positioned by Gilbert at obtuse angles for maximum *Batman* effect (and safety). The cinematographers' variation of lens choice and frame speed produced a visual gut impact not felt in a feature chase since William Fraker's *Bullitt*. Each car leapt through the air at 52 MPH and sailed 20 yards before landing.

Continuing the chase, Mickey next reverted to a classic western stand-off: the bad guy surrounded by the posse, with no way out. Gilbert placed Lance (as Pastorelli) behind the wheel doing a long sliding stop to appraise a police roadblock. Following behind and in front, Troy (as Willis) and other pursuing cops pulled to a stop as well. The police loudspeaker orders for Pastorelli to exit the car were ignored. Then his vehicle shifted into reverse, directly towards Willis and the line of cops. An order to fire came from the ranks. With bullet-hit squibs exploding across the auto's rear end and trunk, the car suddenly blew through a gap in the roadblock as it gained speed. Smashing backward through a parking lot fence running along an elevated freeway underpass, Lance (as Pastorelli) dropped onto parked cars below and drove off.

It was orchestrated like an action comic book. Mickey would have vehicles fall ten feet and drive away. In *real* life, wheel struts would pop and engine mounts disintegrate on impact. Not to mention spinal compression.

Troy (doubling Willis) caught Lance (Pastorelli), the two racing side by side until gunfire "blows" the bad guy's tire. The crippled car skids into Willis', sending both down a hill (and getting *Dukes of Hazzard* air in the process). Via hidden launch ramps, the vehicles were thrown into space off the steeply pitched embankment, flying side by side in slow-motion splendor.

25

The Fat Lady Sings

Finishing out Mickey Gilbert's extraordinary career history is like fast-forwarding a favorite film to its end: bittersweet. While I had the questions, memories of the last pictures he crewed have ebbed from his sharp retention. Perhaps it was boredom. Then again, who among us (lawyer, doctor, priest or cop), can remember *every* case, patient, soul saved, or arrest? Mickey is no different. While other pictures like *The Soft Kill, Last Man Standing, Spy Hard, Liar, Liar, Dragon Fly, After Midnight* and *The Amazing Panda Adventure* all had the "Gilbert touch," he remembered some others better. Therefore, we shall focus on those.

For Mick, *City Slickers II* began with a middle-of-the-night call from Billy Crystal, asking him to head the second unit. The following morning, discussions of the picture's biggest sequence began: a massive horse stampede. It mirrored the first movie while swapping steers for mares, and a poor calf for a beautiful white stallion.

There was also a runaway wagon sequence with Jon Lovitz. A hidden Teamster, Joe Finnegan, piloted the rig, allowing Mickey to let the actor do some of his own stuff. It was one of the film's funnier moments. Mickey had fun with Lovitz: The actor had to ride in the "out of control" wagon while his rubber face was filmed from every angle. Being pulled by horses through the desert horrified him, even though he had been assured that Finnegan wouldn't let him get hurt. Gilbert's actions had the actor otherwise confused: He purposely brushed against or bumped into the out-of-place New Yorker every chance he got. Two days of rehearsal ended with Lovitz's breaking, protesting that Mickey was mean. Crystal finally revealed the joke after the actor openly expressed fear about being around Gilbert alone. "He pointed a shaking, stubby finger at me," Mickey laughingly recalled, "and said I was out to get him. Hugging away the hurt, I kissed Jon's face a wet one to let him know I loved him."

Mick picked a trainable batch of animals with help from Jack Lillie. There were many dry runs teaching the horses how to move from place to place as a group; the 200 head were tutored to move as one on cue. Production time and money was saved by filming the stampede sequences *before* principal photography started. Cut-in gags featuring Crystal *et al.* were easy to plan and shoot.

In Moab, Utah, scenes were backgrounded by majestic rock formations, puffy clouds and pastoral canyons with space-rock features. Scouting for a location for the picture's white stallion capture sequence, Mick and cinematographer Don McCuaig found a canyon that was made for the movie: a mile long and 30 feet deep with a sandy bottom. The continual rock formations created a back-lit field of stone and the clay walls were perfect to showcase the beautiful white horse. "Staking out" camera positions by time of day and angle, the two envisioned a beautiful, mounted dance between man and horse.

Performing the actual capture bits (when the stallion is first roped), Gilbert nailed the initial throws as well as teaching Crystal basic lariat handling.

Mickey signed for epic duty on *Waterworld* in late '94. Hollywood's biggest miss since *Ishtar*, the picture was parallel to Orson Welles' *Citizen Kane*, by way of new generation actor turned successful producer-director. Kevin Costner had scored multiple Oscars five years previously via *Dances with Wolves* and he was continuing to rise as this project became his dream. Or obsession, depending upon how one views spending $20,000,000 on a sci-fi movie. Shot on the water, no less! It was costly because everyone required boat service; the time and effort to film on water has long been cost-prohibitive.

Mick turned down the picture due to schedule conflicts (*The Amazing Panda Adventure*) but later got a second call from its director Kevin Reynolds, who was in dire need. When they met the following day, Mick was serenaded with tales of gluttonous spending by a harried associate producer. Seeing Reynolds' six massive storyboards, Mickey found fault with most of them by meeting's end. Agreeing to make the picture in conjunction with him, Gilbert undertook the second unit responsibilities.

In Hawaii, Mickey met with line producer Steve Traxler to get the production ball rolling. Calling a crew meeting the following morning, Gilbert invoked his best George Patton "greeting the troops" demeanor, including an overt call to the assembled to "get to work!" His boys Lance and Tony warned the stunned attendees that the paid vacation was finished; everyone reported on time the following day. The stunt department made a Herculean effort in difficult and often dangerous circumstances throughout the 157-day shooting schedule, and became the driving force of the film. The production was plagued by gale-force winds and rain (destroying sets and crew morale), and scores of folks quit or were fired. Before Mick took the helm, nerves were sometimes rubbed raw and production came to a standstill.

Listed as second unit director, Gilbert's expanding role on the picture became evident as he scouted the "bone-pile" for a suitable picture craft.

A collection of partial masts, motors, deck planking, discarded sheet metal, bulkheads, hulls and boats in all degree of disrepair testified to the picture's lack of direction. According to Mick, "Without a proper shooting boat, you can't make movies on the water, much less open ocean." He found an intact Boston Whaler 14 feet in length and only six feet wide, and asked marine guru Ransom Wallrod to make bow modifications. Ports were torch-cut, allowing "low-water" shooting angles. The Whaler was also equipped with able motors to smoothly ride the ocean's swells in coverage of the action. The first of many dynamic choices Mickey brought to the otherwise disjointed project, the "shooting vessel" proved invaluable. A nautical workhorse, "Captain Mick's" boat was the backbone of waterbound coverage, serving without mechanical failure. It was required to keep pace with the film's "hero" vessel, a catamaran called the *Mariner*. Its French-engineered tri-hull was based on the genius of Jeanneau Advanced Technologies of Lagoon. Constructed by Marc Van Peteghem and Vincent Lauriot Prevost, the 60-foot crafts were great for speed and dynamic sailing shots.

Confronting the need for more "on demand" speed, Gilbert again dispatched Ransom Wallrod. He supplied production with a 500-horsepower Chris-Craft to tow the large Trimaran via submerged cable. The motorboat had a steel ring and rod catch plate-welded to the bow two feet below sea level. Combined with 200 feet of heavy line, the tow rig remained "invisible" while supplying Gilbert the constant velocity required to pull the Trimaran. The system performed well enough to add ten knots. At one point, the boat was propelled so fast that its stunt pilot was launched ten yards overboard by the wake. Not anticipating the dunking, his angry reaction was authentic.

Retrieval divers in fast skiffs were positioned to fish out anyone swept off deck while shooting. Extraordinary images of Norman Howell (stunt double for Costner's Mariner) were brilliantly captured by cinematographer Gary Capo. Positioned in the picture boat's bow, he was strapped in while shooting hand-held. The sequences were beautifully fluid.

Beyond his job description, Mickey solved other miss-shot sequences, where "in the can" footage was useless. One such scene was Mariner's high fall from the mast peak. The scene has him firing a crossbow in an attempt to blast loose an airplane tethered to the trimaran, circling in ever tighter turns. The violent swaying of the ship's mast nearly caused the vessel to capsize, its sides dipping below the water's surface in the process. Tasked with Costner's high fall, double Norman Howell performed a 70-foot plummet in mid-whip. No easy task. Realizing previous footage to be off-frame useless or otherwise uncuttable from their angled specifics, Mickey redesigned the shot using a 120-foot construction crane. Positioned over the Trimaran's main mast with the hull anchored in temporary dry-dock just above the water, a camera was mounted to the basket of the boom lift, looking downward—past the crow's nest. Attaching cables to the top of the mast, Gilbert pitched the craft at a cantilevered 45 degree angle, raising the left pontoon 12 feet out of the sea, pre-setting the boat for its reverse action. Howell was in the crow's nest (ten feet from the mast's peak), tethered by a descender rig as the camera looked straight down. Action called and the Catamaran's cable released, the boat whipped upright, returning to its normal position. Surviving the frenetic re-alignment of the mast, he was thrown away from the boat, deep into the surrounding water. Howell's cable provided an extra margin of safety in case he was unable to launch himself clear of the pontoon, should something go wrong in the fall. There was no shortage of apprehension, however. First tested by dropping a weighted bag matching Howell's heft, the rig worked perfectly, sending the duffel like a cannon-shot into the water upon the mast whipping back into position. "It gave Norman the confidence he needed," Gilbert revealed.

Mickey was ultimately handed the first unit reins after the two Kevins (Costner and director Reynolds) were no longer speaking. Universal honchos were impressed with his dailies containing clean dialogue, minimal takes and dynamic camera movement, and they said he'd soon direct a picture of his own. Corporate realignment dashed his chances; the executive who liked him was reassigned to Seagram's.

Mickey wound up doing Eddie Murphy films in his final career stages. Following stints as coordinator on several pictures, including Ron Howard's *Apollo 13*, opportunities such as *Metro* and *The Nutty Professor* came his way.

For the latter, Mick was hired by producer Jim Brubaker. Eddie Murphy's reboot of the Jerry Lewis masterpiece was directed by Tom Shadyac and laden with makeup effects and physical gags. Murphy brilliantly played five characters, Buddy Love, Sherman, Grandma Klump, Ernie and Papa. The picture worked well on many levels, and was full of gags to keep Mick busy. He coordinated a large night exterior with a Corvette ripping through Los Angeles streets. Gilbert utilized longtime action mate Don McCuaig to shoot the sequence (20 cars and drivers). Two days later, the bit was wrapped except for the Viper gag finale. The plan was to have Eddie's Buddy Love character park a Dodge Viper by way of a 180-degree spin-move between two parked high-end cars. But no capable driver of color could be found. Alan Oliney—one of a handful of candidates unable to take the job—provided the replacement. But the sub was unable to handle the Viper's power, and ran over parking cones every attempt during instruction. Gilbert had to tell the director that he was not able to find an African American driver to do the stunt. Doing the wheel work himself, Mick refused to double Murphy wearing blackface. Instead, tinted windows and subtle lighting obscured his identity. He nailed the move in one take. In the next shot, Murphy stepped from the vehicle and strutted around the Viper to the amazement of onlookers.

Night was turning to dawn because of a late start owing to Murphy's makeup particulars. Brubaker phoned Mickey with bad news: The latter stuff didn't match, and would need to be reshot. *And*, they had been reported to the NAACP. Alan Oliney contacted the organization and explained what had happened. And Gilbert repeated the driving magic after Brubaker reminded him of his professional obligation to make the shot complete. Gilbert would never again double anyone of a different race.

This author worked as a grip on this show. Some of Murphy's makeup changes took hours, so the working crew members (grips, electricians, etc.) could walk around Universal's park freely. So did Murphy, in character as Granny Gump. Crossing the park from wardrobe to stage in the floral print nightgown, the comedian propositioned gawkers. Pulling the hem of his flannel gown, Eddie would effect Granny's scratchy voice while muttering curses, wriggling his knees and asking males for dates. Not one realized that Granny as a fake. Barely able to keep himself from laughing, Murphy would shuffle away from his gaping "victims."

Mick spent 11 broiling weeks in Canton, Mississippi, filming Joel Schumacher's *A Time to Kill*, then answered a call from helmer Thomas Carter with an offer to do Eddie Murphy's next big picture, Disney's *Metro*. He initially turned down the job owing to past experiences with Murphy, but acquiesced when Carter offered $5000 a day. As second unit director and stunt coordinator, Gilbert had a free hand to dream up an interesting chase involving a runaway San Francisco cable car.

Mick was partnered with longtime pal Don McCuaig to shoot the action sequences. They scouted locations along San Francisco's California Street imagining the master chase, to feature a runaway cable car smashing through a dozen automobiles while a life-and-death fight rages within. They were unable to use actual track lines in the city owing to the expense of closing major streets along the chase route, so a mock-up car was constructed with tracks painted on nearby Jones Street. Hydraulic aircraft brakes were installed so that it could stop on a dime.

Taking place on a series of steep hills, the cable car action sequence saw the vehicle running for nine blocks as Murphy and the heavy fistfight inside. The "blind driver" was hidden wheel man Joe Finnegan. The action coverage was first-rate.

A rollercoaster ride of crashing autos and cliffhanger fisticuffs, the sequence was hailed by *Hollywood Reporter* and *Variety* as one of the best-ever car chase–fights. But the public didn't buy Murphy as a hostage negotiator, no matter how serious he looked holding a telephone.

After stunt-coordinating Universal's *Liar Liar* with Jim Carrey, Gilbert received a message from Robert Redford. He was directing a film for which Mick was perfect: *The Horse Whisperer*. Redford was right. Mickey Gilbert was born to make that movie.

Based on real-life horse whisperer Butch Brannaman, the screenplay contained its share of challenges. Namely, a truck incident with a horse; then subsequent rehabilitation techniques as the filly was restored to health.

One difficult sequence involved a horse struck by a tractor trailer. The storyboards were less than spectacular. Mickey scouted location for the complicated shot: two girls horseback riding in freshly fallen snow, crossing a highway as one horse slips with a logging truck approaching; the semi slamming into the animal and rider. In Mammoth, California's, June Mountain area, he found the perfect spot: a secluded ski resort surrounded with pine forests, with a convenient spot where the truck could turn around. It was picture-postcard perfection. He sent photos to Redford via FedEx the same afternoon.

A phone call a couple of weeks later confirmed Gilbert's suspicion of something rotten in Denmark: The producer's associate hid the 4 × 6 glossies from the director and instead suggested a spot of his own, Sonora, California. Mickey was forced to accept the location despite having some issues with it.

Gilbert gave flip-over pro George Sack, Jr., the job of jackknifing the logging truck on cue. That footage was combined with multiple shots of the mare's loss of footing on ice; final impact was painlessly achieved via an animatronic horse built by Neil Trifunovich. Capable of believable equine action such as rearing on hind quarters, front legs pawing, tail flicking and head turns with living eyes, gaping jaws and clenching teeth, the mechanical colt was covered from forelock to tail in real hide.

The character of Judith was stunt-doubled by Shelly Boyle and the character of Grace by Julie Adair covering. Mickey ramrodded the road-edge horse missteps with the animal fighting for traction. Gilbert employed special wranglers to keep the colt afoot before camera rolled. Cowboys Michael Boyle and Rex Peterson assisted in the tricky business of tethering foot to stirrup for the saddle drag to come.

There was a camera providing the truck driver's point of view and another roadside looking past the horses with the semi bearing down on the terrified girls. Gilbert combined majestic beauty with the horrifying reality of imminent doom. The scene climaxes with the horse rearing as the jackknifed truck hits. Tight framing increased the feeling of impact, and the sound department's addition of a foley crunch made it truly sickening.

In the homestretch of his career, Gilbert signed for an eclectic mixture of projects starting with Disney's *My Favorite Martian* in the summer of '97. It featured Jeff Daniels in the Tim O'Hara role, Chris Lloyd as Uncle Martin, the original Martian Ray Walston as Armitan, and plenty of stunts. A tentpole picture for Disney, it was shot near Owens Valley Radio Observatory. A cantilevered crane platform was erected in a ravine to provide a "spaceship" flyover.

In 2000, Mickey signed with producer Brian Grazer to coordinate Eddie Murphy's *Nutty Professor 2: The Klumps* despite past rubs with the up-and-down star. He was responsible for stunt-training Janet Jackson's double Kelsee King-Devoreaux; with help from Murphy's stunt double Alan Oliney, she was schooled in everything from martial arts to driving. She went on coordination work on the television series *Half and Half* in 2002. Her arc continued with featured stunts in *The Italian Job* and doubling Jada Pinkett Smith in *The Matrix Reloaded*.

Now feeling his age, Mickey Gilbert began to awaken with more desire to tend his ranch than run off to distant places to make motion pictures. He referred more projects to others, including his son Troy. Mick was now in a mentoring-teaching phase of his career. But he did *National Security,* an action flick with Martin Lawrence and enough stunt talent for *three* pictures. It was coordinated by Mickey, Charlie Picerni and Joel Kramer, with Troy Gilbert also in the mix.

It contained car collisions, helicopter gags, fights, high falls and some water work. Gilbert had a cameo as a driving instructor. He also taught his son the finer points of stunt leadership like crew direction, producer relations and keeping others alive by being aware. Young Troy would soon be ramrodding his own big shows. Troy again followed in his dad's footsteps as Robert Redford's double in *The Old Man & the Gun*.

With three sons in the business and 1000 movies to his credit, Mickey felt that the family's beautiful Santa Barbara acreage was whispering to him that the stunt road should come to an end. Among his last hurrahs: second unit direction on Tom Shadyac's *Bruce Almighty*. The director tasked Gilbert with envisioning "God-sized" gags to play off Morgan Freeman's transfer of power to a mortal (Jim Carrey). After installing Troy and Tim Gilbert on his team, Mick coordinated the stunt crew of nearly 50 with the precision of a big band leader. From water-walks to Saleen S7 car gags with "Red Sea" parting of traffic, the stunt group worked as one the entire picture. Totally on his "A" game from first frame to last, Mickey Gilbert wrapped *Bruce Almighty* with little left to accomplish, and even less reason to explore. His physical blood, sweat and tears formula had given way to CGI and stars young enough to be his grandchildren.

As he devoted his new "personal time" to raising horses and romancing his wife, Mick was always a phone call away for family and professional friends seeking stunt advice. Without asking for or expecting credit, he would troubleshoot others' action-scene dilemmas and thereby stayed connected to what he adored: making movies.

Gilbert waxed poetic at interview's end: "When you get to a point where the audience *knows* shots are rendered by computers, it's time for folks who knew the smell of horse-sweat and high falls to return to civilian life."

Offering a final thought, Mickey laconically mused, "The more you watch CGI, the more you long for a simple saddle-drag."

Glossary

Action player, extra—Stunt term for day player stunt worker, usually a person who gets shot, run over, blown up, or otherwise dispatched in short order. Westerns and war pictures rely on such performers.

Air-bag—Inflated device used to reduce impact of high falls from 10 feet to 200 feet in height. "Bag-sizes" vary in fall abatement rigs as figured by their cubic footage and depth to accommodate the person(s) or object landing upon it.

Air ram—Hydraulic catapult, invented by Joe Finnegan, used to simulate cannon blasts with "flying" stunt performers.

Animatronics—The craft of building and or operating mechatronic puppets (lifelike to exacting detail) that double for real animals, from snakes and hamsters to horses and buffalo, in the making of motion pictures or television works to spare living animals from harm while filming.

Arrow-hit—Stunt craft involving the appearance of being shot by an arrow. Old school methodology entailed a wooden backboard hidden beneath wardrobe with a property-expert actually firing a real arrow (somewhat blunted) into the stunt player's back.

Arrow-hit fall—Standard stunt saddle-fall as arrows wound the rider and he or she falls from the saddle.

Arrow rig—Wooden backboard secreted beneath stunt player's costume allowing for real arrow hits without injury to the upper body.

Back-flip—(1) A backward somersault done in the air with arms and legs stretched out straight from a standing, riding, or sitting position. (2) A somersault over a standing railing. (3) A reverse somersault off a moving horse with heels over head in order of fall.

Balcony fall—A flip, fall, or other type of plummet from an elevated porch or balcony.

Balsa wood—Super-light wood material fashioned into break-away sets or furniture like chairs to facilitate a smashing effect for motion picture and stage while sparing the stunt-player injury of a heavier wood.

Batman effect—Super sized stunt coordination often involving big gags with hot camera work to capture the cutting edge motion picture action of the day.

Black-hatters—Bad guys in Westerns.

Blind riding—A rider is asleep in the saddle but the horse is so familiar with the route that it is self directed.

Blob launch—High upward trajectory on air-ram or ramp to sail the stunt-player in a steep but controlled arc, similar to a golfer's chip shot.

Bounce-pit rig—Berm of earth is built up to form an organic ramp to allow a rolling log to completely travel over the gap with a stunt player crouching safely beneath.

Britchen harness—Large strap system that supports a horse with a connected halter that encapsulates legs and under-belly into a portable package moved by an overhead crane.

Bronc riding—Rodeo skill of riding a bucking horse from a chute for a timed course of seconds.

Bucking bull—Wood constructed horse-dummy suspended between two vertical stanchions and rigged to move by wire and or ropes to practice bronc riding.

Bucking straps—A halter applied to a horse's loins causing it to buck wildly.

Buddy leap—A high fall or leap by two stunt performers together, requiring perfect coordination.

Bulldogging—Rodeo skill of leaping off a galloping horse upon roping a fleeing steer, then reducing the steer by the horns via head-lock twist to subdue and rope-tie three of the animal's legs while on its back.

Bumped—Being purposely struck by way of collision by mounted riders with those on or off horses while filming stunts.

Bump(s)—Pay incentive and or increment of additional payment given stunt players for additional takes of a given stunt.

Burn specialist—Stunt player with the highest level of fire experience and expertise in employing partial or full-body burns in special effects on a motion picture set or live stage.

Butkus tackle—Fabled middle linebacker for the NFL's Chicago Bears, Richard Marvin Butkus was an eight-time Pro Bowl member and Hall of Fame football player known for savage hits on opposing running backs during his playing years, from 1965 to 1973. Remembered for reducing the occasional half-back to a quivering heap of bones limping back to the huddle, a "Butkus tackle" was often open-field with the driving legs of the tackler pounding the ball-carrier into the ground for good measure, accompanied by a series of vicious growls and snarls using the ball carrier's name to eliminate any chance of accidental identity.

Buy the farm—To be fatally injured in the process of doing a stunt.

Cable-controlled—Stunt mechanics usually rigged to a harness or object with stunt performers attached: the release of most gags is performed "by wire" and therefore articulated (released, tethered, or controlled) remotely by another stunt person.

Cable-jerk—Violent wrenching of stunt player from a standing or horseback position, as though shot, via a cable rigged under costume and pulled by a second source outside camera frame.

Car to car transfer—The movement of a stunt player from one moving automobile to another without slowing down.

Catcher rig—Structurally reinforced metal basket approximately 10 by 10 feet square employed for radical high-fall arrest (often used on cliffs or high buildings where nothing else can be rigged).

Catch pen—Corralled area where cattle or horses are temporarily held and or separated for movement.

Central Casting—Original Hollywood entertainment industry casting bureau, which opened in 1926 and was originally located in the Hollywood & Western Building in Hollywood. Today has offices in several cities.

Centrifugal force—An inertial force acting with energy on a body moving around a center, directing it outward from the axis.

Cheating perspective—Photographic principle by which foreground objects and figures can be made to seem closer, taller, broader, shorter, farther-away, or slimmer when incorporating lens selection, lighting, and or specific sets in the making of motion pictures or teleplays.

Chitwood, Joie—Race-car driver who became a master of stunt-gags with his Denison,

Texas–based Joie Chitwood Thrill Show beginning in the 1940s. Capable of driving vehicles on two wheels pitched up on one side.

Chopper snatch—Moving transition in which a helicopter "swoops-down" to pick up a stunt player who boards quickly via the landing skids.

Click-clack—Stunt sword fighting.

Continuous dismount—Riding half in and half out of saddle while neither dismounting nor settling back into the saddle in the course of action like fighting or shooting.

Cork bomb—A special effects explosive mortar device, fixed or floating, which replicates dynamite type blasts with limited, controlled destruction to set or subject.

Cowboy crew—Members of a stunt team focusing on all things equestrian with expertise in roping, saddle falls, horse dismounts, and other techniques through actual experience in the cowboy craft as ranch hands or rodeo jocks.

Decelerator—Invented by stunt legend Dar Robinson, a mechanical flywheeled mechanism employing dragline cables with a huge circular gimbal that incorporated remote-controlled friction brakes allowing a stunt performer to vertically free-fall (from buildings or other high points) while being filmed from above without a telltale air-bag showing in the camera frame below.

Deep focus—Cinematic art of holding focus with a long lens on far away subjects as they slowly move forward. A famous example is the Super Panavision 70 footage of Omar Sharif coming from the far-off desert with elongated vertical lines shimmering in the searing desert heat, captured by Freddie Young in 1962's *Lawrence of Arabia*.

Dive-under—Stunt move to leap beneath a rolling object, falling tree, hurtling log or other hazard utilizing an under-pit to safeguard the player from crushing injury.

Down and dirty—Stuntman's reference to the simplest type of action performance without all the bells and whistles of a more extravagant presentation—simple, old-school, without pretense.

Drifting—Automotive term to describe aggressively driving (or racing) in a continuous, controlled skid sideways through a turn.

Drop chute—Large wooden platform rigged over a body of water or dump tank that safely "drops" a horse into the water by way of a set of big, hinged floor joists that open on cue.

Dutching camera—A purposely crooked framing of camera to induce a feeling of confusion in the viewer.

Elevated pommel vault—Gymnastic exercise employing leather pommel rig with trampoline or spring board to increase speed and height of move.

Empty cardboard boxes—Standard fall padding for medium falls and stunt gags going into the late 1960s when inflatable air-bags came into use.

Extra action-player—"Off the streets" hires (with little or no practical stunt movie experience) employed by production companies (producers) primarily to crew movie fights. Often rough-guy brawlers with boxing, military, or street skills, they were an uncontrolled lot whose time ended with the formation of the Stuntmen's Association in 1961.

Extreme high fall—An untethered vertical drop from a building, helicopter, bridge or other highly elevated point. Whether landing into a net, sofa, airbag, or water, all falls are high falls by stunt classification.

Fireman—Stunt personnel assigned to provide safety for burn gags. Often in control of putting out the flames.

Flip-ramp—A ramp used primarily to turn cars over at fast speed for motion picture stunts, typically approximately 10–15 feet long and reaching 3–6 feet in height.

Glossary

Flop over—A move in which a shot but still riding stunt-player assumes a forward posture over the horse's neck while loosely remaining in saddle.

Flying W harness—A stunt harness of leather strapping used with a control cord to trip a galloping horse; see also **Running W**.

Forced tripping—Antiquated stunt method of tripping a galloping horse by use of ground-ropes and or cowboy riding.

Forward fall (front-roll)—A riding maneuver in which a stunt player mimics being shot off a horse with a downward and forward lean past the horse's neck, continuing into a full tumble from saddle to the ground.

Frontal bump—Riding one horse into another.

Full body burn—Special effect action in which a stunt player is completely engulfed in flame for the length of the shot.

Funnel line—Corral fencing forming a "Y" built from wide to narrow at opening for concentrated movement of cattle or horses, producing a sluice effect with the heaviest concentration of animals passing before camera.

Galloping horse-fall—Stunt rider transition from saddle to ground while horse is in full stride.

Galloping horse-fall, rear flip off—Stunt rider transition from saddle via reverse-somersault (over the horse's flank) into the ground as though shot, whacked, or otherwise removed from the mount while in full stride.

Gun-blast jerk—Simulation of being pulled backwards rapidly off a saddled horse, as though hit by a shotgun or large-bore pistol blast. The rider is violently wrenched via cable (rigged beneath costume).

High fallers—General term for stunt folks who handle falling from great height such as 60 feet and above.

High-priced talent—Reference to actor, animal, or any property that works for the highest contract in the motion picture world. Also known as "A" listers. Often meant as a derogatory profile: "high priced talent" is a warning verb to cast and crew alike to tread carefully when approaching.

Hobbling—Temporary tying two of a horse's legs together to retard forward movement.

Holding pen—A fenced in corral (generally of split rail construction) for protecting livestock on ranch and back country locations.

Hollywood brawlers—Amateur "action-extras" employed by the studios for fight scenes in Westerns throughout the 1950s.

Horse fall—Any type of horse-stunt where the rider is removed from the saddle while in motion.

Horse to horse transfer—Moving or transferring from one moving horse to another without stopping or slowing.

Human ladder gag—Physical stunt involving three or more players forming a vertical ladder via standing upon each other's shoulders (with a wide base of two or more folks supporting the structure), providing a "hero" performer skyward rungs of thighs and arms on which to climb.

In and out—Quick stunt job. Short duration, one day only.

Inflatable air-bag—Square landing bladder constructed of specialized nylon and filled with air, of various dimensions and thicknesses (20 feet by 20 feet with a six foot side-wall is routine). Provides impact-reduced "soft landings" from great heights of free-fall.

Inverted parabolic arch—A path like that of a cannon shot, golf chip shot from sand, or vehicle launched from a ramp: low to high to low in trajectory.

Ironing boards—Hidden planks rigged to a horse's harness in a six-horse team to facilitate horse to horse transfers as safe walking planks for the stunt player.

Jerk—Pulling effect for "blowing" a victim off his feet or yanking a mounted rider out of the saddle from behind as though shot, utilizing a cable pulled by a grip and removed from sight in post.

Juggler's cradle—Medieval circus mechanism constructed of a stout wooden pole (15 feet high) with a 24-inch bowed sitting bar bolted to its top forming a crow's nest for performers to climb and do feats of aerial gymnastics. Held up by two strong assistants, the cradle rig was usually part of a troupe act which played the streets to the amusement of gathered crowds, who then threw them money.

Log-gag, run-away—Use of large flaming "tapers" rolled downhill toward stunt players, such as in *Spartacus* (1960) and *How the West Was Won* (1963).

Log rollover—Dynamic location stunt incorporating fast moving felled trees (logs), as they roll over victims. Using trenches with berms of soil bulldozed before them (creating a lift ramp for the deadly trees to impact and fly over), the stunt requires great care.

Low budget quickie—Film produced by smaller producer or big studio going cheap with none of the tools of a major production. From sparse catering to forced calls and all night shoots to minimal equipment, conditions are difficult and pay is generally low.

Marine training—A level of personal proficiency effected by the United States Marine Corps that teaches and instills such skills as hand to hand fighting, esprit de corps, unit preservation, and overall intensity of training beyond that of other military branches .

Mechanic—Horse-fall expert with wide variety of ways to fall from saddle.

Milkman sleep schedules—Reference to working shifts of Hollywood film crews that require rising before dawn as sun-up is often the first shot of the day.

Mini trampoline—Smallish, portable, low-slung trampoline with tiltable base allowing for horizontal flight as well as forward boost in a concealable size.

Multi-link communication—The use of radio microphone devices (walkie talkie) to keep in contact with several separate but integrated departments working on the same film; e.g., a helicopter pilot on a closed link with the director and a special effects person dispersing cork-bomb explosive devices on live location. The use of multi-link radios allows for vital departments to give cues while still providing access to the entire crew's radio channels on demand.

Peckinpah violence—Named for director Sam Peckinpah, a high energy, stamped in blood, graphic brand of violence with slow-motion details intertwined with the personal agony of the victim played against the cold reality of the shooter, elongating combat into a hyper-extended ballet of death.

Pelican connector—Steel ring and cotter pin actuator welded to steel plate for Running W workings.

Plane ticket home—Euphemism for dismissal from a movie project, usually accompanied by "Pack your stuff and catch a van outta here."

Pony Express mount—Leaping onto a running horse (mid trot) before one lands in the saddle and settles into the ride as the horse gains speed.

Powder man—Special effects explosives expert capable of setting various types of charges for motion pictures while keeping crew and talent safe during the process.

Pratfall—A staged tumble or trip, usually onto one's buttocks (often for comedic use), while acting for stage or film. Taken from burlesque or vaudeville theatre.

Primacord—A brand of detonating cord used in blasting that explodes at a rate of 6400 m/s.

Prop-chase—The use of helicopter rotor blades to fly over a herd or object (controlling its movement with downdraft), while pushing it in a desired direction.

Ramp launch—Inclined portable roadway constructed of wood or steel and angled to produce a jump-effect (and or lift) with a moving automobile or motorcycle.

Ramrod—Unofficial movie set fixer; a person in charge of positively driving all crew members (stunts, grips, camera, etc.) to keep the pace moving forward while shooting a film. Sometimes there are multiple ramrods and mixtures of craft like stunt and grip or camera and UPM with ramrods of their own in each department.

Rear flip-off—Reverse somersault from saddle to ground by stunt rider enacting being shot or knocked from horse; see also **Rearward somersault**.

Rear projection—Motion picture process by which an image is projected on the back of a special translucent screen to be viewed from the front as it renders a perfect real-life diorama to be photographed with foreground elements such as pastoral hills, parched deserts, or cityscapes manifesting nearly seamless backgrounds.

Rearward somersault—Stunt player falling backwards from saddle (head over heels), as though shot; see also **Rear flip-off**.

Reverse blind fall—A high fall in which a stunt player (facing camera with back to open space) is unable to see the landing pad below owing to the back-first orientation of the stunt. It is necessary to launch oneself facing upwards throughout the fall (back toward the ground), hold the angle of descent and land accurately without benefit of ever seeing the bag below.

Roll cannon—A device made from a welded steel mortar tube that attaches through the underside of a vehicle to produce a controlled flip or roll by way of an explosive charge firing a wooden slug into the ground.

Roman style riding—Stunt player stands upright on the flanks of two abreast horses, controlling each by long halter strap reins.

Roof to roof leap—Stunt action with player jumping from one elevated rooftop to another, often captured in full-frame. Few if any precautions can be employed (like air-bags or harness) because they will show in the shot. Often occurs in a pursuit sequence with two or more combatants converging on the hero. Many near-misses, scraped knees and raw hands of stuntmen attest to the gag's requirement of focus to succeed.

Rotoscope—Special effects animation technique originally devised for transfer of newsreels (or other film footage) to existing stock to allow for manipulation. A portion of the existing print is cropped closer than shot. Its use in transition of old films to play on television screens is standard practice. The technique is often visible to viewers by wide-shots cropped to medium; many a "third cowboy" was cut from the shot owing to the process.

Running mount—Type of moving launch into saddle as horse and rider bolt as one: The cowboy places both hands on the saddle horn while sprinting several strides alongside the horse, then suddenly vaults into the saddle using forward momentum and inertia. The move is instantaneous, like an accelerating race car.

Running W—Rider controlled rig for front tripping horses that incorporates a hidden wire harness from saddle to foreleg and down to the hoof which folds the animal's foreleg beneath it while running.

Saddle fall (general)—Any fall from a horse (moving or not), where the rider leaves the saddle and hits the ground.

Saddle fall (running)—Any fall from a horse while galloping.

Saddle jerk—Any wire-controlled dismount from a mounted horse, simulating e.g. a rider being shot off or hit by an arrow, or blown off by an explosion.

Saddle somersault, reverse—Backwards dismount from horse with heels over head and the stunt player falling over the horse's flank, as if struck by a tree-branch while galloping or shot off by a high-powered gun.

Shoot offs—Various ways a stunt-player is shot from a horse while sitting, standing, running, or riding from the saddle.

Side fall—A lateral drop from a horse's saddle (either still or running) as though wounded.

Sidewalk fillers—Background extras on Westerns who walked in and out of scenes.

Single overhand grab—A pipe-grasp handhold technique employed by elite old-school stunt players during an elevated stunt, without the safety of an additional wire.

Six ways from Sunday—Favorite description of a violent death by hard-core helmer Sam Peckinpah, meaning to overdo; a frequent example involved multiple bullet hits to one stunt-player, sending his body into a dancing squib-hit orgy before crashing to the ground.

Spear strikes—Standard stunt saddle fall whereupon an aggressor uses a spear or long lance to fatally stab a mounted rider, producing a death fall.

Springboard—Trampoline-like device with foot-base and heavy spring to propel stunt players through space as though flying.

Squib, squib-hit—Special effects explosive device that replicates a bullet impact on human flesh by way of hidden make-up and or wardrobe sourced blood-packs, ignited by stuntman or by remote control.

Stair fall—Physical stunt involving a fall down stairs from a balcony or upper landing set piece. May involve multiple stairwells or flights of stairs, and be initiated by stabbing, gunshot, blow to the head, trip, push, or accidental fall. All require the trade trick of transition from step to step without faltering as well as landing with control of one's head.

Sticky landing—Dismount from moving or stationary object (car, horse, roof, etc.).

Stirrup drag—Specialized mounted stunt in which the rider's foot remains "stuck" in the saddle-stirrup, (after being shot or otherwise dispatched), and the wounded fellow is dragged by the horse as it runs out of frame.

Stirrup wire—Cable running from horse's hoof to rider for pulling Running W move.

Stunt mortar—Custom made platform with steel tube canister employing an explosive charge to simulate cannon or mortar hits to stunt personnel.

Superman gags—Stunt-driven trampoline launch or springboard-powered vertical leap through space that places the body in a "flying" horizontal position, like Superman in flight.

Superman style—Forward leap or jump with body in vertical alignment to ground while doing "camera friendly" action like tackling an adversary, "flying" head-first out of a window, or diving into a pool.

Sword punctures—Stabs to padded area of stunt players with blood-packs beneath costumes.

Tandem horse transfers—Moving from one galloping horse to another while side by side.

Teamster gags—Stunt work involving stage coaches, buckboards, and covered wagons as driven by qualified personnel.

Tentpole picture—Major, high-budget motion picture that is expected to earn a large profit, supporting the studio's production of other pictures with lesser earning potential.

Toe tapper—Device attached to Flying W rig that activates the trip mechanism controlled by the rider, through stirrup to boot.

Torso turn, mid-air—Gymnastic exercise and pommel horse routine used to build lateral strength and quickness of upper body; the stunt version came to be another tool to exit a horse when shot, or transition from one mount to another in mid-stride.

Train fall—Stunt description of any fall from a locomotive or train car, including subway gags, train robbers shot off roofs, and folks jumping from a train attempting to land on a galloping horse; all qualify as train falls.

Trampoline, double-angled—Pitch-adjustable steel frame with live springs covered by mesh skin; in effect two trampolines set at divergent angles, allowing for vertical expansion of live-action jumps from 6 feet to 20 feet (depending upon size of platform and distance of fall). Set in 30 degree pitched trajectories, multiple angled trampolines can be used in "ricochet tandem" to get Superman type flying results without harness or wires.

Transfers—Moving stunt from one object to another in motion; e.g., from car to car, horse to horse, or from aircraft to open bed truck.

Transition beneath a horse—Stunt rider maneuvering beneath a horse while in full gallop.

Trip—Fall of a stunt rider and horse, felled as though gun shot. *See also* **Trip wire**.

Trip wire—Low tech stunt device employed by pre-protocol wranglers to knock horses and cattle to the ground, making them appear to naturally trip over rough terrain during a stampede or to have been shot.

Tripping pit—Shallow earthen trench employed by wranglers to automatically trip horses or cattle for action stunts, primarily used before animal welfare was protected during motion picture production.

Tuck-flip—Forward frontal somersault (bending at the waist and thighs) while landing to shorten the flip-over move.

Two-handed trapeze grip—Safety grasp employed by stunt professionals whereupon one's palms face downward (thumbs facing each other), as fingers close together around a horizontal object, such as grabbing an elevated water pipe and hanging on while a vicious dog passes below.

Variable speed equation—Loren Janes' favorite tool for figuring time and distance of objects crossing paths such as trains, planes and moving cars: the rate at which two moving objects converge on a given course, with speed times distance divided by time accounting for exact points of intersection.

Water-dragging—Old time water-gag with two mounted heavies pulling a victim by ropes attached from saddles to his outstretched arms while their horses run through a shallow river or rocky stream bed, pulling the stunt-player violently behind.

Water shows—Summer family entertainment of the 1950s with high-diving exhibitions, swimming demonstrations, and audience challenges, including speed and duration competitions.

Index

Abbott, L.B. 142
ABC TV 13
Aberdeen Hotel 50
Above the Law (1988) 179
The Abyss (1989) 122
A.C. Cobra 161
accents 141
action horror 121
Adair, Julie 195
Addams, Nick 26
Advance to the Rear (1964) 40, 41
The Adventures of Jim Bowie (1956) 13
aerial gags 42
Aerospatiale helicopters 112; Gazelle 178; SA-330 111
Africa: Texas Style (1967) 134, 137
Africa U.S.A. 134, 135, 137
African Queen (1952) 158
African sharpshooters 137
After Midnight (2019) 191
Agoura Hills North Ranch 12
Air Force One 107
air ram 17, 96, 121, 141, 147, 181
airbag 63, 83, 97, 155, 179; landings 153
aircraft cable 182
Alabama Hills (Lone Pine, California) 15, 17, 29, 31, 149
The Alamo 12
Alamosa, Colorado 97
Albert, Eddie 13
Alberta, Canada 76
Albertson Ranch (Triunfo, California) 19
Aldrich, Robert 169, 170
Alexander, Jane 170
All About Eve (1951) 40
All the Marbles (1981) 171
Allegheny River Frontage 189
Allen, Irwin 97, 156
Almeria, Spain 151, 152, 157
Alonzo, John 98, 178
Alta, Utah 170
Altamont, California 163
Altman, Robert 13, 61
Alvarez Kelly (1966) 131, 132, 133, 138
The Amazing Panda Adventure (1995) 191, 192
Ambassador Hotel (Los Angeles, California) 124

American Consulate 95
American Humane Association 161
American International Pictures 166
American Sweetheart (2001) 125
Amurri, Franco 124
Anderson, Eddie "Rodchester" 37, 38
Anderson, Lloyd 142
Anderson, Michael 43, 44, 45
animals in productions 24, 25, 27, 123, 134, 135, 136, 137, 160, 169
Animas River Gorge (Durango, Colorado) 142, 143
animation 109
animatronics 161, 195
Annakin, Ken 24
Ansara, Michael 14
antique desk 149
Apollo 13 (1995) 193
Apone, Allan 122
Arapaho 147
archery 60
Archie 110
Argo, Victor 80
Arizona State Prison (Phoenix, Arizona) 171
Arkansas Jail Reformist 170
Arkoff, Samuel 166
"Armitan" (character) 195
Arnett, Jim 123, 144, 145, 146, 149
Arnold, Jack 16
Arnold, Newt 170
arrows 13, 29, 30, 73, 74, 77, 159, 160, 186
Arting, Fred 5
Ashby, Hal 163
Askins, Monroe 19
Astaire, Fred 156
Astoria, Oregon 119
Atlanta International Raceway 165
Atlantic Ocean 155
Attack (1956) 13, 61
Aykroyd, Dan 98

B-17s 35
Babcock, Billy 15, 35
Babich, Frank 64
Bachrach, Howard 176
Back to the Future (1985) 112
Backus, Jim 42, 96

Baer, Hanania 121
Baffin Island (Nunavut, Canada) 155
Bahamas 122
Bail, Chuck 161
Baker, Joe Don 82, 151
Baker, Oregon 72
Baker, Ox 107
Bakski, Ralph 109
Bakunas, A.J. 163
Balchowsky, Max 65
Bald Head Island, North Carolina 121
Ball, Lucille 154
The Ballad of Cable Hogue (1970) 147
Ballard, Lucien 44, 48, 139, 140, 159
balsa wood 179
Baltimore Black Theatre 171
bamboo viper 52
Bancroft, Anne 12
bank robbery 171
Barbeau, Adrianne 107
Barbour, Bruce 124
Bare, Richard 19
bareback riding 128, 160
barnstorming 156
Barringer, Danial 124
Barris, George 16
Barron, Allen 26
Barry, Gene 19
Barrymore, John 8
Bartica Airfield (Cuyuni-Mazaruni, Guyana) 81
Barty, Billy 121
Basehart, Richard 96
Bass, Bobby 100, 105
Bat Masterson (1958–1961) 19
Batman effect 189
Baton Rouge, Louisiana 131
batwing chaps 158
Bauer, Chris 163
Bauer, Frank 163
Baxley, Craig 99
Baxley, Paul 19, 21, 36, 38, 61, 64, 68, 69, 77, 80, 172
Bay Area 80
bayonets 186
Beau Geste (1966) 133
Bebermeyer, Pamela 89, 90, 92
Beechcraft C-18 39

205

Index

Beeson, Paul 135, 137
Behar, Kip 42
The Being (1983) 177
Bell, Peter 120
Belushi, John 98
Ben-Hur (1959) 19, 42, 134
Beneath the Planet of the Apes (1970) 149
bentonite 40
Bergman, Candice 157
Berman, Pando 9, 15, 48
Bernardo, Tony 100
Bernsen, Corbin 119
Berringer, Tom 97
"Best Cinematography" Oscar 21, 163
Best Men (1996) 125
Beverly Hills Cop (1984) 111, 121
Big Bear Lake, California 72
The Big Brawl (1980) 107
Big Shots (1987) 177
Big Sky Ranch (Simi Valley, California) 83
The Big Valley (1965–1969) 174
Billings, Montana 73, 86
Billy the Kid 184
The Birds (1963) 97
Bishop, California 84
Bisoglio, Val 80
Black, Terry 121
black-and-white rotoscope 109
"Black Tigers" 94
Blackboard Jungle (1955) 8, 15
blackface 38, 194
Blade 121
Blake, Robert 15
Blangsted, Folmar 36
Blazing Saddles (1974) 81, 154, 162
blind backwards fall 179
blizzard conditions 116
blob launch 165
blow-offs 181
Blue Desert (1991) 122
Blue Thunder (1983) 177, 178
The Blues Brothers (1980) 170
boat chases 189
Bob's Country Bunker 170
Bochco, Steven 119
Bogart, Humphrey DeForest 158, 183
Bogdanovich, Peter 77
bolas 161
Bonanza (1959–1973) 82, 161
Bonaventure Hotel, Los Angeles 124
Bond's Aston Martin 175
Bonneville Dam (Portland, Oregon) 119
Borgnine, Earnest 19, 107, 139
Boride Mines (Whittier, California) 121
Boss, May 81, 98, 108, 121, 125, 175
The Boston Strangler (1968) 153
Boston Whaler 192
Bottoms, Timothy 155
Bouillet, George 165
bounce pit rig 149
Bound for Glory (1976) 163

Bovee, Brad 110
bowie knife 120
Boy Scouts 5
Boyle, Michael 195
Boyle, Peter 89, 95, 110
Boyle, Shelly 195
Bradley, Dan 121, 122
Brady, Buff 128
Brady, John 147
Braga, Sonia 125
Brahma bulls 136, 171
Branch Brothers 100
Brando, Marlon 87
Brannaman, Butch 194
Breakheart Pass (1976) 159
Brennan, Walter 28
Brenner, Yul 22, 36
Brest, Martin 111
Bridges, Jeff 91, 179
Bridges, Jimmy 109
bridle 168
Britchen harness 182
"British Colonel Munro" (character) 186
British Redcoats 96
British West Indies 23, 24
Broken Arrow (1956) 14, 15
Brolin, James 42
bronc riding 5, 127, 128, 150, 151, 168, 171
Bronson, Charles 19, 22, 61, 151, 152, 159
Bronson Canyon Cave (Los Angeles, California) 109
Bronze Stars 36, 49
Brooks, Mel 81, 154
Brooks, Richard 9
Brown, George Stanford 96, 171
Brown, Jim 61
Brown, Jophery C. 89, 90, 92, 123
Brown-Bess infantry rifle 96
Browning automatic rifle 52
Brubaker (1980) 170
Brubaker, Jim "Mean Jim" 193, 194
Brubaker, Tony 126
Bruce Almighty (2003) 196
Bruckheimer, Jerry 111
Bruebaker, James D. 184
Brynner, Yul 36, 85
The Buccaneer (1958) 16
Buck (dog) 88, 115
buckboard 12, 17, 29, 31, 77, 89
Buckle, Ken 25
Bud and Otto 110
buddy leap 142
"Buddy Love" (character) 193
buffalo 27, 161; gags 159; hunt sequence 161
Buffalo Bill Wild West Show 128
building-to-building leap 102
Bujold, Genevieve 89
bull riding 150
bulldogging 128
bullet-hit squibs 189
Bullitt (1968) 65, 77, 80, 112, 189
bumps 21, 25, 65
Burbank, California 72, 96, 99, 133, 142

Burgess, Don 116
Burn-Jell 98
Burnett, Steven "Steve" 64, 154, 156
Burns, Bobby 123, 126
Burroughs, Edgar Rice 5
Burrows, Brian 123, 185
Burton, Hal 125
Burum, Stephan 123
Busby Berkley Dancers 81
Busey, Gary 161
Butch and Sundance: The Early Years (1979) 96
Butch Cassidy and the Sundance Kid (1969) 141, 144, 145, 146
Butkus Tackle 42
Butler, William 87
Butler Aviation 39
Butte, Montana 117
Buttercup Valley (Yuma, Arizona) 133

Cabeen, Boyd 72
cable jerk 45
cactus 33
Cadillac 39, 172; convertibles 77, 78, 174
Cage, Nicolas 177
Cain, Dean 125
Caine, Michael 97
Calabasas, California 63
calculus 7
calder 88
calf-roping 128
Calhern, Louis 9
California Gold Rush 27
California Institute of Technology (Cal-Tech) 5
California Polytechnic State University (Cal-Poly) 7
California Street (San Francisco, California) 194
Call, Ed 82
The Call of the Wild (1972) 88, 123
calves 5, 160
Camaro 161
Camas Prairie Railroad (Lewiston, Idaho) 159
Cambridge, England 35
Camelot (1967) 59
cameras 31, 42, 43, 70, 182, 184; operators 170; positions 139, 191
Cameron, James 122, 124
Camp Pendleton 7
cancer 100
Candy, John 98
Cannon, Dyan 19
cannonballs 132, 181
Canoga Park, California 177
Canutt, Joe 60, 63, 72, 81, 139
Canutt, Tap 13, 60, 139
Canutt, Yakima 19, 21, 23, 24, 30, 60, 159
"canyon stew" 10
Cape Fear (1962) 42
Capo, Gary 193
Captain Bligh 139
capture nets 21

Index

car crashes 119
car races 161
car-to-car transfer 161
carabiners 120
cardboard cutouts 163
Carpenter, John 107
The Carpetbaggers (novel) 48
Carradine, David 163
Carrey, Jim 194
Carson, Fred 15
cart wrangler 167
Carter, Thomas 194
Caruso, Fred 183
Casey, Bernie 153
Casino (1995) 124
Casino, John 116
Cassidy, Butch 97, 145
Castle Ranch "Shea's Lodge" (Bakersfield, California) 19
castles 166, 167
Cat Ballou (1965) 68, 82, 154
Catalina Island, California 6, 57, 94
catamaran 192
catch-pen 160
catcher rig 187
Catching, Bill 47, 172, 174, 175
Cattle Association Party 98
cattle drive sequence 185
catwalks 117, 126
cavalryman roles 15, 73, 159
CBS TV 15
Central Casting 130
centrifugal force 161, 162, 174, 193
CGI 118, 196
chainsaws 149
Chamberlain, Richard 97
Chan, Jackie 107
Chandler, Jeff 17
Chandler, John Davis 72
Chaney, Lon 141
Chaney, Norman 119
Channel Road (Santa Monica, California) 111
Chapelle, Dave 123
Chapman, Graham 110
Charriere, Henri 81
Chase, Chevy 120
chateau set 61
Cherokee Nuclear Power Plant 122
Chevrolet 10, 16
Cheyenne Autumn (1964) 41
Cheyennes 41, 42, 73, 77, 147
Chiang Kai-Shek 50
Chicago, Illinois 99
Chimney Rock Park, North Carolina 187
chimpanzees 135
China 50
China Light Mission School 52
Chinese dragon 78
Chingachgook 188
"Chino" (character) 152
Chino (1976) 151, 157,
Chong, Tommy 110
chopper snatch 174
C.H.U.D. II (1989) 121

Chupaderos, Mexico 43
church steeple explosion 70
Churubusco Studios (Churubusco, Mexico) 22
The Cincinnati Kid (1965) 43
Circle of Power (1981) 171
The Cisco Kid (1950–1956) 10
Citizen Kane (1941) 192
City Slickers (1991) 185
City Slickers II (1994) 191
City View Apartments (Los Angeles, California) 22
"The Civil War" (episode) 27
CL Ranch (Alberta, Canada) 148
Clarence the Cross-Eyed Lion (1965) 134
Clark, Earl 145
Clark, Roydon 14, 17, 77, 125
Cleese, John 110
Cleopatra (1963) 27
Cleopatra Jones (1973) 153
Cleveland Dam (British Columbia, Canada) 183
click-clack 186
cliffhangers 117, 194
Close, Glenn 179
close-quarters gunfire 187
Clothier, William 40
Clouse, Robert 107
clubs 109, 115, 121, 186
Cobb, Lee J. 27
Coburn, James 22, 26, 184
Cody, Iron Eyes 52
Cold War 15, 42
"Coleman" (character) 50, 51
Coleman, Ben 176
Colorado 142
Colorado P.I. (1978) 164
Colorado River 42
Colt .45 (1957) 128
Colt M1911 141
Colton, California 122
Columbia Pictures 26, 98, 171; Burbank Ranch 170
Columbia River Gorge, Oregon 119, 149
Combs, Gary 61, 77, 98, 99, 105, 139
comedic stunts 68
comedic Western 72
coming-of-age stories 165, 177
compression-ramp technology 176
computer-animated video 188
computer scientist 82
The Concord...Airport '79 (1979) 170
Confederate Beefsteak Raid (1864) 132
Confederate soldiers 13, 132; colonels 146
Connery, Sean 19, 95, 157, 158
Connors, Chuck 137
Continental Divide, Colorado 164
continuous dismount 73
control harness 159
controlled flight 165
Convict Lake Work Camp 50

Coogan, Jackie 16
Coogan's Bluff (1968) 64
Cooper, Gary 13
Cooper, Jackie 26
Coos Bay, Oregon 127
"Cora" (character) 188
Coral Gables, Florida 184
Corbin, Barry 171
Corey, Jeff 97
Corey, Phil 106
cork bombs 158
Cork County, Ireland 95
Corman, Julie 124
Corriganville Ranch (Simi Valley, California) 15, 19
Cortez, Stanley 17
Corvette 193; convertible 161
Cossack 36
Costner, Kevin 161, 192
Cottonwood, California 26
Couch, Bill 54, 55, 60, 91, 133
Couch, Chuck 53, 54, 55, 58, 60, 61, 133
counterweight 78, 172
Coupe De Ville (1990) 182, 184
Courtney, Chuck 24, 25
Cowboy in Africa (1967) 137
cowboys 131, 134, 162, 169, 185
Cox, Monty 176, 177
Cracking Up (1985) 166
Crane Beach (Ipswich, Massachusetts) 64
cranes 69, 143, 182, 193; cantilevered platform 195
Crawford, Michael 72
Creach, Everett 133
Creber, William 63
Creed, Roger 168
Crendon, John 35
Crenna, Richard 42, 51, 52
Crichton, Michael 95, 153
Crlenkovich, Helen 6, 7
Crockett, Davey 12
Cronenberg, David 110
Cronenweth, Jordan 145
Crow roles 73, 77, 147
Crystal, Billy 185, 191
Cundley, Dean 107, 109
Curtis, Howard 143, 153, 156
Curtis, Tony 36
Custer, Gen. George Armstrong 147
Cypher, Jon 121

Dafoe, William 122
Daheim, John 35, 77, 83, 155
dam breaking sequence 155
Damski, Mel 110
Dances with Wolves (1990) 161, 192
Daniels, Jeff 195
Darby O'Gill & the Little People (1959) 19
Darin, Bobby 26
Davenport, Bob 35
Davidson, Steven 120
Davis, Andrew 179
Davis, Bud 86
Day, Doris 39

Dayton, Nevada 35
DC-3 12, 43, 72
Dead Heat (1988) 121
The Dead Zone (1983) 110
Deadrick, Vince, Jr. 125
Deadrick, Vince, Sr. 26, 111
DeAlessandro, Mark 112
Death of a Gunfighter (1969) 132, 138
Death of a Salesman (1949) 171
Death Valley Days (1952) 128
Death Valley National Park, California 37
decelerators 182, 183
deep-core rig 122
De Havilland Tigermoth 156
De Laurentiis, Dino 110, 151
De Longis, Anthony 121
DeLorean 112
Del Ruth, Thomas 145
DeLuise, Dom 163
De Mille, Cecil B 13, 16
De Niro, Robert 183
Denver International Airport 164
Der Kaag, Paul (rafter) 120
descender rig 193
Devis, James 183
DeVito, Danny 119, 123, 163
Dexter, Brad 15, 22
Dial, Dick 61
dialogue coaches 139
Dick, Andy 125
Dillman, Bradford 97
Dimitri, Nick 77, 80, 82
The Dirty Dozen (1967) 61, 169
Dirty Harry (1971) 64, 80
Disney, Walt 19, 23
Disney Studios 43, 195
Disney's Golden Oaks Ranch, California 36
ditch turn 165
Dixie Dynamite (1976) 86
Dmytryk, Edward 128, 132
Dobbins, Bennie 155, 156
Dobson, Tamara 153
Dr. Zhivago (1965) 116
Dodge 16, 161
Doff, Red 26
The Don Is Dead (1973) 80, 153
Donno, Eddie 111, 161
"Doodlebug" (character) 153
Dooling, Lucinda 107
"Dot, Flo and Dick" (act) 171
Doucette, John 43, 52
Douglas, Kirk 19, 42
Douglas, Michael 80
Douglas, Paul 17
Dove, Phil (canoeist) 120
Dragon Fly (2002) 191
Dragon Parade 79
drawbridge 166
dressage folks 154
drifting 164
Drilling, British 186
drive-in 165
drivers 139
drop chute 170
drowning 109

drugs 164
Drunken Monkey Kung Fu 186
dry-suits 183
Dublin Station, Ireland 95
The Duke 158
The Dukes of Hazzard (1979–1985) 108
Dunaway, Faye 156
Dunne, Joe 167
Duran, Larry 22
Durango, Colorado 77, 145, 185
Durango, Mexico 139, 164; airport 43; plate 143
Durock, Dick 82, 97, 109
Duvall, Robert 149
Dye, Dale 186
dynamite 149, 157

E Gee La Ha Da 77
Eakins, Bud 36, 65, 86, 98
earthen bridge sequence 133
Earthquake (1974) 83, 155, 156
Eastwood, Clint 64, 72, 123, 149, 164
Eaves Movie Ranch (Santa Fe, New Mexico) 97, 147, 184
Ebsen, Buddy 13
Echo Park, California 114
Edwards, Anthony 177
Edwards, Blake 39
El Guapo 120
El Paso, Texas 52, 80
Elam, Jack 14
Elder, Patty 78
The Electric Horseman (1979) 168
elevated pommel-vault 133
Elias, Louie 42, 53, 139, 140
Ellis, Bob 110
Elmore, Richard 26
Epper, Garry 123
Epper, Jeannie 73
Epper, Stephanie 154
Epper, Tony 139
Epper, Tony, Jr. 114
"Ernie" (character) 193
"Errol Flynn" landings 110
Escape from New York (1981) 107
Eskimo Tribe, Inuit (Nunatsiarmiut) 155
Essequibo River, Guyana 81
Estevez, Emillio 110, 184
"Etta Place" (character) 146
"Eula Goodnight" (character) 158
Evans, Robert 95
Every Which Way but Loose (1978) 164
Everything's Ducky (1961) 26
explosions 12, 17, 57, 71, 96, 111, 113, 119, 146, 149, 157, 181, 187
express office shootout 140
Eye of the Tiger (1986) 177
eye patches 141
eyelashes 161

face-slapping 156
Fairbanks, Douglas 8
The Fall Guy (1981–1986) 108, 171, 172, 173, 174; official truck 175

falls 12, 14, 15, 18, 19, 22, 35, 40, 42, 47, 59, 83, 95, 97, 98, 108, 114, 125, 131, 132, 138, 184; high falls 142, 147, 155, 163, 172, 181, 195, 196; off horses 26, 30, 41, 43, 82, 96, 121, 133, 154, 157, 159, 170
false teeth 141
Fapp, Daniel 67
Farfan, Fredrico 111
Fargo, James 164
Farnsworth, Richard 15, 72, 77, 81, 111
The Fast and the Furious (2001) 164
Fast Times at Ridgemont High (1982) 177
The Fastest Guitar Alive (1967) 52
Faulkner, Lee 63, 64, 72
Faulkner, Ralph 55
Fawcett, Farrah 174
The F.B.I. (1965–1974) 14, 46, 47
Federales 141, 181
Feitstans, Buzz 111
Feldman, Phil 141
fencing 21, 60
Ferrari 161
ferris wheel stunt 98
Fields, Freddie 99
Fifer, John 122
fight stunts 26, 64, 77, 80, 119, 153, 154, 159, 163, 172, 186, ; with fists 39, 98, 107, 108, 163, 177, 185, 194
Figure Eight Island, North Carolina 121
filly 152, 194
Filoon, Mike 122
Finnegan, Joe (teamster) 141, 191, 194
Fire and Ice (1983) 109, 110, 120
fire-hose effect 160
fireballs 106, 111, 145
The First Great Train Robbery (1979) 95
The First Texan (1956) 12
Fisher, Tommy (special effects supervisor) 185
Fisk, Jack 108
F.I.S.T. (1978) 94, 95
Fix, Paul 45
Flaming Star (1960) 25
flare guns 120, 189
Fleischer, Richard 80, 153
flintlocks 186
flips: backward 58, 147, 153, 154, 170; off rear 159; over banister 14; over railing 108; with ramp 155; reverse dismount 41; with tuck 153
Flipper (1964–1967) 134
flop-overs 133
Flowers, A.D. 45, 83
fluid breathing sequence 122
flying circus 156
Flying W rig 36, 160; *see also* Running W
Flynn, Errol 59, 89
Foley crunch 195
Fonda, Henry 27, 97

Fonda, Jane 180
Forbes, Scott 13
forced tripping 157
Ford (vehicles) 166, 169, 172, 174
Ford, Glenn 8, 9, 40
Ford, Harrison 169
Ford, John 27, 32, 41, 42
Forrest, Frederick 87, 151
forward momentum (inertia) 161, 189
fox-hunt sequence 154
fractured coccyx 108
Fraker, William 65, 72, 98, 189
Francis, Anne 9, 77
Frank, Billy Butch (military consultant) 113
Frankenheimer, John 82
Frazee, Logan 83
Frazetta, Frank 109
Fredricks, Ellsworth 13
Freeman, Morgan 170, 196
Freiberg, Rick 124
The French Connection (1971) 80, 112
Friedman, Dave (stills photographer) 105, 145
Friendly Persuasion (1956) 13, 14
Fright Night (1985) 112
The Frisco Kid (1979) 154, 169
Fritz, Ford 26
From Hell to Texas (1958) 15
front rolls 157
Frost, Lee 86
The Fugitive (1993) 179
full-body burn 110
full-size pirate ship 123
Fuller, Clem 12
Furth, George 145
Fussen, Bavaria 35

G-force 138, 189
Gable, Clark 15
Gabriel, Roman 146
Gaffney, South Carolina 122
Gailbraith, Bruce 35
gal stunters 175
Garner, James 36, 77, 80
Garr, Teri 42
Garrett, Pat 184
garrote 64, 80, 153
Gary, Davis 164
"Gary Owen" battle hymn 148
Gatlin, Jerry 22, 77
Gaudi, Antoni 64
Gehrke, Tom (pilot/aerial) 111, 112
geldings 144, 166
The General (1926) 116
General Lee (car) 175
General Motors Co. (GMC) 172, 175, 176
George, Dan (chief) 148
"George Woodcock" (character) 145
German forces 157
"Geronimo" (character) 12
The Getaway (1972) 80
Ghost Ranch, New Mexico 185
G.I. Bill 7

Gibbs, Joe 148
Gilbert, Fred, Jr. 127
Gilbert, Frederick, Sr. 127
Gilbert, Jenavive 127
Gilbert, Lance 181, 184, 185, 187, 188, 189, 190, 192
Gilbert, Tim 173, 181, 185, 188, 189
Gilbert, Troy 181, 183, 184, 184, 185, 186, 188, 189, 190, 192, 195
Gilbert, Yvonne 180, 181
"Gilbert touch" 191
Gill, Andy 108, 121, 123
Gill, Jack 98, 123
The Gill Brothers 123
Gilligan's Island (1964–1967) 96
Gilroy, Frank 125
gimbals 156
giraffes 136, 137
Gittings, Al (underwater) 122
gladiators 21
Gleason, Jackie 39
Globus, Golan 114
Globus, Yoran 120
Goddard, Gary 121
The Godfather (1972) 80
Goin' South (1978) 95
Golan, Menahem 120
gold coins 140
gold heist 52
Goldblatt, Mark 121
The Golden Child (1986) 177
Golden Oak Ranch, Newhall, California 138
Goldstone, James 89
Goldstone Studios 120
The Good Guys and the Bad Guys (1969) 72
Good Guys Wear Black (1978) 94
Gordon, Leo 40
Gossett, Lou, Jr. 155
Goulding's Lodge, Monument Valley, Utah 42
"Grace" (character) 195
gradating light 122
Grade, Lew 96
The Graduate (1967) 63
Graham, Fred 27
Grand Junction, Colorado 164
"Grandma Klump" (character) 193, 194
Granger, Stewart 27
Grant's Pass, Oregon 28, 158
gravitational pull 161
Grazer, Brian 195
greased platforms 170
The Great Bank Robbery (1969) 66, 67, 68, 69
Great Britain 61
The Great Escape (1963) 35
Great Sand Dunes National Monument, Colorado 109
The Great Waldo Pepper (1975) 156
The Greatest Story Ever Told (1965) 36
Greed (1924) 17
Green, Nigel 135
Green Goblin 126
Greenwood, Mississippi 72

Gregory, James 43, 45
Greystone Mansion, Beverly Hills, California 126
Griffith, James 12
Griffith Park, Los Angeles, California 123
Griggs, Loyal 38, 43
grips 56, 139, 162
Grumman, Francis 109
Guardino, Harry 26
Guastini, Vincent (prosthetic makeup) 186
Guillerman, John 83, 93, 156
Gulf of Mexico 92
The Gumball Rally (1976) 161
gun-blast jerks 76
gunfights 184
The Guns of Navarone (1961) 42
Gunsmoke (1955–1975) 19, 161
Guthrie, Woodie 163
gypsy 132

Habberstad, Jeff 126
Hackett, Buddy 26
Hah-Ka-Nah (horse) 5, 76
Hairpiece, Huron 186
Hale, Alan, Jr. 41
Half and Half (2002) 195
Hall, Conrad 145
Halloween III: Season of the Witch (1982) 109
Halty, James 87
"Hambone" (character) 158
Hampton, Maj. Gen. Wade III (Confederate army) 132
Hancock, John 96
hand to hand combat 181
"Hank Stamper" (character) 149
Hard County (1981) 171
Hargitay, Mickey 16
Harlan, Russell 15
Harris, Ed 122
Harris, Richard 60, 159, 160
Harry and the Hendersons (1987) 177
"Harry Tasker" (character) 124
Harthorn, Tony 137
Hartman, Elizabeth 48
Harvey, Orwin 123, 164
Haskin, Byron 12
Hassett, Marilyn 84
Hatari (1962) 134
Hathaway, Henry 27, 28, 43, 44, 48, 49
Hatswell, D.R.O. 133
Hauss, Harry (pilot) 111, 112, 116
Hawaii 192
"Hawk" (character) 158
"Hawkeye" (character) 188
hay wagon 172
Hayes, Isaac 107
Hayward, Chuck 40, 43, 77, 81, 133, 149, 169
H.B.O. 121
head-on runs 165
Hearst Castle, San Simeon, California 21
Heckerling, Amy 177

heifers 185
Helfer, Ralph 134
Helfer, Tori 134
helicopters (choppers) 111, 114, 115, 117, 155, 162, 176, 178; gags 195; play 174; transfer to trucks 137
Hell Is for Heroes (1961) 26
Hello Dolly (1969) 72
Helpern, David 121
Hepburn, Katharine 158
Herrington, Rowdy 188
Herron, Bob 14, 72, 82, 120, 133, 139
Hertfordshire, England 35
Heston, Charlton 63
Hewitt, Ted (railroad coordinator) 116
Heyes, Douglas 133
Heyward, Chuck 26
Hibbs, Jesse 12
Hice, Eddie 110
Hickman, Bill 65, 78
Hickory Nut Falls, Rutherford County, North Carolina 188
Hicks, Chuck 26, 108, 109, 114, 115
Hidalgo Santa Maria Regla's Canyon of the Prisms, Mexico 180
hidden ramp 164, 165, 190
High School Confidential (1958) 16
high speed chase 164
high-speed overtakes 161
high-speed passes 163, 164
Highway 202, Cascade Locks–Astoria, Oregon 119
Hill, George Roy 97, 139, 141, 142, 143, 149, 154, 156, 157
Hitchcock, Alfred 97
hobo camp 163
Hoch, Winton 19
Hock, Johnny 120
Hodges, Mike 82
Hoffa, Jimmy 95
Hoffman, Dustin 73, 75, 76, 77, 123, 148
Holblit, Greg 119
Holden, William 139, 156
"Holga" (character) 147
Holland, Tom 112
Holliman, Earl 43, 47
Hollywood Reporter magazine 194
Holt, Larry 97, 108, 123, 125
Hong, James 163
Honky Tonk Freeway (1981) 171
hooey 150
Hook (1991) 122
Hooker, Buddy Joe 81, 112, 163
"Hooper" (character) 164
Hooper (1978) 163, 172
Hope, Bob 131
Hopkins, Bo 139, 141
Hopper, Dennis 14, 16, 43
Horack, Peter 179, 180
horse-over-horse move 148
horse-to-horse transfers 163
The Horse Whisperer (1998) 194
horses 14, 28, 130, 135, 149, 150, 157, 169, 172, 181, 184, 186, 191

Horsley, Lee 108
Hoskins, Bob 123
hot-air balloons 68, 69
Housing Authority 101
Houston, John 35, 157, 158
How the West Was Won (1962–1963) 18, 27, 28, 29, 32, 33, 34, 40, 91
Howard, Ron 193
Howard, Ronald 137
Howard, Sandy 159, 160
Howell, Norman 193
Howitzers 133, 157, 166
Hubbard, Bud 141
Hudkins, John "Bear" 72, 132
Hudson, Rock 146
Hughes, Whitey 19, 139
Hulu handle 136
human ladder 54
human pyramid 60
Hume, Alan 114, 117
The Hunter (1980) 99, 100, 106
hunting sequences 159
Huron 186
Hutchins, William 14
Hutchinson, William 61
Hutton, Ed 145
hydraulic brakes 194
Hyman, Kenneth 61
Hymes, Gary 122

Ibbetson, Arthur 166
Ice Station Zebra (1968) 67
Idle, Eric 110
Imada, Jeff 109
In Harm's Way (1965) 42
In the Line of Fire (1993) 123
Indian Dunes, Valencia, California 185
invasion paranoia 98
inverse action 180
invisible escape sequence 148
Inyo National Forrest (Bishop, California) 48, 49
Irving, David 121
Irwin, John 119
Ishtar (1987) 192
Isleton, Oregon 163
The Italian Job (2003) 195
It's a Mad Mad Mad Mad World (1963) 37, 38
Iverson Ranch (Chatsworth, California) 13, 16, 19, 130
Iwo Jima 36

jack-knife 195
Jack the Bear (1993) 123
Jackson, Janet 195
Jackson, Jerry 88
Jackson, Terry 115, 117
Jackson Hole, Wyoming 88
Jacoby, Scott 165
Jaeckel, Richard 13, 61
Jaguar (car) 164, 172
Jailhouse Rock (1957) 15, 26
"James Bond" 164
Jamison, Jerry 96
Janeczek, Homer 26

Janes, Loren 103, 150, 156
Janss Conejo Ranch (Thousand Oaks, California) 12, 25, 40, 138
Japanese Gardens, Woodley Park (Van Nuys, California) 121
javelin 21
Jeanneau Advanced Technologies (Lagoon, France) 192
Jensen, Soren (pilot) 116
"Jesse Cole" (character) 49
Jewison, Norman 64, 95
Joe Kidd (1972) 149
"Joe Lefors" (character) 144
"Joey Chitwood" (character) 189
"John Chism" (character) 184
John Deere 151
John Goldfarb, Please Come Home (1965) 42
"Johnny Hooker" (character) 154
Johnson, Ben 19, 97, 139, 146, 151
Johnson, Don 96
Jones, Deacon 137
Jones, J. David (pilot) 68
Jones, James Earl 89
Jones, L.Q. 26, 139, 147
Jones, Melvin 109
judo 30, 61
juggler's cradle 56
jumps 154, 152, 174
Junction City Prison, Ohio 170
Junior Bonner (1972) 141, 149, 151
Jupiter's Darling (1955) 6, 7, 9, 15

Kane, Carol 163
Kane, Jim 149
Kasznar, Kurt 53
katana 83
Katt, William 97
Katz, Stephen M. 165
Kauai, Hawaii 91
Kaufman, Phil 155
Kavanagh, Hermine T. 19
Keaton, Buster 116
Keelung River, Taiwan 52
Keith, Brian 19, 49, 157
Keith, David 170
Kelly, David E. 125
Kelly, Gene 72
Kelly, Wallace W. dp
Kennedy, Burt 72
Kennedy, George 43, 44, 72
Kent, England 35
Kent County, Ireland 95
Kentucky long rifle 13, 96, 186
Kenya 134, 135, 136
Kerns, Hubie 94
Kerns, Hubie, Jr. 121
Kershner, Irwin 159
"The Kid" (nickname) 151, 196
The Killers (1946) 64
King-Devoreaux, Kelsee 195
King Kong (1976) 91
Kingi, Henry 123
The King's Pirate (1967) 53, 54, 57, 58, 59, 60, 80
Kinjite: Forbidden Subjects (1989) 180
Kinmont, Jill 84, 86

Kirk, Tommy 43
Kleven, Max 82, 84, 95, 107, 114, 115, 117, 125, 162
Kline, Richard 80, 153
knives 186; fights with 147; throwing 185
knocked unconscious 149
Knuckles, Paul 86, 153
Koenekamp, Fred 97, 156
Konchalovsky, Andrey 114, 115, 116, 117
Korman, Harvey 154
Koslo, Paul 149
Kotcheff, Ted 121
Kotto, Yaphet 170
Kovacs, Ernie 27
Kovacs, Laszlo 77, 97, 149
Kramer, Joel 124, 195
Kramer, Stanley 38
Krasner, Elliott 86
Krasner, Milton 40, 149
Krotz Springs, Louisiana 50
Kubrick, Stanley 21
Kulik, Buzz 99
Kurosawa, Akira 22

L.A. Law (1986–1994) 119
La Goma, Mexico 139
La Hood, Gary (canoeist) 120
Lake Cumberland (Clinton County, Kentucky) 27
Lake Piru, California 5
Lakes, Ken (jet boat) 120
Lakota Sioux 147
Lame Deer, Montana 73
Lancaster, Burt 15
Lancaster, California 99
Lancelot 60
lances 186
Land Rover 134
Landau, Martin 49
Landis, John 120, 170
Landon, Michael 16, 82
Lane, Charles 42
Lang, Charles (cinematographer) 22
Lang, Walter 35
Lange, Jessica 91, 94
La Plata Airport, Boulder, Colorado 142
Laramie (1959–1963) 11, 19
lariat 137, 185
Larson, Glen A. 108, 172, 174, 175
Las Vegas, Nevada 124, 125, 168
LaShelle, Joseph 31
Last Man Standing (1996) 191
The Last of the Mohicans (1992) 185, 188
Laszlo, Ernest 88
latex facial prosthesis 63
Lathrop, Philip "Phil" 43, 154
Laughlin, Frank 83
Laughlin, Tom 83, 84
launch ramp 46
LaVigne, Emile 36
Lawrence, Martin 195
Lawrence of Arabia (1962) 187
LAX 61, 120

leaden chaps 158
Lean, David 157, 181
leapfrog 144, 148
leaps 184
leather halter 134
LeBell, Gene 47, 82, 94, 107, 108, 109, 121, 123, 164, 179
Lee, Bruce 107
Legionnaires 133
LeMani, Tanya 60
Lemmon, Jack 125
Leonard, Terry 80, 81, 98, 108, 123, 125, 157, 158, 159, 160
Lerner, Fred 113
Lester, Richard 96
Levine, Joseph E. 48
Lewin, Al 6, 7
Lewin, George 6
Lewis, Geoffrey 157
Lewis, Jerry 16, 35, 193
Lewiston, Idaho 159
Liar, Liar (1997) 191, 194
Light, George 130
Lilley, Jack 82, 191
limousine 59, 134, 188
Lincoln 39, 134; convertible 128
Linson, Art 183
lions 134, 135, 136, 169, 176
Littieri, Al 80, 153
Little, Cleavon 154
Little Big Horn (Big Horn County, Montana) 147
Little Big Man (1970) 73, 75, 76, 147, 148
Little House on the Prairie (1974–1983) 82
Little Nikita (1988) 177
Lloyd, Chris 195
Loftin, Carey 38, 65, 66, 68, 80, 86, 110
log roll-over 25
Logan, Josh 15
Logan, Joshua 59, 72
Logan's Run (1976) 88
Lomax, Joe 168
Lone Pine, California 27
long rifles 186
The Longest Day (1962) 134
Lord Baltimore 144
Los Angeles 81, 96, 119, 150, 154, 159, 181, 193; downtown 178; eastern area 110; tags 150
Louise, Tina 72
Lovely but Deadly (1981) 107
Lovitz, John 191
Low, Warren 44
Lowery, Hunt 188
Lucas, Billy 124
Luce, Ami 60
Luke, Keye 121
Lumet, Sidney 179
Lundgren, Dolph 121
Lupino, Ida 151
Lykins, Ray 119
Lyons, Cliff 66, 68

MacArthur, James 23, 24
MacDonald, Joseph 52

MacDonald, Peter (aerial) 111
MacGraw, Ali 86, 95
machine guns 67, 111, 141, 153
Maclaine, Shirley 42
"Macmuid" (character) 42
Madison, Guy 96
"Madman" (character) 140
Mae West Vegas Stage Show 42
The Magnificent Seven (1960) 22, 26, 67
"Magua" (character) 186
Majors, Lee 108, 172, 174, 176, 177
Mako 52
Malden, Karl 28, 80
Maldonado, Bill 155
Malibu, California 46, 63, 83, 98, 121, 131
Malkovich, John 123
Malta 122
Mame (1974) 154
Mamet, David Alan (writer) 183
Mammoth, California 84
Mammoth Lakes (Mono County, California) 195
The Man from Uncle (1964–1968) 64
Man Trouble (1992) 123
Mangine, Joseph 108
Mann, Michael 185, 188
"Manny" (character) 114, 115, 117
Marine Corps 19, 67; 1st division 7; training 49
"Marshal Cogburn" (character) 158
Marshall, George 17, 27, 33
Marta, Jack 83
Martin, Dean 43, 44, 95
Martin, Pepper 82
Martin, Quinn 46, 164; productions 80
Martin, Steve 120
Martin, Strother 13, 139, 147
Marton, Andrew 134, 136
Marvin, Lee 13, 61, 68, 72, 149, 154
Mason, James 110
The Master Gunfighter (1975) 83, 84
Masters of the Universe (1987) 120
The Mating Game (1959) 17
The Matrix Reloaded (2003) 195
Matthews, Eddie 126
Maui Bay, Hawaii 81
May, Jodhi 187
Mayberry, Russ 96
McBride, Robert 159
McClarty, Gary 160, 170, 177
McClure, Doug 53, 56, 58, 80, 96, 133
McColm, Matt 180
McCord, Kent 42
McCrea, Joel 12
McCrostie, Hamish (rafter) 120
McCuaig, Don 191
McCuaig, Doug 193, 194
McDermott, Dylan 123
McDonald, Joe 36, 133
McEnroe, John 96
McGavin, Darren 121

McGregor, Roy (rear admiral) 15
McLaglen, Andrew 40, 139, 146
McLarty, Gary 133
Mclintock! (1963) 40
McMurry, Fred 97
McQueen, Steve 9, 15, 22, 26, 35, 36, 39, 48, 49, 50, 51, 52, 64, 65, 72, 80, 81, 83, 86, 98, 99, 100, 101, 102, 103, 104, 105, 150, 151, 156; Best and Last 98
mechanical animals 159, 171, 195
Medearis, Jim 98, 99
Media, Augustino (gypsy wrangler) 152
Mellor, William 38
Men at Work (1990) 185
Meredith, Burgess 80
Metro (1997) 193, 194
Metty, Russel 21
Metz, Rexford 149
Mexican soldier 43, 141, 147
Mexico 142, 147
Mexico City 180
Meyer's Manx Dune Buggy 64
MGM 7, 9, 15, 17, 67, 91, 157; casting books 61; studios 48; tunnels 64
Miami Vice (1984–1990) 179
Michaels, Lorne 120
midair torso turn 163
Midler, Bette 119
The Milagro Beanfield War (1988) 177
Milius, John 157
Millar, Henry (effects genius) 155
Miller, Charlie 189
Miller, Robin 114
Miller, Stuart 77
Mills, John 25, 135
Mineo, Sal 42
miniatures 118
Mirisch, Walter 14, 166
The Misfits (1961) 35
The Missouri Breaks (1976) 86, 123
Missouri River 87
Mitchell, Cameron 97
Mitchum, Robert 72
Moab, Utah 36, 38, 191
mock-up 165
Mohawk 186
Moio, John 97
Mojave Desert 99, 178
Mok, Harry 112
Money Play (1998) 125
Monkey Trouble (1994) 124
Monongahela River, Pennsylvania 188
Montrose, Colorado 28
Monty the Mustang 127
Monzetto, Hank 54, 60
Moore, Demi 183
Moore, Dudley 99
Moore, Michael 52, 154, 158, 159
Morales, Mexico 22
Moran, Dicky (key grip) 162
Moreno, Rita 19
Morgan, Bob 12, 91
Morgan, Harry 42

Morgan, John 159
Morgan, Red 43
The Morning After (1986) 179
Morocco 157
Morrow, Vic 9
mortar explosions 181
Mostel, Zero 68
motorcycles 35
Mount Baldy, California 7
Mount Washington, Pennsylvania 188
Mounties 163
Move Over Darling (1963) 39
MP-40 grease gun 61
Muller, Robby 110
Mullholland Canyon 10
Mulligan, Richard 73
multi-link communication 111; by radio 116
Mungai, Njoroge (M.D.) 137
murder 162
Murphy, Audie 12
Murphy, Eddie 111, 193, 194, 195
Murphy, Geoff 184
mustaches 141
Mustang (car) 35, 65, 166, 173
My Favorite Martian (1997) 195
Myopia Hunt Club (Long Island, New York) 64

Nairobi, East Africa 137
Nannuzzi, Armando 152
Nanyuki Airfield (Kenya, East Africa) 137
Napier, Charles 170
"Napo" (character) 110
Nardini, Tom 135, 137
narrow-gauge track 32, 145
Nastase, Illie 96
National Bank (Dublin, Ireland) 95
National Collegiate Championship 128
National Football League 16
National Security (2003) 195
Navajos 27, 36
Nazas River, Northern Mexico 141
Nazis 36
NBC Studios 64, 82
Nederlander, Ned 120
Needham, Hal 17, 19, 40, 68, 73, 81, 132, 133, 146, 147, 163, 172
Neilson, Leslie 133
Nelson, Craig T. 171
Nelson, Ralph 39
Nero, Franco 60
neutral density filter 57
Nevada Smith (1966) 48, 49, 50
New England 64
New Zealand 120
Newhart, Bob 26
Newman, Paul 97, 141, 142, 143, 144, 149, 156
Nichols, Kelly 92
Nichols, Mike 63
Nicholson, Jack 86, 87, 95, 123
"Nico Toscani" (character) 179
Nimoy, Leonard 15

1941 (1979) 98
99 and 44/100 % Dead (1974) 82
Nordberg, Jim 176
Norris, Chuck 94
North and South (1985) 113
North to Alaska (1960) 27
Notre Dame 42
Novak, Kim 68, 69
The Nutty Professor (1996) 193
The Nutty Professor 2 (2000) 195

Oates, Warren 139, 155
O'Brien, Hugh 77, 80, 134, 135, 136
Ogden, Morry 55
Ohio River 27
Old Gringo (1989) 180, 182
Old Gringo Rides 172
"Old Lodge-skins" 148
The Old Man & the Gun (2018) 196
Old Tucson, Arizona 40, 138
Oliney, Alan 162, 193, 195
Oliver, Bud 121
Olsen, Merlin 146
Olsson, Axel 156
Olympic Coliseum, Los Angeles, California 128, 129
Olympic trials 52, 127
Olympics (1936) 6
Olympics (1956) 21
The Omega Code (1999) 126
O'Murtin, Thomas 170
180-degree spin 193
O'Neal, Ryan 77, 78
Orbison, Roy 52
Orrison, Bob 160, 161
The Other Side of the Mountain (1975) 84
Our Winning Season (1978) 164
Out to Sea (1997) 125
Outer Limits (1963–1965) 80
outlaws 27, 32
Overbeck, Bob 28
Owens Valley Radio Observatory (Big Pine, California) 195

Pacific Coast Highway (Malibu, California) 174
Paducah County, Kentucky 27
Page, Arizona 38
Paint Your Wagon (1969) 72
Palance, Jack 13
Palen, Cole 35
palm to palm body lift 56
Palmdale, California 99, 122
Palmisano, Conrad 123
Panorama City, California 127
Papanickolas, Pete (grip) 31
Papillon (1973) 81
Paramount 72, 91, 95, 111, 134
Paramount Pond 143
Paramount Ranch (Agoura Hills, California) 19
Parke, Fess 26
Parsons, Phil 83
Parton, Regina 47
Parton, Regis 16
Parys, Steve 189

Pasadena, California 127
Pasadena High School (City College) 6, 8
Pastorelli, Robert 189
A Patch of Blue (1965) 48
Patton, George 192
"Paul Morelli" (character) 165
Pawnee 73
Payton, Douglas 109
Pearl Harbor (Oahu, Hawaii) 42
Peck, Gregory 27, 180, 181, 182
Peckinpah, Sam 80, 139, 140, 141, 147, 149, 151
Peerce, Larry 84
"Peg-leg Bates" (character) 91
Pena, David 26
Penn, Arthur 73, 87, 139, 147
Penn, Sean 177, 183
pentathlon 21
Peppard, George 28
Perkins, Anthony 13
Perkins, Gil 82
Peru, Bobby 122
Peteghem, Peter 192
Peters, Kelly Jean 147
Peterson, Preston 16
Peterson, Rex (cowboy) 195
Peterson, Wolfgang 123
phallus swords 37
Philadelphia Enquirer 149
Phillips, Lou Diamond 184, 185
Picerni, Charlie 53, 55, 60, 64, 195
Pickens, Slim 14, 97, 147, 154
Pierce College (Woodland Hills, California) 128
Pima, California 86
Pirate City 58
Piscopo, Joe 121
pistol 21
pitch of launch 172
Pitons 120
Pitts, Zasu 163
Pittsburg, Oregon 163
Pittsburgh, Pennsylvania 188
Placer Creek (Whittier, Alaska) 115
"The Plains" (episode) 27, 29
Planet of the Apes (1968) 27, 63
plastic wrap 115
Players (1979) 95
Pleasence, Donald 107
Pleshette, Suzanne 50
Pocket Money (1972) 149
"Po-Han" (character) 52
Point Loma (San Diego, California) 67
Point Park (Pittsburgh, Pennsylvania) 188
Poitier, Sidney 9, 48, 171
Pollack, Sidney 168, 169
polo matches 64
Pontiacs 100, 105
Pony Express 128, 147, 184; tricks 132
Pony Express (1959–1960) 19, 130
Porsche 119, 161, 175
Portage, Alaska 115
Porter, Bobby 123
Porter, Jean 128, 130

Post, Ken 155
Post, Ted 94
post–Civil War western 87
Powers, Gary 42
The Practice (1997–2004) 125
Preminger, Otto 42, 43
Prentiss, Paula 43
Prescott, Arizona 150, 151
Presley, Elvis 15, 25, 26, 43, 52
Preston, Robert 27, 28, 30, 151
Prevost, Vincent Lauriot 192
Price, Vincent 121
Priestly, Tom 189
Primacord explosive 145
Prisoner of Zenda (1979) 166
Problem Child (1990) 184
Professional Bull Riders Association 35
prop chase 68
prop guys 139
propane heaters 155
prosthetics 186
Pryor, Richard 99, 171
Puenzo, Luis 182
Puller, Chesty 7
Pyramid Lake, Castaic, California 109
Pyramid Lake Indian Reservation, Nevada 37
Pyun, Albert 108

Quaid, Dennis 164, 165
Quaid, Randy 87
Quantas Airlines 120
Queen Kelly (1929) 17
Quinn, Anthony 80, 153

Radford's Backlot (Studio City, California) 96
Raggedy Man (1981) 108
"The Railroad" (episode) 27, 33
rain towers 185
Raisch, Bill 21
Raise the Titanic (1980) 96
Rall, Tommy 12
Rambo: First Blood Part II (1985) 111
ramp launches 17
ramrod 147
Randall, Corky 35
Randall, Glenn, Jr. 71, 73, 81, 119, 154
Randall, Larry 157
Randall, Tony 17
Rangitaiki River (South Island, New Zealand) 120
Raw Deal (1986) 119
Rawhide (1959–1966) 82, 130
Ray, Aldo 183
rearview mirror gag 65
The Rebel Breed (1960) 19
The Rebels (1976) 96
receiving brackets 160
Red Hills (Tucson, Arizona) 83
Red Rock Canyon State Park (Cantil, California) 149
Red Rock State Park (Yavapai County, Arizona) 19

Reddish, Jack 72
USS *Redfish* 15
Redford, Robert 97, 141, 142, 143, 144, 154, 156, 168, 170, 194, 196
Redmond, Harry, Jr. 137
Rees, Danny 54, 58, 60
The Reivers (1969) 72
Relyea, Jack 72
Renaldo, Duncan 10
Rennahan, Ray 19
Repo Man (1984) 110
Republic Pictures 15, 128
respiratory failure 97
retractor 157
retrieval divers 193
The Return of a Man Called Horse (1976) 159
Reynolds, Burt 163, 177
Reynolds, Debbie 17, 18, 27, 28
Reynolds, Fez 25
Reynolds, Kevin 192
Reynolds, Reynolds 29
Reynolds, Ross (pilot) 100, 111
Rickles, Don 15
Ritter, John 184
"The Rivers" (episode) 27
Road House (1989) 188
Roadhouse Junction (Redondo Beach, California) 43
Robards, Jason 96, 147
Robbins, Harrold 48
Roberson, Chuck 35, 41, 43, 44
Roberts, Eric 108, 114, 116, 117
Roberts, Julia 123
Robertson, Chuck 40, 43, 149
"Robin Hood" (character) 124
"Robin Hood Meets the West" 141
Robin Hood, Men in Tights (1993) 123
Robinson, Dar 81, 83, 108, 128, 156
Robinson, John 15
rock hammers 120
Roddenberry, Gene 61
rodeo 150
Rogue River, Oregon 158, 161
Roizman, Owen 159, 169
Rolle, Ester 153
Rolls-Royce 161
Romans 19, 21, 36
Rome 151
Romito, Victor 49
Rondel, Ronnie, Jr. 53, 57, 59, 123, 133
roof rolls 14
roof-to-roof leaps 101
Rooney, Mickey 26
Rooster Cogburn (1975) 158
Roots: The Next Generation (1979) 96
rope ladder 176
rope swing 120
Rosales, Tommy 101
Rosenberg, Stuart 149, 171
Ross, Katherine 146
Roth, Joe 184
round-house punch 156
Rourke, Mickey 98

Index

Rowland Ranch (Canoga Park, California) 13, 19
Ruben, Joseph "Joe" 164, 165, 166
run-away log gag 149
Run Silent Run Deep (1958) 15
Runaway Train (1985) 114
runaway wagon sequence 191
Running W 159; *see also* Flying W rig
Russell, Kurt 14, 107
Russo, Barry 153
Ruthless People (1986) 119
Ryan, John P. 114
Ryan, Robert 139, 140
Rydell, Mark 72
Ryusaki, Bill 109

sabers 147, 181
Sack, George, Jr. 195
saddle stunts 45, 124, 130, 131, 154, 158, 185
safety cable 155
safety handle 159
Sai-Kung River (Hong Kong, China) 50
St. Laurent Du Maroni, French Guyana 81
St. Louis, Missouri 107
Saipan 36
Saks, Gene 154
Salomon, Michael 122
Salt Lake City, Utah 125
Salton Sea 15
San Fernando Valley, California 177
San Francisco, California 52, 65; airport 65; city hospital 79; synagogue 169
San Francisco Bay 77
San Juan Mountains, Colorado 97
San Pedro Harbor Freeway 110 112
San Quinten Prison, California 114
sand gag 157
The Sand Pebbles (1966) 50, 51
Sandoval, Miguel 110
Santa Barbara, California 169, 196
Santa Clarita, California 81, 126; hospital 177
Santa Cruz, California 6
Santa Fe South Artist Colony (Los Angeles, California) 122
Santa Fe Train Station (Prescott, Arizona) 151
Santa Monica, California 98
Santillo, Frank 151
Santos, Joe 80, 153
Sarrazin, Michael 161
Saturday Night Live (1975) 120
Saunders School 7, 13, 16, 22
Savalas, Telly 42, 61, 133
Savannah, Georgia 96
Sawaya, George 80, 170
Sawaya, Rick 47, 172
scalping 186, 187
Scheider, Roy 125
Schueneman, Karl 99, 100
Schumacher, Joel 194

Schwarzenegger, Arnold 119, 124
Schweig, Eric 187
Scorsese, Martin 124
Scott, Walter 87, 112, 119, 119, 121
Screen Actors Guild 125, 130
script supervisor 139
Sea Hunt (1958–1961) 134
Seavers, Colt 172, 174, 176
Segal, George 82
Segal, Steven 179, 180
Sellers, Peter 167
Semler, Dean 184
Serling, Rod 149
Seven Arts 11
707 gag 66
The Seven Samurai (1954) 22
The Seven Year Itch (1955) 40
Shadyac, Tom 193, 196
Shaffner, Franklyn J. 63, 81
Shamroy, Leon 27, 42
Shanghai Costume Company 79
Sharpe, Dave "David" 47, 72, 154
Shatner, William 61
Shaw, Robert 89
Sheeting, Lexan 189
Shelden, David 107
Sheppard, Sam 108
"Sheriff Bledsoe" (character) 97
"Sherman Klump" (character) 193
Sherman Oaks, California 182
Sherwood, Jim 35
shiv 114
shoot-offs 131, 147, 169, 184
Short, Martin 120
Short Circuit (1986) 119
Shreeve, James 151
Siebert, Tim 10
Siegel, Don 26, 64, 138
Sierra Madre, California 5
Sierra Nevada Mountains, Cromberg, California 120
Silence of the Hams (1994) 124
Silver Streak (1976) 154, 162, 163
Silverheels, Jay 12, 13
Silverman, Ron 170
Silverton, Colorado 145
Simba 176, 177
Simpson, Barlow 35
Simpson, Don 111
Singapore Lake (Universal Studios, California) 89
single over-hand grip 103
Sinise, Gary 123
Sioux 159, 161
The Six Million Dollar Man (1976–1978) 174
skateboard play 177
skid plates 176
Skidmore, J.D. 15
skiing 21; gags 164
Slater, Christian 184
Smailes, Marjorie 5
smelling salts 156
Smith, Brian 126
Smith, Dean 47, 80
Smith, Irby 185
Smith, J. Lewis 35
Smith, Jada Pinkett 195

Smith, William 169
Smits, Jimmy 180
Smokey and the Bandit (1977) 163, 174
Smolek, Jeff 122
Snickner, Roy 139
Snow White and the Three Stooges (1961) 35
Snyder, William 54, 58, 60
S.O.B. (1981) 171
The Soft Kill (1994) 191
Solberg, Russell 114, 115, 117
Soldier in the Rain (1963) 39
Soledad State Prison, California 114
sombrero 139
somersault 7, 12, 41, 49, 57, 72, 100, 108, 110, 112, 133, 144, 150, 181,
Sometimes a Great Notion (1971) 149
Sonnenfield, Barry 125
Sonora, California 195
Sonora Desert 184
The Sons of Katie Elder (1965) 43, 44, 48
Sony Stages (Culver City, California) 123
soundmen 139
Spacek, Sissy 108
spaghetti cinema 80
Spain 157
Spanish stuntmen 167
Spartacus (1960) 16, 19, 22, 42
Spelling, Arron 77
Spider-Man (2002) 126
Spielberg, Steven 98, 122
Spinotti, Dante 186, 188
springboard 186
Spy Hard (1996) 124, 191
Squaw Valley, California 94
squibs 95, 119, 153
stabbing 186, 187
Stader, Paul 25
stagecoach hijacking scene 147
stairs 14, 22, 154
Stallone, Sylvester 95, 111, 112
stampede 132, 160, 191
Stanley, Frank 99
Stanton, Harry Dean 19, 87, 107, 110
"The Star-Spangled Banner" 43
Star Trek (1966–1969) 61
Starrett, James 153
Steadman, Bob 95
Steadman, Robert 180
Steal Big Little Sister (1995) 124
steel cable 119
Steele, Tom 81
steep-grade descents 97
"steer-arounds" 161
Stephens, John 67, 80
Stetsons 182, 185
Stevens, George 37
Stevens, Leslie 80
Stevens, Stella 40, 147
Stevenson, Robert 19
Stewart, James 27, 28

Index

Stine, Clifford 55
The Sting (1973) 154
Stir Crazy (1980) 171
stirrup drags 75, 110, 124, 131, 132, 133, 140, 147, 158, 181, 182, 184, 185
Stockton, California 163
Stockwell, Dean 133
Stoltz, Art 88
storm washes 110
Strader, Paul 83, 97, 156
Stradling, Harry, Jr. 77
Streets of San Francisco (1972–1977) 80
Streisand, Barbra 78
Striepeke, Dan 149
Striking Distance (1993) 188, 189
Strode, Woody 16, 19
Strong, John 42
Stroud, Don 149
studded tires 164
Studi, Wes 186
stunt dummy 163
Stuntfest 146
The Stuntman (1980) 172
Stuntman's Association 11, 26, 33, 47, 59
Sturges, John 22, 67, 149, 151
submerged cable 192
substratum 176
Sugarfoot (1957–1961) 14
Sullivan, Grant 130
Sundance 97
Sunset Blvd. (1950) 17
Superior, Arizona 32
Superman 17, 38, 42, 116; gags 176
Support Your Local Sheriff (1969) 77
Suppose They Gave a War and Nobody Came? (1970) 77
Surtees, Robert 156
Sutherland, Keifer 185, 195
Swamp Thing (1982) 177
The Swarm (1978) 97
Swashbuckler (1976) 89, 93
Swenson, Bo 156
Swenson, Jeep 107
Swiss Family Robinson (1960) 23, 24, 25
The Sword and the Sorcerer (1982) 108
swordfighting 60, 133, 159, 186
Sydney, George 6
Sykes, Brenda 153

T-boned 111
Tales of the Texas Rangers (1955–1958) 128
The Tall Stranger (1957) 14
Tallman, Frank (aerial genius) 39, 156
Talmadge, Richard (stunt coordinator) 7, 8, 13, 15, 17, 25, 27, 31, 32, 36, 42, 59,
Tamblyn, Russ 16
Tangiers Expatriate 157
Taos, New Mexico 97
Taras Bulba (1962) 36

Tarruella, Tony 152
Tarto, Richard 62
Tashlin, Frank 35
Taurog, Norman 43
Taylor, Don 26
Taylor, Dub 139, 151
Teamsters 67, 95, 97, 142, 148, 176
Teconapa Jungle, Mexico 111
Telluride, Colorado 97
The Ten Commandments (1956) 13, 16
Tennessee River 27
Tent Rocks (Cochiti Reservation, New Mexico) 97
Terhune, Bob 14, 22, 53, 54, 55, 58, 60
The Terminal Man (1974) 82
Teton Village, Wyoming 89
USS *Texas* 51
Texas longhorns 24, 49, 132, 147
This Rebel Breed (1960) 19
The Thomas Crown Affair (1968) 64
Thompson, J. Lee 36, 42
Thorson, Ralph "Papa" 99
Thousand Oaks, California 12, 75
Three Amigos (1986) 120
Thunder in the Sun (1959) 17
Tibbs, Casey 151
ticket booths 172
Tickle Me (1965) 43
Tillman Water Reclamation Plant 121
"Tim O'Hara" (character) 195
A Time to Kill (1996) 194
Timoteas 167
Tinian 36
Tinseltown 13, 157, 163
To Live and Die in L.A. (1985) 112
Tobago Islands 23
toe-tappers 157, 158, 182
Toltec Railway, Chama, New Mexico 97
Tom Horn (1980) 98
Tomahawk 186
Tombstone Territory (1957) 128
Topanga Canyon Road, California 175
Tora! Tora! Tora! (1970) 153
Tors, Ivan 134, 137
The Towering Inferno (1974) 83, 86, 154, 155, 156
traffic signals 165
trains 162
trampoline 17, 47, 56, 57, 113, 132
transference 161
trapeze 102, 138
Traxler, Steve 192
Trejo, Danny 114
tridents 21
Trifunovich, Neil (mechanical genius) 195
Trimaran 192
Trinity Collage, Dublin, Ireland 95
trips 97, 131, 185; with wire 160
Triumph TR-6 Thunderbird 36
True Lies (1994) 124

Tryon, Tom 42
Tuchman, Barbra 157
Tucker, Forrest 96
Tucker Farms System 170
"Tucker McElroy" 170
Tucson, Arizona 12
tundra 149
20th Century Fox 15, 25, 27, 35, 42, 50, 63, 108, 122, 123, 141, 146, 149, 151, 156, 170, 172, 175; Mission Ranch 52
twisted half-gainers 170
Two Mules for Sister Sarah (1970) 64
Tyree, Jack 108

Ugland, Rudy 152, 182
The Ultimate Warrior (1975) 85
"Uncas" (character) 187
"Uncle Martin" (character) 195
The Undefeated (1969) 146
underwater charges 149
Underwood, Ron 185
Union Army 132; officer 148
Union Station (Los Angeles, California) 163
United Arab Emirates 42
United Artist Pictures 95, 159
United Kingdom 95
United Methodist Church (La Vern, California) 63
U.S. Army 147
U.S. Navy 42; gunboat 52
Universal Pictures 19, 21, 53, 64, 80, 83, 108, 120, 130, 133, 138, 149, 153, 155, 170, 194
Universal Pictures Gladiator Camp Backlot (Universal City, California) 19
Universal Studios, Six Points of Texas 158
Universal Theme Park 194
University of California–Los Angeles 42, 112
Unsworth, Geoffrey 95
Ustinov, Peter 42, 183
Uzi 111

V-1 rocket launch 89
Valentino prototype 163
Van Cleef, Lee 19, 107
Vancouver (British Columbia, Canada) 163, 183
Van Doren, Mamie 16
Van Horn, Buddy 72, 89, 110, 123, 132, 149, 164
Van Nuys, California 121, 127, 128, 177; junior rodeo 128
vans 79, 177
Van Sickel, Dale 26
Vargas, Antonio 153
Variety Magazine 194
Vaseline 24, 115
Vasquez Rocks (Aqua Dulce, California) 15, 81, 121
Vaughn, Robert 22
vehicle work 164
Velez, Eddie 110

Index

Veluzat Ranch (Los Angeles, California) 121
Verbois, Jack 80
VHS camcorder 177
Viet Cong 111
Vigoda, Abe 80, 153
Vilas, Guillermo 96
Vincent, Jan Michael 146
Vincent, Sailor 12
Vincent Thomas Bridge (Los Angeles, California) 82
viper gag 193
Viva Zapata (1952) 52
Vladimir Central Prison, Russia 42
Voight, Jon 114, 116, 117
Voightlander, Ted 137
Von Stroheim, Erich 17
Von Sydow, Max 38

Wagner, Robert 156
wagon flip-overs 14, 133
Wairoa River (North Island, New Zealand) 120
"Waldo" (character) 156
Walk the Proud Land (1956) 12
Walken, Christopher 110
Walker, Clint 68
Walker, Greg 97
Walker, Rock 97
Walker, Tracey 106
Walker Ranch (Santa Clarita, California) 15
The Walking Dead (2010) 121
Walking Down Broadway (1938) 17
Walking Tall (1973) 82
Wallace, Tommy Lee 109
Wallach, Eli 22, 28
Wallis, Hal B. 80
Wallrod, Ransom (marine guru) 192
Walston, Ray 195
Wanted Dead or Alive (1958) 15
The War Lover (1962) 35
Ward, Richard 171
Warden, Jack 15
"Warden Rankin" (character) 117
"Warden Walter Beatty" (character) 171
wardrobe gals 139
Warehouse District (Chicago, Illinois) 179
Warlock (1959) 129, 132
Warlock, Dick 47, 107, 122
Warner, Jack 10
Warner Bros. 14, 41, 68, 80, 81, 97, 98, 107, 108, 139, 153, 154, 161, 164, 179
Washington, George 117
Washington, Richard 108
Washington, D.C. 124
water-dragging (river-drag) 48
water pots 181

Waters, Chuck 164
Waterworld (1995) 192
Waugh, Freddy 72, 133, 149, 165
Waxman, Harry 25
Waxman, Michael 188
Way, Guy 26, 42
Wayne, Jesse 26, 47
Wayne, John 27, 40, 43, 48, 134, 146, 147, 158
Weatherwax, Frank "Rudd" (trainer) 13, 88
Weekend at Bernie's (1989) 121
Weintraub, Freddie 107
Weis, Gary 99
Weiss, Don 53, 59
Welles, Orson 192
Wells, George 7
Wendover, Nevada 125
Wenger, Clifford, Jr. 111
We're No Angels (1955) 183
We're No Angels (1989) 177, 183
West, Artie 9
West, Red 42
West Side Story (1961) 16
Western spoof 154
Westworld (1973) 153
Wexler, Haskell 64, 163
whale 155
What's Up Doc? (1972) 77, 78
wheelchair 143
When I Was King (1981) 171
When Legends Die (1972) 151
Whimpy, Rex 35
Whiskey Row 151
Whitaker, Forrest 177
White, Doug 122
White, Teddy 35
The White Dawn (1974) 155
White Water Summer (1987) 120
"The Whiz Kid" 170
Who'll Stop the Rain, (Dog Soldiers) (1978) 164
Wholly Moses (1980) 99
Wiard, William 98
Wick, Charles 35
Wickman, Karl (pilot) 111
Widmark, Richard 28, 41, 97, 129, 132, 138, 151
wig 161
Wilcots, Joseph M. 96
Wild at Heart (1990) 122
The Wild Bunch (1969) 139
Wild Wild West (1999) 125
Wild Women (1970) 77
Wilder, Billy 17
Wilder, Gene 154, 162, 163, 169, 170, 171
Wilder, Glen 26, 42, 52
Williams, Ester 6, 7
Williams, Jack 22, 29, 30, 43
Williams, Mary 130
Williams, Paul 47
Williams, Robin 123

Williams, Treat 98, 121
Willingham, Calder 147
Willis, Bruce 188, 189
Wills, Chill 16
Wills, Henry 19, 22, 36, 43
Wills, Jerry 164
Wilmington, North Carolina 121
Wilson, Henry 10
Wilson, Luke 125
Winchester rifle 42, 98, 141, 158
The Wind and the Lion (1975) 157, 166, 167
wind shear 112
Winters, Shelly 153
Winton Flyer 72, 73
wire wedges 120
Wise, Robert 15, 16, 52
Wisnievitz, David 181
Wizan, Joe 82, 150
Wolfe, Robert 151, 158
World Rodeo Championships (1955) 129
World War II 5, 13, 26, 42, 110, 127; Bronze Star 49; postwar 39, 171; snipers 36
The World's Greatest Lover (1977) 163
wound brackets 160
Wrangler Jeep 177
wrap party 163
Wrightsville Beach, North Carolina 121
Write to Kill (1991) 122
Wyatt, Al, Sr. 80, 81, 154, 164
Wyler, William 13

Yangtze River, China 50, 51
Yanks, Al 154
"Yellow Hand" (character) 161
Yellowbeard (1983) 110
Yerkes, Bob 83, 123
YMCA 5, 151
Yost, Paul Edward (balloon captain) 71
Young, Freddie (master shot) 116, 187
Young, Jack N. 35
Young Guns II (1990) 184
The Young Lions (1958) 52
Yrigoyen, Joe 12, 43, 72, 81, 130, 131, 132, 133, 135, 136, 137, 139, 140, 141
Yrigoyen, Yvonne 130
Yuma, Arizona 133

Zebras 134, 135, 136, 137
Zemeckis, Robert 112
Ziker, Dick 153
Zimbalist, Efrem, Jr. 14, 47
Ziv Studios 19
Zorro (1957–1961) 82
Zucco's Troupe 53, 54

www.ingramcontent.com/pod-product-compliance
Lightning Source LLC
Chambersburg PA
CBHW080804300426
44114CB00020B/2825